Lacan on Love

Pour Héloïse, mon amour

As for what it means to love [. . .], I must at least, like Socrates, be able to credit myself with knowing something about it. Now if we take a look at the psychoanalytic literature, we see that this is what people talk about the least. [. . .] Isn't it astonishing that we analysts – who make use of love and talk about nothing else – can be said to present ourselves as truly deficient when compared to [the philosophical and religious] tradition? We haven't made even a partial attempt to add to – much less revise – what has been developed over the centuries on the subject of love or provide something that might be not unworthy of this tradition. Isn't that surprising? (Lacan, 2015, p. 16)

Lacan on Love

An Exploration of
Lacan's Seminar VIII, *Transference*

Bruce Fink

polity

First published in 2016 by Polity Press

Reprinted 2015, 2016 (twice), 2017, 2018, 2019 (twice), 2021, 2022 (twice)

Polity Press
65 Bridge Street
Cambridge CB2 1UR, UK

Polity Press
350 Main Street
Malden, MA 02148, USA

ISBN-13: 978-1-5095-0049-9
ISBN-13: 978-1-5095-0050-5(pb)

A catalogue record for this book is available from the British Library.

Library of Congress Cataloging-in-Publication Data

Fink, Bruce, 1956- , author.
  Lacan on love : an exploration of Lacan's Seminar VIII, Transference / Bruce Fink.
    p. ; cm.
  Includes bibliographical references and index.
  ISBN 978-1-5095-0049-9 (hardcover : alk. paper) -- ISBN 1-5095-0049-9 (hardcover : alk. paper) -- ISBN 978-1-5095-0050-5 (pbk. : alk. paper) -- ISBN 1-5095-0050-2 (pbk. : alk. paper)
  I. Title.
  [DNLM: 1. Lacan, Jacques, 1901–1981. Séminaire de Jacques Lacan. Livre 8, Transfert : 1960–1961. 2. Love. 3. Transference (Psychology) 4. Psychoanalytic Theory. WM 62]
  RC454
  616.89--dc23
                              2015009802

Typeset in 10.5 on 12 pt Times NR MT by Servis Filmsetting Ltd, Stockport, Cheshire
Printed and bound by CPI Group (UK) Ltd, Croydon, CR0 4YY

For further information on Polity, visit our website: politybooks.com

Contents

THE REAL

GENERAL CONSIDERATIONS ON LOVE

Preface

Whether to vilify and bury love once and for all or, rather, to praise it – the dilemma has preoccupied poets and philosophers for millennia. Whether to celebrate the incomparable joy love brings or denounce the intense pain and desperation one suffers in its wake, whether to glorify its life-giving virtues or expose its cruelty and illusions – that is the question certain psychoanalysts, too, have weighed in on, following in the footsteps of the bards and literati.

Relations between Eros, the Greek god of love (Cupid to the Romans), and psychoanalysis have not always been cordial, to say the least. Freud at times reduced love to the dependency of a child on its mother, the child's affection for her deriving essentially from her ability to satisfy the child's hunger for food, warmth, and closeness. Jekels and Bergler, well-known first- and second-generation analysts, decried love as nothing more than the wish to be loved – hence a narcissistic project.[1] Driving a further nail in the coffin, they alleged that we seek love from someone toward whom we feel guilty, reasoning that we will feel less guilty if we can make that person love us.[2] Wilhelm Reich, on the other hand, who was to become a pariah of the psychoanalytic establishment, conceived of the achievement of utter and complete love as the foremost aim of treatment.[3]

It seems that psychoanalysts have long been divided over the question whether to condemn love as a form of self-deception – a mirage, a cover for something else, a simple narcissistic project parading as altruism – or as the holy of holies, the greatest of all possible psychical accomplishments. Erik Erikson attributed to Freud the well-known formulation that psychoanalysis strives to restore the patient's ability to "love and work"[4] (at least one of them making the considerable assumption that the patient had such an ability at some prior point in time). And yet kissing was at times described aseptically by the father of psychoanalysis as the rubbing together of "mucous membranes,"[5] "affectionate love" as resulting merely from the inhibition of sexual desire,[6] and the more sublimated forms of so-called selfless love for others (charity, for example) as often but a poor disguise for self-aggrandizement and condescension toward others.

Nevertheless, the early analysts were hardly the first to propose conflicting appraisals of love. Centuries before Plato and Aristotle held court in Athens, Hesiod taxed women with generally being "bad for men," warning men that:

> A bad [wife] makes you shiver with cold;
> A greedy wife roasts you alive with no help from a roaring
>   blaze,
> And tough though you be brings you to a raw old age.
>   (Hesiod, trans. Wender: 1973)

But he also opined that "No prize is greater than a worthy wife." Love, in his account of it (in the context of marriage) and depending on the character of one's beloved, could give rise to the worst of evils or the very best life can offer.

In ancient Greece and Rome, it was common to characterize love as an attack, Cupid being depicted as physically burning the lover with a torch or shooting the lover with arrows, even as Love was celebrated as a great god.[7] In the early Middle Ages, Andreas Capellanus provided an apparently spurious etymology for the word love itself, deriving *amor*, the Latin for love, from *amus*, meaning hook: "He who is in love is captured in the chains of desire and wishes to capture someone else with his hook." This medieval chaplain referred to love as a form of suffering of which "there is no torment greater," but went on to say, "O what a wonderful thing is love, which makes a man shine with so many virtues and teaches everyone, no matter who he is, so many good traits of character!"[8]

Hélisenne de Crenne, the Renaissance author of *Torments of Love*, depicted love as a "lamentable illness" and a most cruel calamity. It is "a passion in the soul that reduces us to perplexity and sadness because we cannot enjoy what we love."[9] She went so far as to anticipate certain analysts' views that there is something rotten in the State of Love, some paradox baked into human desire. And our sixteenth-century novelist foreshadowed Freud by introducing the term "libidinous" and by maintaining that "one who is capable of loving ardently is also capable of hating cruelly" – leaving it to Sigmund, following in Kierkegaard's footsteps,[10] to add that hate is the flipside of love and to Lacan to invent the term *hainamoration* (combining *haine*, hate or hatred, and *énamourer*, to become enamored). Yet, as tormenting and calamitous as love is in her novel, Crenne's characters live only for the enlivening sensations it brings.

For the nineteenth-century Stendhal, love and its attendant uncertainties and palpitations are the leisure classes' antidote to boredom, and the less contact one has with one's beloved, the more deliciously sublime one's love can be. His British contemporary, Jane Austen, prefers the language of attachment to that of Stendhal's *coup de foudre*, the "thunderbolt" of love at first sight that so preoccupied him. Charlotte's pronouncement in Austen's novel *Pride and Prejudice* is decidedly pessimistic:

> Happiness in marriage is entirely a matter of chance. If the dispositions of the parties are ever so well known to each other or ever so similar beforehand, it does not advance their felicity in the least. They always continue to grow sufficiently unlike afterwards to have their share of vexation; and it is better to know as little as possible of the defects of the person with whom you are to pass your life. (p. 17)

Yet Austen's overriding view rejects both Charlotte's cynicism and Stendhal's quintessentially Romantic-era celebration of love at a distance (consider Marianne's gradual attachment to Colonel Brandon in *Sense and Sensibility*).[11]

To round out this thumbnail sketch of contrasting appraisals of love with a jump to the twentieth century, we need but juxtapose Carole King's 1976 conclusion that "Only Love Is Real" with the J. Geils Band's 1980 assessment that "Love Stinks."

The situation becomes far more complex when, instead of simply giving love the thumbs-up or the thumbs-down, instead of praising love as a munificent marvel or skewering it as a pestilent affliction, we raise the thorny question, "What is love?"

For one person, to discuss love is to discuss theology, love being sent to us by the gods; for another, it is an investment in someone whose value should be ascertained conclusively before one becomes enamored; for a third, love is what resolves differences among partners in a sort of musical harmony; for a fourth, it is the attempt to find and fuse anew with our other half; for a fifth, love is peaceful and just, moderate, temperate, and sound-minded; for a sixth, love is a messenger between mortals and immortals, and is tantamount to the worship of beauty – and all six of these views of love are found in but one of Plato's dialogues, the *Symposium*!

In the seventeenth century, Spinoza defined love as a joy

accompanied by the idea that the pleasure comes from something outside of ourselves. In the thirteenth century, Saint Thomas Aquinas distinguished concupiscence-type love (better known as lust) that comes from inside us and seeks to penetrate the beloved's heart, from friendship that brings the beloved into one's own heart. For Aristotle, "to love is to wish someone well,"[12] that is, to take a genuine interest in his welfare; for Erich Segal, "love means never having to say you're sorry," a horse of a different color.

For some, love involves dependency and shameful submission to another's will; for others, both partners must be self-actualized, independent beings for true love to exist between them. For some, love is sweet surrender and steals upon us like God's miraculous grace; for others, love seeks to subjugate and possess the beloved. Love is blind; love is clairvoyant, piercing our social masks. Love is ephemeral; love is everlasting. Love is grasping and envious; love is guileless and giving. Love is incompatible with desire and marriage; love and desire can and must fuse in marriage. Love enriches both parties; love enriches the beloved at the lover's expense – it is a rip-off. Love is tragic; "love is a comical feeling."

How could love be so many different things to people, and even to one and the same person at various times? Could it be that love is different for the beloved than it is for the lover? Different for men than it is for women? Different for the ancient Greeks than it is for our contemporaries? Is love merely a product of culture and history, being something totally different for a Chinaman of the Ming Dynasty, a noblewoman of Imperial Rome, an eighteenth-century Austrian musician like Mozart, and a twenty-first-century American country singer like Sara Evans trying to figure out "what love really means"?

Rather than immediately assume that different cultures define love differently, or that love has been experienced in opposing manners in different historical periods, let us note that virtually all of these varied notions of love can be found in our own culture and era. Many rock musicians depict love as an attack; blues singers often cast love as pain, agony, and torture; and other songwriters represent love as the greatest of pleasures ("you get too much, you get too high"). If love were nothing more than a cultural/historical product, it would seem that most everyone within one and the same culture would experience love in the same way. Nothing, however, could be further from the truth.

What do we mean by the simple word "love"? Do we mean passion? Affection? Concupiscence? Attachment? Lust? Friendship? Each language divides up the amorous sentiments in different ways.

The Greek tradition provided us with the well-known term "Eros," which seems to cover a vast spectrum of experiences, much like Freud's term "libido" which, as Lacan suggests, is "an extremely broad theoretical entity that goes well beyond the specialized sexual desire of adults. This notion tends rather toward 'desire,' antiquity's Eros understood very broadly – namely, as the whole set of human beings' appetites that go beyond their needs, the latter being strictly tied to self-preservation."[13]

Freud strove to define some of the components of libido, and was led to use widely diverse terms at different times in the development of his theory – love, attachment, desire, affectionate love, cathexis, sensual love, and drive – and even to define each of these terms somewhat differently from decade to decade. There is, in my view, no singular theory of love to be found in Freud's work or in Lacan's work: there are only multiple attempts to grapple with it at different points in their theoretical development.

In this book I shall explore and compare and contrast some of the different attempts to discuss love by both authors. In order to do so, it will be necessary to introduce a number of terms from their work, including "narcissism," "ideal ego," "ego-ideal," "imaginary," "symbolic," "real," "demand," "desire," "drive," and "jouissance," to mention but a few. Much as the reader might like it if I were to somehow clean up the enormous mess in the Augean stables of our philosophical and psychoanalytic literature, and come up with a clear, compelling, and all-encompassing theory of love, this is not possible and probably not even desirable! The reader will instead, I hope, glean a number of important insights that will lead to a deeper appreciation for the complexity of the human experience of love and passion, as we work our way through first a portion of Freud's work, then a portion of Lacan's, then another portion of Freud's, and so on, relying all the while on Lacan's registers of the symbolic, imaginary, and real.

There is no need to have read in advance all of the texts by Freud and Lacan that I delve into here, but it will be helpful to have at least reread Plato's *Symposium* by the time we get to Chapter 8, and it will certainly not be disadvantageous to read the first 11 chapters of Lacan's Seminar VIII as we proceed through Chapter 8. The exploration of literature from a wide range of periods and languages in Chapter 7 relies on the reader's general knowledge.

Note on Texts

In this book, I cite the eminently readable translation of Plato's *Symposium* by Alexander Nehamas and Paul Woodruff that is found in C. D. C. Reeve's (2006) volume entitled *Plato on Love*. References to Seminar VIII, *Transference*, are to my recent translation of it published by Polity Press (2015). Note that virtually all translated citations by French authors here (Lacan, Stendhal, Rougemont, and so on) are either by me or have been modified by me; page numbers followed by a slash and a second number refer first to the original French edition and then to the available English edition.

Small portions of Chapters 2, 4, and 5 originally appeared in Volume 2 of my collection of papers entitled *Against Understanding* (London: Routledge, 2014); and about two pages of Chapter 5 appeared in Volume 1 of that same collection; everything has been significantly expanded and reworked for inclusion here. An early, condensed version of Chapter 6 appeared in *Sexual Identity and the Unconscious*, published by École de Psychanalyse des Forums du Champ Lacanien in 2011, and much of Chapter 3 appeared separately in *The Psychoanalytic Review* 102/1 (February 2015): 59–91.

Introduction

Love is blind, and lovers cannot see
The pretty follies that themselves commit;
For if they could, Cupid himself would blush . . .
                    Shakespeare, *The Merchant of Venice*, II. vi. 41–3

In the Beginning Was Love

All of contemporary psychotherapy finds its origin in a love story. A well-respected Viennese nerve specialist – not Freud – is called in to treat a young woman whom he finds exceptionally vivacious, intelligent, and beautiful. Not only is she charming and exceedingly attractive, she also speaks several foreign languages and is highly creative. Her case is a very unusual one, and she becomes terribly difficult for her family to deal with if the dashing young doctor does not meet with her frequently. As it is 1880, he makes house calls, coming to see her almost every day, often for several hours at a time. Eventually, he begins coming both morning and evening.

The neurologist grows impassioned about their work together and speaks about nothing else, even at home. His wife becomes bored with such talk and grows increasingly unhappy and morose. She does not come right out and complain and, as so often happens, it takes her husband quite a long time to fathom what is fueling her changed mood. When it finally dawns on him that she feels neglected and is jealous, he realizes the tenor of his own feelings for his patient and becomes guilt-ridden.

The fine-looking physician abruptly resolves to put an end to the treatment, sensing that he has been doing something morally reprehensible, despite the patient's obvious improvement. Announcing to her the next morning that their work together is finished, he is urgently called back by her family that very evening to find that the young woman is going through an hysterical childbirth, presenting all the signs of a real childbirth, having imagined that she is pregnant with the doctor's baby!

He manages to calm her down, but is profoundly shaken by the seemingly sudden amorous turn of the patient's fantasies. The good doctor professes to have had no idea she was in love with him. And far be it from him to fully admit to himself the degree to which he was enamored of her! He refuses to recommence treatment (referring her instead to the Bellevue Sanatorium in Kreuzlingen founded by Ludwig Binswanger) and whisks his wife off with him to Venice soon thereafter for an impromptu second honeymoon.

Psychoanalysis might well have been stillborn, for the love-struck doctor, Josef Breuer by name, vowed never again to employ the technique his patient Bertha Pappenheim had spontaneously invented – christened "the talking cure" by her – clearly finding its side effects too hot to handle.[1] If not for the curiosity of Sigmund Freud, who encouraged Breuer to go over the details of the case with him again and again, psychoanalysis might never have been anything but the story of one unfulfilled, unconsummated, and even largely unacknowledged love affair. Instead, thanks to Freud's lively interest in the case, Bertha (known in the psychoanalytic literature as Anna O.) ended up giving birth to talk therapy, which was to make the twentieth century, perhaps even more than "the space age," "the therapeutic age." (We might even call it "the therapeutic space age.")

Freud was not deterred by patients' expressions of love. A female patient of his once threw her arms around his neck and kissed him affectionately, upon coming out of hypnosis; but rather than consider himself irresistible – indeed, he thought himself far less prepossessing than Breuer – Freud tried to figure out what it was about doctor–patient relationships that elicited such reactions. Strong emotions had been part of such relationships since time immemorial, even with less than charming or handsome physicians. Rather than feeling guilty for having aroused amorous feelings in his patients, or simply running away from them like Breuer, Freud came to view them as part and parcel of what he called "transference love" – love transferred onto the physician from some other real or idealized figure in a patient's life.

Transference was, he hypothesized, a case of mistaken identity: the love his patients expressed was not love for him, but rather love for the role he played, love for what he agreed to represent – the helpful, healing Other who listens to us and seems to know what ails us. Feelings stirred up in patients engaged in the talking cure were incommensurate with what their doctor said or did, but those feelings could, he found, be harnessed and made to serve as the motor force of the therapeutic process.

Now, not only is love the mainspring of psychoanalytic work, it also turns out to be the number one source of complaints addressed to analysts, therapists, and counselors of every ilk even today. People more often than not enter therapy seeking help with or relief from what the minstrel calls "this crazy little thing called love"[2] and what writers go so far as to call a malady.[3]

Complaints about Love

For I have sworn thee fair, and thought thee bright,
Who art as black as hell, as dark as night.

                              Shakespeare, *Sonnet 147*, lines 13–14

Love has often been viewed as an illness of sorts and is experienced by people as debilitating for a wide variety of reasons. Some of the major complaints about love one hears, whether they are proclaimed over the airwaves, online, or on the couch, include:

- I never manage to meet anyone who measures up to my exacting standards or fits my criteria; or, if I do, that person is already involved with someone else.
- When I do manage to find someone to love who is available, my love is unrequited or never adequately returned.
- I can never achieve the kind of fusion that I seek with my beloved; and if, by some miracle, I am able to do so momentarily, love quickly fades.
- My beloved cannot handle the intensity of my feelings – passion, rage, jealousy, fury – and cannot stand what I most enjoy.
- My beloved is deceptive, fickle, unfaithful, disloyal, jealous, possessive, toxic, and unfair – in a word, impossible – bringing me nothing but pain.
- The person I am crazy about has fallen in love, not with me but with someone else: my best friend or my sibling.
- My best friend has fallen in love and forgotten all about me.
- I am constantly wracked by thoughts that someone will steal my beloved from me; night and day I worry my beloved will meet someone new, someone better.
- I walk on eggshells, fearing lest an unthinking comment I make may cool the fires of my partner's passion for me – if my beloved knew me as I truly am, all would be lost.

- I am never loved for myself but only for my appearance, what I represent, or what I possess; what my beloved loves seems to have nothing to do with me.

These are just a few of the complaints about love that we hear, and many of them are as old as writings about love itself, going back well before Ovid's *Art of Love*, published in 1 B.C.

But are they all of a piece? Do they all involve the same facet(s) of love? To frame the question differently, are they all situated at the same level? Hardly. Some of them concern love triangles (for example, "I'm in love with her but she's in love with him"), which, I will suggest, are best understood from the *symbolic* or structural standpoint (for readers who are not already familiar with these Lacanian terms, I will give an account of what they mean as we go along).

Others involve looking for someone who fits a vast array of pre-established criteria, which is often a screen for seeking a "soul mate" – that is, someone believed to be just like us (or just like the us we prefer to imagine we are). These can perhaps be understood as *imaginary*-order phenomena, involving as they do a search for someone who is a perfect likeness, mirror image, or reflection of ourselves.

Still others involve being captivated by another person the way one is when one falls in love at first sight, like Kierkegaard did with Regina, knowing little or nothing about the beloved in advance. This may signal a process best situated in the register of the *real*, which short-circuits desire and the doubts and second-guessing often endemic to it.

Words, Words, Words

To speak of love is in itself a jouissance.

Lacan, 1998a, p. 83

Encompassing, as it does, such diverse things, our language of love needs to be refined if we are to grasp the complexity of love triangles (they primarily involve desire, which is a thing of language), the choice of partners based on how similar they are to ourselves (key here is narcissism, which is organized on the basis of images), and the experience of being thunderstruck upon first encountering someone with whom every joy seems instantly possible (the first glimpse of the person is perhaps somehow immediately associated with satisfaction of the drives).

I will attempt to explore some of the myriad facets of love by situating them at their corresponding levels: symbolic, imaginary, or real. The reader may be aware that Lacan's early work focused on what he referred to as the imaginary, his middle work in the 1950s and early 1960s on what he called the symbolic, and his work in the mid- to late 1960s and the 1970s on what he defined as the real. The imaginary, briefly stated, involves sensory images, above all, visual images of the self and others. The symbolic, on the other hand, concerns language and structure. And the real centers on the body and its range of possible satisfactions.

Lacan's focus on the various components of what we rather over-simplistically call "love" (and what the Greeks more generally called "Eros") tends to involve shifting vocabularies: at times he speaks of love where we might feel it clearer to speak of desire or even more specifically of sexual desire, and at other times he speaks of desire where it might seem it is actually love that is at issue. But such is our language of love in both French and English, or so it seems to me. As a first step toward clarifying things, I suspect many readers would agree that to tell someone, "I want you," is not exactly the same as to say, "I love you."

Eschewing chronology, the first part of this book, "The Symbolic," takes up Freud's and then Lacan's discussions of love as something tied to the symbolic register of experience since they are, perhaps, the easiest to grasp. The second part, "The Imaginary," covers imaginary phenomena and the third part, "The Real," the facets of love that can be characterized as real in the Lacanian sense of the term. In the fourth part, "General Considerations on Love," I review and examine a few of the many varied languages and cultures of love, found in the work of such authors as Aquinas, Aristotle, Augustine, Capellanus, Crenne, Gide, Kierkegaard, Rougemont, Stendhal, and others; then I provide a detailed exploration of Lacan's commentary on Plato's *Symposium* and, using Lacan's formulations as a springboard, my own further interpretations of the dialogue. In the final chapter, I enumerate a few conclusions that I believe we can safely draw from Lacan's discussion in Seminar VIII and highlight a number of still unanswered questions.

Although the later parts of the book generally build on the earlier parts, much of the fourth part can be followed without having read the second and third parts, and certain readers may prefer to return to those parts after reading the fourth part.

THE SYMBOLIC

I

Freudian Preludes

Love Triangles

One might wonder whether anything in psychoanalysis could better illustrate what Lacan calls the "symbolic order" – an order characterized by language and structure – than love triangles. Freud devotes several papers to discussing the kinds of love triangles in which specific groups of neurotic men and women, whom he refers to as obsessives (or obsessional) and hysterics (or hysterical), all too often find themselves entangled. We shall see to what degree what we learn from these subsections of the population is applicable to human beings more generally.

Obsessives in Love

There are certain men, Freud tells us in "On the Universal Tendency to Debasement in the Sphere of Love,"[1] who are incapable of falling in love with a woman unless she is already involved with another man. A woman is uninteresting to such men in the absence of this formal, structural, symbolic condition – a condition that obviously harks back to the Oedipal triangle where, right from the outset, boys had a rival for their mothers' affections in the form of their fathers (and/or siblings).[2] Freud indicates that such men need to feel jealous of and have "gratifying impulses of rivalry and hostility" toward the other man, the man who was already involved with the woman before he came on the scene.[3]

Men who love in this way often end up having a whole series of triangular attachments, proving that it is not the particular women they fall for who are important but rather *the structural situation itself*: a situation including a woman who is already "taken" and the man who "possesses" her. Should the woman in question leave her boyfriend, fiancé, or husband, the triangle collapses and the woman is no longer of any interest to our lover, who can no longer fancy himself an interloper or invader of the other man's territory. It is only the continued *impossibility* of the situation – the enduring hopelessness of ever possessing the other man's woman – that keeps him interested; as soon as the obstacle to possession disappears, so too does his love for her.

This is an obsessive configuration insofar as the obsessive's desire is always for something impossible: to attain an unattainable status (e.g., perfection, omniscience, or immortality), to complete an uncompletable project, or to possess what he cannot possess. In saying that the obsessive is characterized by an impossible desire, Lacan goes so far as to add that his desire is for impossibility itself.[4] A relationship with a woman is not in and of itself appealing or gratifying enough to our obsessive: it must be mediated by a living, breathing, third party who renders his quest unrealizable, allowing him to go on dreaming "the impossible dream" (as the Broadway musical *Man of La Mancha* put it).

This third party may be no older than our lover, even if older men are the most enjoyable targets of his rage and shenanigans. The obsessive is most intrigued when the Other man is clearly designated, in socially recognizable linguistic terms of the historical era and culture, as having an official status as a boyfriend, lover, partner, fiancé, husband, or whatever the other terms of the time and place may be (for example, *mignon*, *favori*, "favorite," or "servant"). Yet even when the third party simply is someone who occasionally hangs around the woman (actually or virtually), having some sort of nebulous, vague, undefined relationship with her, our obsessive can often imagine that he is far more substantial than he appears to be or than she lets on – that is, that he is a genuine father-like rival.

Although it may appear outwardly that our lover is captivated by another man's woman, it is the Other man himself who is of libidinal centrality to him – for it is the obsessive's competition with this Other man that gets his juices flowing, so to speak, that gets him angry or stirred up, feeling, by turns, inferior or superior to him. Consciously he believes that it is the Other man's woman who fascinates him; unconsciously it is the battle with the Other man that fascinates him.[5]

The ostensible goal here seems to be to defeat this man (and get his girl), just as one wished, but failed, to defeat one's own father back in the day. Perhaps at age three to five, the young would-be father slayer felt he knew what he would do with the prize of such a glorious victory (he would be with her always, cuddle with her, and take his father's place in the conjugal bed with her); but at age 20, 30, or 40, he no longer wants her once he wins her, should he ever – whether accidentally or inadvertently – win her.

It should be kept in mind that, although such obsessive love triangles are currently most common among men, they can also be found among women, many of whom are hardly strangers to obsession.

Let us turn now to hysterics and their triangles.

Hysterics in Love

There are certain women, Freud tells us, who are especially attuned to any expression by their beloved of even the slightest interest in another woman (the prime example he gives is that of the witty hysteric in *The Interpretation of Dreams*).[6] Should he seem to appreciate, esteem, or compliment a woman he knows from work or some other context and express this in even the most tepid of terms, a chain reaction is set off: our lover becomes jealous – sometimes insanely so – and insistently inquires about this woman, seeking to discern what her beloved could possibly see in her. (Just as certain women are no strangers to obsession, certain men are no strangers to hysteria, and one can thus find such acute attunement to expressions of the partner's interest in another in both men and women, in heterosexual and homosexual couples alike.)[7]

The question that spurs the female hysteric on is, according to Lacan, "How can another woman be loved?"[8] – in other words, how can this man, who professes to love *me*, find something to love in another? He claims to be well satisfied with me and yet along comes someone who is *nothing* like me and he finds plenty to praise in her! This proves that I am no longer the be-all and end-all of his existence – I must find a way to reclaim my rightful place.

"How can another woman be loved?" might be more colloquially formulated as, "What's she got that I ain't got?" Perhaps if I study her carefully and get to know all about her, I can fathom her secret, plumbing simultaneously the secret cause of this unsuspected desire in my beloved.

It is not terribly difficult to discern a parallel here with the little girl's question: "Why does Daddy love Mommy more than me?" (after all, he shares his bed with her, not me, and he talks with her about my misbehavior but not with me about hers).[9] What does he see in her? What can she give him that I can't? One of the classic answers is a baby, explaining at least in part little girls' interest in baby dolls, which they imagine to be babies they have had with Daddy.

Just as a little girl may observe her mother to learn how a woman must walk, talk, dress – in short, be – in order to attract Daddy, the hysteric becomes fascinated with the infamous "other woman"

to learn what she must do and how she must act to captivate her
beloved. Her fascination with this other woman at times goes so far
as to easily surpass her interest in her beloved.

Women who can charm her man (and perhaps enchant other men
as well) sometimes become so intriguing to the hysteric that the man
himself becomes secondary – no more than a vehicle, vertex on a triangle, or traffic sign that points her desire in a certain direction. She
begins to emulate these alluring women. Without thinking about it
in most cases, she finds herself becoming like them in certain ways,
even in ways that are of no interest whatsoever to her partner. She
may well become fixated, for example, on clothing, hairstyles, and
body shapes that are not attractive to him and that even turn him
off.

Women's preoccupation in recent decades with a look that has
been fostered in the media by fashion designers and photographers
for the most part – skeleton-like thinness – has rarely, if ever, been
appreciated by the kind of men who are actually excited by women.
A vast swath of the current female population seems to have come
to believe that, since such undernourished women were finding
their way to the covers of magazines, men must find such boniness
glamorous and attractive, failing to realize that the fashion industry
has long been dominated by men who are *not* especially attracted
to women (and who are often even disgusted by the mature female
figure, especially insofar as it differs from a prepubescent boyish
figure). Men who *are* sexually attracted to women, like the husband
of the witty hysteric in Freud's early example, generally prefer fuller,
more feminine forms to boyish figures.

Try as a man might to convince a hysterical partner that, although
he finds certain women in their entourage vaguely interesting in one
way or another, he is not turned on by their thinness, she may nevertheless latch onto their shape as something to imitate – after all, can
he be trusted when he says he does not find that appealing? Perhaps
he is just saying that to mollify me. Isn't that the most obvious,
visible difference between them and me? Perhaps he does not know
his own mind and will find himself inexplicably drawn to me if I
become thin like them.[10] In any case, it is not the specific qualities or
personality traits of the other woman that are so important to her;
what is crucial is her *structural position* as someone who finds a way
to elicit a desire in a partner whose desire may well be experienced
by the hysteric as flagging if not altogether dead.

Now what happens if the hysteric's love triangle collapses? Recall
that the obsessive who inadvertently succeeds in breaking up the
Other man's relationship – or who witnesses the splitting up of the
couple through no doing of his own – suddenly has no more use for

the woman of his purported dreams than a fish for a bicycle. Unless there is a chance of her getting back together with her partner, in which case the regular intervention of the former partner can fuel the obsessive's continued interest. What happens if the hysteric's partner loses all interest in the other woman? Will the hysteric feel triumphant at having bested her rival? Perhaps momentarily, but it is likely that she will seek to discern an interest in yet another woman on her partner's part, failing which she may go so far as to introduce a new woman to her partner in the hope of eliciting a desire in him that she may then explore.

For when there is no desire in her partner to excavate, she feels that he is dead – and then she might as well be too. Desire is, as Spinoza tells us, the essence of humankind,[11] and we must ever be looking for something or engaged in a quest of some kind. Just as the obsessive must always have a rival rendering his desire impossible, the hysteric must always locate a desire in her partner for something outside of or beyond herself, suggesting that he is dissatisfied or suffers from a lack of satisfaction. If he wants something it must be, as Socrates would have it, because he feels that he does not have it and longs for it.[12] It is not enough if she detects a desire in him for something he does not have in a realm that does not involve her – work, sports, hobbies, or the like – for he will still be dead as concerns herself. If he does not have, or no longer has or expresses, a desire for something that involves or otherwise concerns her – as is very often the case, especially when the relationship has gone beyond the initial stages of infatuation – she may attempt to incite one in him.

It should not be thought that her goal, in detecting or eliciting such a desire in her beloved, is to satisfy him – to help him obtain, for example, whatever or whomever he wants – for once satisfied his desire would disappear and she would need to begin the whole process anew. He must continue to be wanting – feeling deprived of something – for it is his wanting that gives her a project and place in life.

She may consciously believe that his wanting troubles and frustrates her greatly, and that she would like nothing more than to be able to give him precisely what he wants (were such a thing even possible, but more on that later). Yet were she to do so, there would be nothing left to be desired, for him or for her. And a life without desire is to be avoided at all costs, for it is tantamount to nonexistence, death.

Hence, should she like nothing more than to give him what he wants (and it is not always clear that she does), she must frustrate this tendency in herself; she must resist her own temptation. She must frustrate her own want and leave unsatisfied her own desire. This is, in part, what leads Lacan to view the hysteric as characterized by unsatisfied desire, whereas the obsessive is characterized by impossible desire.

Note that the parallelism between obsession and hysteria is not absolute: whereas the obsessive is ostensibly interested in *another* man's woman, but is actually engrossed in rivaling with and undermining the Other man himself, the hysteric ostensibly seeks to divine the reasons for her *own* man's interest in another woman, but is actually more interested in unearthing the secret of femininity through this other woman so that she can become like her, thereby becoming the very essence of Woman. The obsessive wishes to defeat and replace the Other man, the hysteric to study, imitate, and become like the other woman – at times to the point of virtually falling in love with she whom the hysteric believes holds the secret of her own femininity.

Moreover, the obsessive does not select as his rival a man who seems to catch the fancy of the obsessive's pre-existing girlfriend or wife (his choice of a partner would then have been possible, not impossible), whereas the hysteric's quest involves the very woman who seems to catch the fancy of her pre-existing boyfriend or husband (or even father, as in the case of Dora, where Dora becomes fascinated with Frau K. who is the mistress of Dora's father).[13]

The Oedipal connection seems clear enough in both cases: in his rivalry with his father for his mother's affections, the boy undoubtedly attempts to grasp what his father has that he does not have that makes his mother prefer his father to him (the ability to earn money, physical strength, social status, a larger penis, a sense of humor, or whatever the case may be, assuming she *does* prefer his father to him) and may well strive to become a man like his father, if not more of a man than his father.[14] The girl, in her rivalry with her mother for her father's affections, similarly attempts to grasp what her mother has that she does not have that makes her father prefer her mother to her.

Although an obsessive may at times adopt a couple he encounters (to serve as parents, as it were) with whom he has no prior connection, and insert himself into it, in the majority of cases the man in the couple is already known to him – either as a friend, boss, or colleague. Indeed, he might never have paid a moment's notice to the woman in the couple had he not been in some way taken with the man.[15]

This friend, boss, or colleague morphs into a father-like rival for the obsessive, just as the other woman noticed by the hysteric's male partner becomes a mother- or sister-like rival for the hysteric. The obsessive is perhaps more likely to compete directly with his rival and the hysteric more likely to emulate or model herself on her rival, but their situations are similar in many respects. In both cases, while the desires of which they are aware revolve around someone of the opposite sex, the desires of which they are unaware revolve around someone of the same sex. And in neither case is much satisfaction found – or, rather, satisfaction is far more likely to be found in the rivalry with the person of the same sex than with the person of the opposite sex.

II

Freudian Conundrums

Love Is Incompatible with Desire

One may well wonder whether either of the triangles outlined in the previous chapter actually has anything whatsoever to do with love. Love for a woman seems, in the case of the obsessive, to be a thin disguise for rivalry with a man; and love for a man seems, in the case of the hysteric, to pale in comparison with fascination with another woman. For such obsessives, love – to whatever degree there can be said to be any – seems of little import compared to the desire for impossibility; for such hysterics, love seems to be eclipsed by the desire for unsatisfied desire.

Are love and desire incompatible? And if so, are they incompatible just for this particular segment of the population? Or are love and desire so different for everyone as to inescapably be at loggerheads? Could it be that this is actually no more than a semantic problem? How have we implicitly defined love and desire to arrive at this impasse? Not every language divides up the amorous sentiments in the same way as English – the Greek term "Eros" might be thought to include both love and desire, for example. Perhaps our conundrum here is no more than a chimera.

Let us consider first what Freud has to say about this conundrum, in papers where he distinguishes love (*Liebe*), as the kind of affection the child feels for its parents, from sexual desire.

"Where They Love They Do Not Desire"

It should be perfectly clear to you that where you find it easy to attain your desire you may be sure there is no love.

Capellanus, 1990, p. 149

Freud notes that certain men choose women as partners who remind them of their mothers, at least to some degree, selecting women whom they consciously or unconsciously believe will provide them with many of the same satisfactions they received as children from their mothers. He refers to this as "anaclitic object-choice," since the choice of life partner is determined by or based on ("anaclisis" literally means leaning up against, propped up by – hence, based on) the self-preservative or life drives – namely, the drives for nourishment, warmth, and care.[1] In such cases, the partner is chosen precisely because the man feels she will be like his mother was and take care of him in the same devotedly selfless fashion.

Such a partner is, as we can easily imagine, likely to be cherished, respected, and perhaps even obeyed. She is given a great deal of consideration, and may well be idealized, idolized, put on a pedestal, and considered saintly, no one else having in her whole body as much goodness as she has in her little finger (in the words of Jonathan Swift). Such a woman is loved as a young boy loves his mother, but sexual arousal with her is virtually impossible, Freud tells us, owing to the incest taboo.

How does the incest taboo enter the picture? The answer is quite complicated, insofar as several different scenarios are possible.

"Normal men" – of whom there are admittedly very few, in Freud's (1912/1957b) view – love their mothers but do not become sexually fixated on them as young children. These males' true sexual awakening (Freud's discussion of infantile sexuality in the *Three Essays* notwithstanding) does not occur until the massive hormonal changes accompanying puberty. As much as they may have loved their mothers as boys, the result of the incest taboo – in the form of the classical Freudian father who makes it clear to his three-, four-, or five-year-old son that he must give up his mother as his primary love object as she already belongs to the father – is simply the *repression* of their love for their mothers.

"Repression," let us recall, does not mean destruction. When one's love for someone is repressed, it becomes hidden – not only from everyone around one but even from oneself. Repression means that the love disappears, revealing itself only in disguised forms. One possible result of repressed love for one's mother is apparent dislike of one's mother, and it is a well-known fact that boys of five and over often manifest displeasure or even disgust when their mothers hug, caress, or coddle them, even when this does not occur in front of other people. Disgust is a sure sign of repression: we manifest outright disgust – as opposed to simple disinterest or avoidance – at the very things that interested and amused us most prior to repression.[2]

Another possible result of repressed love for one's mother is warm dreams or daydreams of women who are disguised mother-figures (they may have several traits or only a single trait of the mother's, like hair color, eye color, or a particular piece of clothing or jewelry); elementary school teachers and babysitters sometimes fill the bill here. A still later result is often the choice of a partner who unwittingly reminds the man in one or more ways of his mother (or of his sister, who may herself be like the mother).[3]

The crucial point here, however, for Freud, is that in the case of such "normal men" the incest taboo leads to the repression of love for the mother, but *it does not lead to repression of sexual desire* since sexual desire played little or no role in their early relationships with their mothers, blossoming only at puberty.

In other words, for boys who grow up to be "normal men," sexual desire for their mothers (or sisters) is never repressed because there was no sexual desire present at the time at which the major repressions in their lives occurred (that is, when the castration complex put an end to the Oedipus complex by around age five).[4] Later in life, such men can feel both love and desire for the same woman: the earlier love for the mother that went underground owing to the father's castration threat is now displaced onto a new woman, and there is no obstacle that would stop the sexual strivings that originated at puberty from electing this very same woman as a sexual object. In such cases, the affectionate and the erotic currents are able to fuse (Freud, 1912/1957b, p. 180) and flow toward the same person. There is no necessary either/or for such "normal men" as regards love and desire.

What is the result of the incest taboo in the other ninety-some-odd percent of men? Sexual stirrings of one kind or another (oral, anal, and/or genital) began for them *before* the incest taboo was driven home to them – that is, before they gave up their mothers – and those stirrings became associated with their mothers. This regularly occurs, as Freud was the first to publicly state, because it tends to be the mother who cares so extensively for the child's body, breast-feeding him, wiping his tushy, washing him, and so on. In doing so, she touches and inevitably stimulates many different sensitive parts of the child's body (the erogenous zones and the skin in general), and sensations in his body thus become associated with her movements, gestures, and caresses. (Not every mother cares for her child's body lovingly, however – some do it only reluctantly, perfunctorily, gruffly, or disgustedly.) The boy's earliest sensual sensations thus become associated with his mother.[5]

Freud hypothesizes that there are two different categories of boys in this context: those who become only partially fixated on their mothers as sexual objects, and those who become totally fixated on their mothers as sexual objects. Those who become totally fixated will never, as Freud sees it, be able to feel both enduring love and sexual desire for one and the same woman. Many practitioners will concur that they have encountered such males in their clinical practice, but Freud's explanation for it seems opaque in certain respects. For if, in the case of such boys, both love and sexual desire for the mother are repressed when the Oedipus complex is brought to a close, why can't the sexual desire that is repressed be displaced onto the same woman onto whom the love that is repressed is displaced (as we saw earlier in the case of "normal men")? Is the effect of repression different upon love than it is upon sexual desire? Freud's answer seems to be a resounding "Yes!"

His contention might be formulated as follows: the boy did not make anything in particular of his wishes for sensual contact with his mother until he learned where babies come from. Knowing nothing of sexuality, he did not think of his mother as a sexual being, nor did his own wishes for physical closeness with his mother seem anything but perfectly innocent to him – or, rather, they simply were what they were, as he did not yet have any notion of corruption or depravity to contrast with innocence. But once he finds out about sex – and this is, in Western culture, almost always accompanied by the idea that sex is "dirty," "bad," or "naughty" – and realizes that his mother must have had, and perhaps even continues to have, sex with his father, something momentous happens. He learns facts of capital importance, and like Adam and Eve in the Garden of Eden, the notion of something like a state of innocence (involving ignorance of sexual matters) is born at the very moment that he loses his innocence by eating of the fruit of the Tree of the Knowledge of Good and Evil.

The boy suddenly realizes that the sensuous feelings he has for his mother are not "good clean fun" or innocent; they are dirty and wicked. Prior to this realization, "clean" and "dirty" applied primarily to the absence or presence of urine, feces, and vomit. Now they begin to apply – at least in a great many Western households – to virtually all sensual experiences. Not just his own: his mother's too.

His mother falls off a pedestal that did not exist prior to this realization. The notion that there are two different classes of women in the world suddenly begins to take shape in his mind: the class like his mother before the Fall – before the boy grasped her sin of preferring his father to him (her granting his father that kind of close physical contact being tantamount to disloyalty, in his eyes) – and the class like his mother after the Fall, the kind who are capable of cheating on him with another man. (We thus have two different images of the boy, too: before the realization, a kind of utopian, innocent, pure, loving, altruistic, asexual image – even if not true; after the realization, a kind of fallen, depraved, selfish, exploitative image.)

The mother herself thus serves as a model for both categories of women: the mother the child believed to grant no particular sensual privilege to the father over himself – let us call her mom$_1$ – is the model for the good girl (or Madonna, as Freud puts it); the sinful mother who betrayed her commitment to her son – we will call her mom$_2$ – is the model for the bad girl (or whore).[6]

The bigger the imagined commitment, the harder the fall. The larger the son's illusion of his mother's absolute fidelity to him (an only child or only son may believe very strongly in such fidelity), the greater his sense of betrayal. Insult is added to injury if he sees that his mother sides with his father in the latter's will to untie their son from her apron strings. The more the boy believed she loved him above and beyond anyone else, appearances to the contrary notwithstanding, the more radical the split between the two kinds of women in the world. Freud postulates that, from that time forward, the boy's affectionate current – love and tenderness – runs only toward the mythically pure, faithful mother (the Madonna, the loyal girl next door), while the sexual current runs only toward the fallen, sinful mother (the unreliable, trampy girl from the wrong side of the tracks). The notion of betrayal might suffice to explain why he can henceforth only *love* someone he considers to be like mom$_1$; but I do not believe it explains why he can only be sexually interested in someone like mom$_2$, for we might well imagine he could no longer be sexually interested in any woman at all (or, indeed, love any woman at all). Freud perhaps believes that the incest taboo explains the exclusive sexual interest in mom$_2$; if so, Freud presumably assumes that the boy interprets his father's castration threat as forbidding sexual contact only with mom$_1$-like women. What is clear is that, to Freud's mind, mom$_1$ and mom$_2$ can never be united in any one woman. Where such a man loves, he does not desire, and vice versa (Freud, 1912/1957b, p. 183).

Few would contest that a great many men categorize women into these two widely divergent classes and pursue very different kinds of relationships, often simultaneously, with the women in these two perceived classes. But they may well wonder whether, in our twenty-first-century families – which tend to be somewhat less prudish about sexual matters than Freud's turn-of-the-century Victorian milieu – the sexual fall of the mother is a plausible explanation for this widely acknowledged social phenomenon. Aren't children today aware of sexual matters much earlier than they were in Freud's time? Don't modern-day children realize from a very early age that their parents have sex? There is perhaps a degree to which it is a class issue, just as it was in Freud's own time: many members of families of modest means may sleep all together in one bedroom,

children in such situations witnessing sexual acts more or less unin-
terruptedly from birth onward.

Perhaps there has never been such a sharp Madonna/whore division for boys raised in such modest circumstances, or perhaps a
similar division comes about due to an emotional, as opposed to
a sexual, fall from grace: the boy perhaps initially believed that his
mother preferred him to all others in almost every respect, and feels
betrayed when he perceives that she aligns with his father's will to
get him to stop hiding behind his mother's skirts and grow up and
be a man.

I say this because we continue today to find the same rescue
fantasy in many a man that Freud observed a century ago: that of
saving a woman who has lost her way; although at her core she is
fundamentally good and pure, he believes, the slings and arrows
of outrageous fortune have reduced her to drinking, taking drugs,
working as a stripper or lap dancer, or even prostituting herself. The
fantasy here seems to be – as in Freud's time – that of turning mom$_2$
back into mom$_1$.[7]

Could there be another reason for such a sharp division? Freud's
theory of the Madonna/whore split precedes any extensive discussion on his part of the castration complex (despite a few early
mentions of it)[8] as putting an end to the Oedipus complex by
confronting the boy with a choice: either he gives up his attachment to his mother or his father will cut his penis off and he will
consequently lose all the gratifying sensations he derives from it.
Bluntly stated, either he gives up his primary love object or he
loses virtually all possibility of sexual satisfaction, love and sex
being weighed against each other in the balance, one of which must
be found lacking.[9] If he obstinately refuses to give up his mother
as the elective object of his love, he loses his capacity for sexual
gratification with women. (He need not literally have his penis cut
off to be emasculated for all sexual intents and purposes – he may
simply become incapable of performing or enjoying himself sexually with women.) If, instead, he stubbornly clings to his penis, he
gives up his primary love object and the question would seem to
arise whether he can ever hope to love again, and if so perhaps not
a woman but only a man like the one who imposed such a categori-
cal choice upon him.

Stated thusly, the Freudian father's castration threat might be
understood by certain boys to constitute an either/or regarding
love and sex, as opposed to simply requiring them to transfer their
love for their mothers onto other females like her. And this brings
out the degree to which it is not so much the exact words the father

(or father substitute) uses that count, but how they are interpreted by the son. The father's intent may be to convey to his son that he must seek out a woman of his own, yet the son may take it as a prohibition of all love for women or even as a prohibition of all love, period.

This possible explanation of the cleavage between love and desire clearly involves no fall on the mother's part. The great divide arises owing to the father's perceived castration threat, which may be understood by the child literally or figuratively – that is, as a loss of the real, physical organ or as a loss of the father's esteem and love.

Setting aside for the moment the more extreme cases, what we see quite commonly is that two different categories of women become well established in men's minds. A man may fall in love with a "good girl" and treat her well, as they say, but he is likely to see her as virtually *untouchable*. Apart from the occasional kiss on the cheek, holding of hands, or grazing of her hair as he helps her into her coat or car, he treats her as though she were sexually off-limits. Similarly, although he can bear certain signs of affection she shows him, he prefers not to see any signs of sexual arousal in her.

For a man who anaclitically chooses a life partner (we will turn to the other major type of object-choice Freud introduces, narcissistic, in the second part of this book, concerning the imaginary), it takes three to love, insofar as his mother is intimately involved in the match – even if his mother never meets his wife or is no longer alive. His wife begins where his mother left off; indeed, she is nothing more than a younger version or reincarnation of his mother in his eyes.

Many men may object that they themselves did not choose a spouse on such an anaclitic basis, but Freud argues that a man often *turns his wife into a mother figure* as time goes on. As different from his own mother as she may have seemed at the outset, in the space of a few months, years, or even decades, he ineluctably seems to cast her ever more in the role of mother – especially if she has become the mother of his children – and to view her as he viewed his own mother. (In my thirty years of analytic practice, the absolutely most common slip of the tongue I have heard made by men involves saying "mother" when they consciously meant to say "wife"; saying "sister" instead of "wife" would probably come in second.) Thus, even a man who selected a woman whom he believed to be as unlike his mother as could be, and who found his partner sexually exciting for several or even numerous years, sooner or later begins to feel about his wife much the way he felt about his mother. Although perhaps initially thinking of his partner as not a terribly "good girl," if not altogether a "bad girl," he gradually begins to act toward her as though she were some kind of untouchable figure.

Should he, nevertheless, attempt to make love to her – perhaps out of a feeling of duty or nostalgia – he is likely to discover that he cannot achieve or maintain an erection with her without fantasizing about other women, looking at porn prior to or even during the sexual act, or taking "performance-enhancing" medications. He may seek to blame this on his advancing age or some physical condition, and the medical establishment – eager to sell him drugs – encourages him to believe this. In general, however, he has no problem achieving and maintaining erections during his dreams at night (during REM sleep), nor has he any such problem when looking at pornography or seducing a woman he does not love. In other words, his impotence – or "erectile dysfunction," as people prefer to call it nowadays to make it sound more antiseptic, no doubt, even if physicians inadvertently alighted upon a medicalized euphemism whose abbreviation, ED, points with poetic justice to oEDipus – is all in his head, he having mentally transformed the woman who shares his bed into his mommy.

He can feel love for her, but not sexual desire. Love and desire seem to operate on different planes for him, planes that are worlds apart.

"Where They Desire They Do Not Love"

[Alcohol], sir, it provokes and unprovokes: it provokes the desire but it takes away the performance.
                                    Shakespeare, *Macbeth*, II. iii. 29–30

Although such a man may feel sexual desire for the "wrong kind of woman" or a "bad girl" – and she may qualify as bad simply because she is willing to engage in an extramarital affair with him, in other words, is willing to transgress moral and/or legal boundaries – he is not likely to ever come to love her, love being reserved for the trustworthy, loyal wife.

Hence the self-deception we see in many a woman who sleeps with another woman's husband: much as she would like to believe that the man's attachment to her is so strong that he will leave his wife for her, his attachment to his mistress is primarily erotic and he cannot be truly said to love her.

Where he desires, he does not love, and never the twain shall meet. The usual configuration of love and desire for such men is as follows:

1. The right kind of woman (a woman of his own bourgeois class, says Freud, referring to the social class of the majority of his patients at the time): love possible, desire impossible.
2. The wrong kind of woman (a woman of a lower social class): desire possible, love impossible.

Should such a man shrug off social conventions and *marry* the wrong kind of woman, choosing desire over love, he has to be vigilant lest she gradually grow into the role of "the right kind of wife" – the kind after whom he cannot lust. He must continually *debase* her in his mind, and perhaps verbally as well, so that she never seems worthy of esteem like his mother.[10] She may be willing to go along with this by role-playing the bad girl during sex, but the more it is transparently "playing," the less convincing it will be to his libido.[11] Things work out for him only as long as love and desire are kept separate, love being discarded.[12] Naturally, this may be less than satisfying to her![13]

Freud's (1912/1957b) conclusion regarding men is as follows: "Anyone who is to be really free and happy in love must have surmounted his respect for women and have come to terms with the idea of incest with his mother or sister" (p. 186). It would seem, in other words, that a man must stop putting women on a pedestal, stop seeing them as Madonna-like figures, for in such cases he cannot desire them sexually.[14] The second part of Freud's sentence would seem to suggest that a man must come to terms with the fact that sexuality with a woman always involves some incestuous component; and incestuous impulses invariably appear in every analysis, assuming it is taken far enough, whether or not there has ever been direct sexual contact between siblings or between parent and child.

If we bring together several of Freud's formulations, then, a man's love and desire can converge on one and the same woman, perhaps even durably, if and only if (1) his feeling of having been betrayed by his mother has been worked through; (2) he is no longer shocked that he might be inhabited by sexual desire for his mother and sister(s) and has seen through the incest taboo insofar as he realizes there is something incestuous involved in his relations with every woman; and (3) has come to grips with castration, that is, has allowed himself to be separated from his primary source of jouissance as a child without constantly striving to get it back. How any of these, much less all three, could be accomplished without a thoroughgoing analysis is hard to imagine!

On Women, Love, and Desire

It is difficult for a woman to always burn with passion for one
and the same man.

Ovid, The Art of Love, I. 328

Anne Elliot: We certainly do not forget you, so soon as you
forget us. [. . .] All the privilege I claim for my own sex (it is not a
very enviable one, you need not covet it) is that of loving longest,
when existence or when hope is gone.

Austen, 2003, pp. 219–22

It is often said that women are more easily able to love and desire
the same person than men are. Is there any truth to this old saw?

In the same paper by Freud that I have been discussing here,
regarding the supposedly "Universal Tendency to Debasement in
the Sphere of Love," Freud (1912/1957b) says that women have
little need to debase their sexual object (p. 186). The only explanation he provides for this is that women do not overvalue men the
way men overvalue women, turning them in their minds into ideal,
Madonna-like figures. Why women do not do so, Freud does not
say. But given what we postulated earlier about the mother's fall
from grace, we can hypothesize that, to Freud's mind, a girl's father
does not fall from grace in the same way as a boy's mother does.

And yet, when a little girl discovers where babies come from,
we might expect to find the same shock in her at learning that her
father has sex with her mother as the little boy has at learning that
his mother has sex with his father. Is it the existence of a double
standard in society, whereby men are not expected to be virginal,
whereas women are (or at least were), which accounts for the difference? Perhaps for a part of it, but wouldn't it still be possible for
the daughter to feel her father has betrayed her by having sex with
her mother, whereas the daughter thought she herself was the most
special to her father (appearances to the contrary notwithstanding)?
Why wouldn't there be, in her case, a faithful father before the fall
(dad$_1$) and a faithless father after the fall (dad$_2$)?

Must one conclude that girls are less likely than boys to dupe
themselves into believing they are preferred over everyone else by
the parent of the opposite sex? The very existence in our culture of
a term like "Daddy's little girl" would seem to contradict this. And
the often encountered project undertaken by hysterics to prop up
"the weak father" would seem to suggest an earlier belief in some
kind of ideal, strong father.[15] An analogy could be drawn here
between the male rescue fantasy (turning mom$_2$ back into mom$_1$)

and the hysteric's wish to restore the weak father to his earlier strong state.

If there is any truth to Freud's claim that women have little need to debase their sexual object, it can perhaps be located in the fact that the father is rarely the young girl's first love object – the mother is. It took Freud some years and prodding by female colleagues to realize that the primary love object for both boys and girls is the primary caretaker, who even today usually is the mother; she is, after all, generally the one who has the lion's share of physical and sensual contact with the children, holding, bathing, feeding, and changing them.[16] The shift of love for the mother to the father that often occurs afterward is hardly straightforward and may be only partial. As Freud described it in his later works (1931/1961c and 1933/1964, Chapter 33), this transition is accompanied in many cases by considerable hatred for the mother. The reasons given for this hatred are numerous, including having breastfed her daughter too little, having deprived her of all kinds of care and pleasure, being responsible for her lack of a penis, and the list goes on and on (1931/1961c, p. 234).

Without going into the relative truth or falsity of these reasons, it seems that as a girl's anger focuses on her mother, she turns away from her and directs her love to her father. The mother is vilified and the father loved.[17] Having begun later in time, her love for *him* has never been subject to two distinct moments or stages: one of innocence – Dad being viewed as perfect – and one of betrayal and depravity.

Now, contradicting Freud's claim that women have little need to debase their sexual object, thus ostensibly skirting the love versus desire divide, is what I will call the "bad-boy phenomenon." This is something Freud either did not see due to a theoretical oversight or bias, or because it did not exist in his milieu a hundred years ago in Vienna. Nevertheless, I would argue that it has existed for at least two centuries, if not considerably more, unless Jane Austen invented *Northanger Abbey*'s Captain Tilney and *Pride and Prejudice*'s George Wickham out of thin air, which strikes me as highly unlikely. Stendhal himself – a good, albeit highly neurotic, boy – complained in 1822 about women's fascination with the bad boys of his time: "One must dare all things with women. Where General LaSalle fails, a foul-mouthed captain sporting a mustache succeeds" (Stendhal, 2004, p. 79/82).[18]

Such "bad boys" – whether yesteryear's undignified, insolent soldiers with mustaches or today's slightly unshaven, unkempt boys with or without earrings and tattoos – presumably do not fit the mold of women's own idealized father figures, and generally show little respect for propriety or for the women they approach. (They at least seem to have, in Freud's previously cited words, "surmounted [their] respect for women.") They want what they want and make no bones about it: they do not pretend that they want love when they want sex, or that they want a long-term relationship when what they want is some quick fun and excitement.

Such boys do not treat women like princesses the way their fathers may well have: they take liberties with them instead of showing them consideration. Does a woman who is fascinated by such disrespectful boys love them, desire them, or both? It would seem that she primarily desires them, and that there must not be much resemblance between her *beloved* father and a man for whom she can feel sexual *desire*. (Unless, of course, bad boys are simply new editions of her own bad-boy-like father who treated her cavalierly and was not a terribly idealizable figure in the first place . . .) Bad boys are more stereotypically masculine, exciting, transgressive, and anything but safe; they are not the kind of boys one is supposed to be with. Such a guy is generally considered to be more experienced sexually than the woman and in no wise interested in being her best friend; the relationship with him is usually a struggle, the woman often thinking she can somehow change him.

Perhaps many a woman, too, cannot so easily love and desire in the same place, cannot so easily love and desire the same object. To be sexually excited, she has to be with the wrong kind of guy, a guy who has been around the block several dozen times, and who does not treat her like a precious jewel the way her father did, for the latter would lead to love, not desire. He must not gaze at her deferentially or reverentially, but rather insolently and lustfully. (Paradoxically, having found such a guy, she may then unwittingly seek to elicit a manifestation of love from him that she would not even want if she received it.)

I shall return to a woman's fascination with bad boys in Chapter 7, but what should already be clear is that she is thrilled by the bad boy's desire for her but likely to be turned off if he eventually declares that he is in love with her. Should she get involved with him in some ongoing way, she will prefer that he give her few if any signs of love, reserving those, if he has any to give, for his mother or grandmother.

Having established that she prefers that he desire rather than love her, we have to wonder what this does for her: does it allow her to desire without any concern about becoming attached to or dependent on him? For attachment might lead her to want to take care of him or prop him up the way she did with her own father. Does it allow her to love him with impunity – in other words, with no chance of being loved in return and hence no trepidation about her love being reciprocated? Or does being desired by him simply make her feel that she is in the precise position she would like to be in with regard to a man and that all is well with the world?

If any of the above apply, and this bad boy begins to profess love for her and expresses a wish to be with her always – proving that his bad-boy stance was (at least in the realm of relationships) merely an act – we might expect to see her adopt a strategy of debasing him in order to be able to go on desiring him. She may feel compelled to make it clear to him, for example, that she finds him beneath her, insufficiently cultured, educated, or successful – in short, not at all a suitable life partner for someone like herself.

Should he persist in loving her, he may degenerate from bad boy into "boy toy" (a less pejorative term than "gigolo," cf. *Breakfast at Tiffany's*), and soon find himself replaced. For certain women, love and desire may be as difficult to reconcile as they are for the obsessive men described earlier.

Although Freud (1912/1957b) did not cast his discussion of women in terms of a love/desire divide, he himself recognized that all is not perfect in the realm of women's desire, for, according to him, women often need there to be a prohibition or "forbiddenness" (p. 186) to get sexually aroused. They can only become truly excited if, for example, they make love in public places where it is not allowed and where there is a risk of getting caught. (French cinema has made a great deal out of this for decades.) Sex in the marital bed is simply boring to them. The mistress of one of my patients was most turned on when she had sex with him in the basement of the church at which her husband worked. It was not enough for her to be cheating on her husband: she had to do it in a church, right under his very nose, and at a time when someone might well walk in and catch her in the act!

For such women, there is, according to Freud, a certain structural condition of desire involving interdiction.[19] As we see here, Freud emphasizes the unsuitability of the situation, whereas the bad-boy phenomenon emphasizes the unsuitability of the partner.

Too Little

Privation is the cause of appetite.

Hélisenne de Crenne, 1538/1996, p. 58

Why do such women need there to be a prohibition? Freud suggests that sexual restrictions placed on girls in our society are so much more extreme and long-lasting than those placed on boys that women become used to suppressing sexual excitation and not satisfying their sexual urges. Hence they need something more than the usual stimulus to become aroused. The presence of a partner who is interested in them may not be enough.

This is related to Freud's larger point about the suppression of the sexual drives in general in society. As he sees it, the education of children, which is supposedly designed to turn them into civilized, productive members of society, leads to the paring down of sensual sensations from the entirety of the body to the more limited erogenous zones. Moreover, it directs us to choose only certain partners instead of all possible available partners, and to approach these partners in only a limited number of ways.

The upshot, to Freud's way of thinking, is that the "education" or socialization of our bodies occurs only at great cost to ourselves, that cost being a considerable "loss of pleasure" (Freud, 1912/1957b, pp. 189–90). He assumes, in a sense, the existence of a mythical moment in time where the infant could experience a kind of "full pleasure," including enjoyment from all parts of its body and all available objects ("polymorphous perversion," as he calls it). Weaning, toilet training, and the prohibition of autoeroticism, homoeroticism, and incest are such that, after early childhood, our pleasures can never again be full, total, or complete – and it is not by simply espousing "free love" that they can become so. Civilization is self-defeating to some degree in this respect: a fundamental loss of what Freud calls satisfaction and what Lacan refers to as "jouissance"[20] is imposed upon us by it.

Since human beings, Freud goes on to tell us, find it hard to deal with such a loss of satisfaction, they try to recoup some of it: they attempt to heighten their pleasure by crossing barriers and contravening prohibitions. Transgressing social mores and even legal strictures (involving where and when sex takes place or what goes on in terms of positions, domination, degradation, force, and even brutality) provides many women a kick they are unable to achieve in other ways, allowing them to obtain a kind of substitute "sexual" satisfaction otherwise unavailable to them. This kick has little if anything to do with love.

Too Much

The only real pauper [is he] who went through life and never felt a need for anything!

Kierkegaard, 1847/1995, p. 10

According to Freud (1912/1957b), it is clear that, even more generally speaking, something is rotten in the State of Eros (or in *la carte
du tendre*):[21] "We must reckon with the possibility that something
in the nature of the sexual drive itself is unfavorable to the realization of *complete satisfaction*" (pp. 188–9). This might be viewed as a
forerunner of Lacan's famous claim that "there's no such thing as a
sexual relationship."[22]

Let us compare the explanation for this rotten Danish state we
have just examined, involving an ineluctable loss of satisfaction
brought about by education, with another way of viewing the
matter found in *Group Psychology and the Analysis of the Ego* – a
text written by Freud nine years after the last one we considered.[23]

Love and desire are not presented here as independent affections
or tendencies, the first deriving from our attachment to the person
who takes care of our earliest physical and emotional needs, the
second from the hormonal changes brought on by puberty. Instead,
love – "affectionate love," as he puts it here – is considered to result
from the inhibition of desire, which he refers to in this context as
"sensual love" and as "earthly love" (Freud, 1921/1955e, p. 112).

Taken by itself, sensual love, Freud claims,

> is nothing more than object-cathexis [that is, the investment of
> one's libido in someone else] on the part of the sexual drives
> with a view to directly sexual satisfaction, a cathexis [that is, an
> investment of libido] which expires, moreover, when this aim
> has been reached. (p. 111)

Libidinal investment in an object – namely, the buildup of excitation
related to someone – is considered to be short-lived here, disappear-
ing as soon as sexual satisfaction is achieved. In other words, when
sexual desire is satisfied, we are no longer interested in the person
with whom we satisfied that desire. (Consider, for example, the
number of men who leave a sexual partner as soon as they possibly
can after completion of the sexual act.)

According to Freud here, it is only by inhibiting or prohibiting
sexual satisfaction that a more enduring investment can be made
in someone. When real sexual satisfactions are thwarted, sexual
desire for that person gives rise to a kind of symbolic idealization
of him or her, leading to *an affectionate current which is secondary*,
not primary. Idealization of the partner and affectionate love itself
(we perhaps see the fullest expression of idealization in courtly love,
as we shall see in Chapter 7) thus involve endless deferral and sublimation of the sexual drives.[24] Affectionate love, which earlier in his
work was either anaclitic or narcissistic (we shall turn to the latter

of these in the second part of this book), here seems to involve idealization of the object, attention being paid to its spiritual merits as opposed to its sensual merits.

Love is not considered here to precede sexual desire, but rather to result from the inhibition of sexual satisfaction. It leads to far greater excitement about the potential sexual partner than would have existed without such inhibition. In other words, *restricted* sexual access to the partner intensifies sexual excitation, ultimately leading to greater sexual satisfaction than would have been possible otherwise.

Education or socialization channels the sexual drives so extensively into narrow pathways that they reach a feverish pitch and the sexual act becomes, in a certain sense, overvalued – this, Freud believes, is especially true of men. The idea here seems to be that the more a certain activity is inhibited or restricted, the more intense our desire for it becomes. As I have put it elsewhere, "prohibition eroticizes."[25]

In the so-called state of nature – which is a theoretical fiction, naturally – in which human beings purportedly behaved with each other just like animals do, the sexual drives were far less inhibited and sexual satisfaction simply was what it was: one of the few pleasures available to primitive mankind. It was, according to certain hypothetical accounts, easily available and thus not prized the way scarce resources generally are: it was not blown out of proportion; it did not lead to intense overvaluation of the sexual partner; nor did it lead to the experience of falling in love. Primitive man could never have said to himself what Freud's obsessive patient known as the "Rat Man" said to himself upon having intercourse for the first time: "This is glorious! One might murder one's father for this!" (1909/1955a, p. 201). This sounds more like an excess of satisfaction than like a loss of satisfaction!

Owing to education, sex leaves the realm of the basic animal instincts and gives rise to a whole art form: the whole set of courting and mating rituals developed by human beings over the past millennia. Freud foreshadows some of Lacan's comments on the courtly love tradition when he says that people create their own barriers to love so as to heighten its pleasures (1912/1957b, p. 187). "If sexual freedom is unrestricted," satisfaction is not full, by which Freud presumably means not as heightened as it can potentially be. In his view, prohibitions (which are expressed in words and thus symbolic, in Lacan's terms) and limitations intensify satisfaction.[26] Freud suggests that at least a certain amount of prohibition leads to greater overall sexual satisfaction,[27] and that where it is lacking, human beings are inclined to create prohibitions of their own "so as to be able to enjoy love" (p. 187) more than they would otherwise.

*

If these two Freudian theses regarding what is rotten in the State
of Eros sound like somewhat unlikely bedfellows, it is because they
are. They come from two different hypotheses that Freud formulates about the effect on sexual life of the education imposed upon us
by civilized society: one that emphasizes a loss of sexual satisfaction;
the other a gain. The second perhaps predominates less in Freud's
way of thinking than in Lacan's or Stendhal's.

III

Lacan's Reading of Plato's *Symposium*

Lacan's most sustained treatment of love from the symbolic perspective can be found in Seminar VIII, *Transference (1960–1961)*, where he devotes about half the academic year to an in-depth reading of Plato's most famous dialogue on love, the *Symposium*. Like many of Lacan's other seminars, Seminar VIII is so rich that one would be hard-pressed to summarize all of its intriguing points in any one book; I shall try to highlight just a few of them in this chapter, turning to more of them in Chapter 8.

But first I would like to make a number of comments about how he reads Plato's dialogue. His discussion of the *Symposium* does not in any way purport to be exhaustive. So much has been said about this one dialogue alone that he would obviously never be able to cover it all; and in any case it is not his purpose to read Plato in that manner. Lacan's way of reading a great many texts, especially literary texts, is not so much to find the author's so-called intended message as to uncover a hidden logic within the text – as he does in the case of Edgar Allan Poe's "The Purloined Letter" – or to use it as a springboard for thought, helping Lacan invent something new of relevance to psychoanalysis.[1]

So far is Lacan from seeking Plato's supposed "intended message" that he dispenses with the assumption that there is any singular truth or claim that Plato is trying to convey here, especially because the form Plato chose is dialogical, in the Bahktinian sense, allowing more than one voice to have its say. Indeed, we are faced, in the *Symposium*, with a cacophony of ideas about love, each vying for expression, and we must, in Lacan's view, take each seriously even as we see them being made fun of by various characters in the dialogue.[2]

Readers of Plato often assume that it is what Socrates says in a dialogue that represents the real truth of Plato's message, but Lacan reads the various speeches in the *Symposium* as a series of psychoanalytic sessions by one single individual, each of which is important in its own right, and each of which retroactively sheds light on the ones that preceded, even as it qualifies or contradicts them in a dialectical unfolding or meandering. Lacan emphasizes the importance of the twists and turns in the text, postulating that love might be understood to consist in the very twists and turns in the *Symposium* – just as the unconscious might be understood (Lacan, 2006a, p. 620) to consist in the twists and turns Freud felt obliged to make as he wrote *The Interpretation of Dreams*. (Freud complained to his friend Fliess that he could not write the book in any more straightforward a manner, feeling forced to proceed as he did by his subject matter.)[3]

Lacan pays close attention to each speech in Plato's dialogue, but still closer attention to the transitions and failed transitions between one speech and the next. When an analysand jumps from one topic to another as he or she free associates, the analyst attempts to discern the logic of the jump, the assumption being that although the analysand may not be aware of the why and wherefore of the next thought that came to mind, free association is anything but free. Jumps like this or failed transitions occur in the *Symposium* when, for example, Aristophanes has the hiccups, and cannot speak when it is his turn to do so; when Alcibiades bursts in drunk, changing the prior purpose of the party, which was to eulogize Eros, the god of love; and when Socrates, who has offered to sing the praises of Agathon, is interrupted by the arrival of revelers. Lacan also notes that when Socrates speaks in the guise of the wise woman Diotima, his usual elenctic method breaks down, and Plato resorts to a different kind of discourse – in particular, myth, the myth regarding love's peculiar parents, Poros and Penia (resource and poverty or lack) – to go further into the nature of love. Dialectic here seems to have to give way to myth, being unable to go any further under its own steam, so to speak.

There is no singular theory of love that grows out of Lacan's reading of the *Symposium* and indeed no singular theory of love in Lacan's work as a whole (which is not to say that he ever repudiates the theory he propounds in Seminar VIII, for I do not believe that he does). There are, in fact, so many different glosses on love in the course of his 50-year writing career that Jean Allouch (2009) devoted 600 pages to discussing each of them in turn. I will do nothing of the sort here, touching instead on just a few of them.

Love Is Giving What You Don't Have

Giving what you have is throwing a party, not love.

Lacan, 2015, p. 357

The first point I will highlight in Seminar VIII is Lacan's ostensibly paradoxical assertion that "love is giving what you don't have" (Lacan, 2015, p. 129), an assertion that explicitly contradicts Aristophanes' claim in Plato's *Symposium* (196e) that "you can't give to another what you yourself don't have." This "unprovoked denial" on Aristophanes' part probably made Lacan's ears prick up and he used it as a jumping-off point for his own thinking.[4]

If we begin with a couple involving a lover and a beloved – which is how male homosexual couples were often conceptualized in ancient Greece – the beloved is the only one in the couple who appears to *have* something, to possess something special and worthwhile. The lover, on the other hand, gives what he does not have: in a matter of speaking, he gives his lack of something, something he would be hard-pressed to account for or explain, for *he does not know what he is missing* (Lacan, 2015, pp. 39–40). He feels a lack or emptiness within himself, and a yearning for something to fill the hollow, to make up for his sense that he is missing something – this is the lack or gap from which desire springs.

In psychoanalytic terms, this lack obviously stems from symbolic castration: from the fact that we are required to express our needs in words, in a language not of our own making (Lacan calls this "alienation"), and from the sacrifice of satisfaction or jouissance each of us has had to make in being weaned, toilet trained, and separated from our primary source of satisfaction – our mothers in most cases. Strictly speaking, all human desire stems from this lack, this lack-in-being or want-to-be (*manque-à-être*), as Lacan puts it. Where there is no lack, there can be no desire.

Desire aspires to make good this lack, to compensate for it. And each desire for something new is but the continuation and displacement of the selfsame desire stemming from the same old lack; this is what allows Lacan (2006a, p. 623) to qualify the ceaseless unfolding and multiplication of human desires as the "metonymy of the want-to-be," as the continual displacement of the lack in being brought about by castration, wrought by our alienation in language and loss of jouissance. Each new "I want" is linked to this original lack by a shorter or longer series of displacements (or metonymic shifts). Someone who has never given up his or her primary source of satisfaction is not driven by a desire to fill a lack as are most of us who *have* given it up.[5]

Now this lack is precious to us. What we gave up defines us, we feel. It goes to the heart of our perceived individuality, to the core of our "subjective difference" – that is, to the core of what makes us different from everyone else. Thus, it is not with just anyone we meet that we are willing to say that he or she has something that corresponds to the lack in us! We may be protective, not wishing to show we feel lacking in any way, that we need anybody, that we are castrated. We may prefer to shroud ourselves in an aura of sublime indifference, and in certain cases that may get us loved by others, but it has nothing to do with we ourselves loving someone else. To love someone else is to convey in words to that person that we lack – preferably big time – and that he or she is intimately related to that lack. We need not suggest that he or she fills the bill in absolutely every respect, that he or she can *saturate* our lack one hundred percent. But we must reveal through speech *that* we lack and that our lack concerns him or her.[6]

In this way we give our lack, we give what we do not have, Aristophanes' claim that such a thing is impossible notwithstanding. Men in Western culture generally seem to have a harder time than women do admitting to lack, a harder time verbally admitting that they are missing something, incomplete in some respect, limited in some way – in a word, castrated. (The reader will, I hope, allow me to momentarily associate men with obsession here, and women with hysteria, in a way that vastly overgeneralizes things, in order to highlight something schematically at first.) I do not mean simply admitting that they do not actually know how to drive somewhere in particular or that they do not know some specific fact about something that has come up in a conversation – I mean a lack that is more far-reaching than that! To love is to admit to lack (Soler, 2003, p. 243), and Lacan even goes so far at one point – and here I am jumping ahead some 15 years in his work – to suggest that when a man *loves*, it is insofar as he is a woman (Lacan, 1973–4, class given on February 12, 1974). Insofar as he is a man, he can admit to *desiring* the so-called partial objects he sees in his partner, but he generally feels that perfectly good partial objects of much the same kind can be found in many different partners. Insofar as he is a man, he contents himself with the enjoyment he derives[7] from the partial objects he finds in a whole series of interchangeable partners, and avoids like the plague showing that he lacks.[8]

But unlike desire, "Love demands love," as Lacan (1998a, p. 4) puts it in Seminar XX; love insistently requests love in return. When one is fascinated by or lusts after a sexual partner, one's desire does not necessarily wither or disappear if one does not feel desired in return. Even if "desire is the Other's desire" (a claim often repeated by Lacan; see, for example, Lacan, 2015, p. 178), in the sense that we wish to be desired in return by the object of our desire, desire can do just fine without being requited. But "to love is to want to be loved" (Lacan, 2006a, p. 853): to love – at least in our times – is to implicitly ask the beloved for love that can make good or somehow compensate one for one's own lack, the hollow or emptiness one feels inside. In this sense, all love seems to constitute a request for love in return.[9] (In Alcibiades' case, this takes the form of a pressing *demand* for Socrates to prove that he returns Alcibiades' passion for Socrates.)[10] Since to love is to show and declare one's lack, love is feminine, as Colette Soler (2003, p. 97) says, following Lacan's statements to their logical conclusion.[11]

As a man, one might easily take umbrage at such comments – they are obviously essentializing, claiming that men are like this and women are like that – but Lacan tempers this by defining things the other way around: to his mind, anyone, regardless of anatomy or chromosomes, who is fixated on partial objects as found in any number of fungible partners, and loath to reveal any lack, is characterized by what he calls masculine structure (akin to obsession), whereas anyone, regardless of anatomy or chromosomes, who is primarily concerned, instead, with lack and love is characterized by what he calls feminine structure (akin to, although in no wise identical to, hysteria). Readers who are familiar with Lacan's work in the 1970s are aware that his definitions of masculine and feminine structure are even more precise than the ones I have just given. They are based on the kind of satisfaction or jouissance one may potentially experience: those who can potentially experience only what he terms "phallic jouissance" are characterized by masculine structure, and those who can potentially experience both phallic jouissance and what he refers to as "the Other jouissance" are characterized by feminine structure. I will not go into that complicated topic here, as I have discussed it at length elsewhere (Fink, 1995a, Chapter 8).

The point I would like to make here is that Lacan's essentializing primarily concerns two radically different forms of enjoyment, two radically different ways of getting off, as we say in the vernacular, and this leads to a rather different way of dividing up the sexes than the usual ones (insofar as it is based on jouissance, it is based on the real, not on the imaginary – *images* of what men and women are, for example – or the symbolic, that is, *ideas* about what women and men are or should be).[12] Freud, for example, insofar as he proposes something beyond the old saw that men are active and women are passive, sometimes talks about masculinity and femininity in terms of the multiple identifications that we each have with our different parents and thus with both sexes. Contemporary discourse has more of a tendency to talk about the social construction of gender and emphasizes sexual identity as something that is polyvalent, multilayered, and perhaps even a performance. Lacan's approach concerns neither identifications nor identities, but people's actual capacities for enjoyment. His notion that love is feminine might be thought to receive support in Plato's *Symposium* from the fact that everything Socrates offers about love is said to have been told him by a woman, Diotima, and she herself concludes that Socrates at first mistakenly "thought love was being loved, rather than being a lover" (204c) – in other words, that everything Socrates initially thought about love, before she instructed him, was tied to a masculine perspective wherein one wishes to simply receive love instead of to actively love by expressing one's own lack to someone else![13]

As I said earlier, to admit and verbally declare that we love is to admit that we lack. But this goes further still, for Lacan suggests that we in fact admit that we are lacking in some way whenever we open our mouths to say something. As infants we opened our mouths to convey that we were lacking in food, nourishment, warmth, or attention, and we learned to speak to express our wants in such a way that they would be less at the mercy of the interpretations of those who cared for us, for our caregivers could not always figure out what it was we wanted and their ministrations often left a great deal to be desired. All speech is a request or demand for something we are missing, or at least to be heard and recognized as missing something, as lacking in some respect. Ultimately, as Lacan puts it, all speech constitutes a demand for love. Whenever we speak, we are unconditionally asking to be heard (Lacan, 2015, p. 356), we are asking for our request to be recognized, we are asking to be responded to, we are asking to be loved.

This is one of the reasons why psychoanalysts must not speak too much during sessions, and should even avoid presenting themselves as the authors of the little they do say when possible, preferring to reiterate and punctuate the analysand's speech. They must not reveal much about themselves, for when they do they are essentially asking or even begging (Lacan, 2015, p. 370) to be loved, which puts the shoe on the wrong foot, as it were; this is one of the many reasons why self-disclosure is such a bad idea. As we shall see, it is not so much in order to refuse to admit to be lacking that analysts must not speak so much, for analysis structurally puts analysts in the position of loving the analysand, and that loving itself reveals their lack. Analysts must not speak much in their own names or talk about themselves *so as not to demand to be loved in return by their analysands*.

Now, insofar as all speech constitutes a request or demand for love and thus indicates that the speaker is lacking in some respect, men in our culture, not surprisingly, tend to be somewhat taciturn, not very loquacious around their partners in relationships. God forbid they should admit to lack! The very thing that their partners in love often most want from them, that men tell them how they love them and that they (like Elizabeth Browning) count the ways – this they are incapable of providing, not knowing, supposedly, what to say or how to say it. Men – insofar as they are men and not women – prefer acting to talking, prefer having sex to making love in the older sense of the English expression where making love meant speaking of love, poetically creating love – in a word, courting.[14]

Men's sexual *desire* for the partial objects that they perceive in their partner stems, they perhaps feel, from a kind of phallic fullness in themselves, a Nietzschean overflowing of some kind (like certain theologians, they perhaps associate lack with imperfection and fullness or overflowing with perfection). To admit to a lack would, they feel, put a serious crimp in their overflowing. Love and desire are often, for them, mutually exclusive, as we saw in the preceding chapter. Hence the divergence of the love object from the desired object, which often gives rise to what Freud referred to as "debasement in the sphere of love," and philandering in the sphere of relationships.

By declaring our love – articulating it aloud in words to our beloved – we give our lack. We declare ourselves to be missing something, to be lacking in being, to be wanting in something at the core of our very being; and yet we manage to thereby bestow being and a feeling of fullness on our partner. In this way, *we give the gift of what we do not have*. Indeed, we turn what we are missing over to another and ask that he or she handle it with care. We hope this other will not spurn our lack or trample it underfoot. Obviously some people are so afraid that the other will reject their lack-in-being or lacking being that they are loath to reveal it, to show it, to give it. This is tied to all the concerns with timing when it comes to declaring one's love, for to say, "I *love* you," is to say, "I lack and you speak to my lack." (It is not to say, "I lack and you complete me," as Hollywood prefers to say, vastly oversimplifying matters.) To say "I love you" is to say, "you bring out the lack in me" or "you are intimately related to the lack in me."

The beloved, too, generally views true love to be giving what one does not have: well-to-do parents who spend gobs of money on their children can easily afford to, and their children will hardly be inclined to take store-bought gifts or large allowances as proof of their parents' love for them. If, however, these same parents are very busy and have little time to spare, but they nevertheless give freely of their time to their children, the latter might well be inclined to view *that* as a sign of love. Giving what you have is easy – anyone can do it. Giving what you do not have is far more meaningful.

This is at least one way of talking about love as "giving what you don't have."[15]

Not Having and Not Knowing

The second point I will take up in Lacan's reading of the *Symposium* concerns the relationship between love and ignorance. In Seminar VIII, Lacan (2015) suggests that the lover is in search of something and yet does not know what it is; the beloved, on the other hand, is thought to have something by the lover, but the beloved does not know what he has that makes him loved by the lover (pp. 38–40). If the lover and the beloved have anything in common, it is that *neither one knows something* that seems to be of very great importance!

This mutual ignorance is perhaps one of the reasons why Lacan suggests that love is a comical feeling (pp. 33, 74, and 109).[16] In any case, he asserts that "there can be no discourse on love but from the point at which [one does] not know" (p. 131) – in other words, love and ignorance are intimately related. For perhaps there is no actual correspondence between what the beloved is believed by the lover to have and what the beloved believes he has. As Lacan puts it, "What the one is missing is not what is hidden in the other. This is the whole problem of love" (pp. 39–40).[17] Not the "whole problem," I would suggest, for many other problems seem to gravitate around love as well.

Let me try to take this problem a bit further than Lacan himself takes it by raising a question. Why do we care what it is we have that we are loved for, as long as we are loved? Isn't it because we do not want to be loved for something our partner might well find in a better form or greater abundance in someone else or in many other people? We do not want to be loved for our hair color if plenty of other people can be found with the same hair color, or for our height and figure, since so many other people probably fill the same bill. Being situated in the position of someone's beloved automatically makes us subject to comparison with everyone our lover might come into contact with. What do we have that those others do not have?

We are, willingly or unwillingly, cast onto the scale of comparison with all other potential beloveds. What we want is to be loved *not* for what can be found in other people besides ourselves (who may be as good-looking, accomplished, or successful as us), *not* for what makes us akin to other people, but for ourselves, for what makes us *different* from everyone else – in a word, for our "subjective difference."

Now, to want to be loved "for myself" raises a thorny question: what is the self, what is it that makes me different from everyone else?[18] What is this self, this highly individual soul or spirit, that I want to be loved for? In psychoanalysis, the answer would seem to have something to do with my unconscious, my symptom or symptoms, and my fundamental fantasy, the fantasy that is at the root of so many of my interactions with other people. In certain cases, this could even go as far as wanting to be loved for being essentially *unlovable*, disgusting, or repulsive (a lazy good-for-nothing or a turd). At the same time, my fantasy and symptoms usually are not things that I am especially proud of or willing to even accept in myself: I see them as my foibles or failings, if not my tragic flaws. So how could I stand to be loved by my partner for the unseemly things I can barely fess up to in myself?

Stated differently, *I want to be loved for the very thing about myself that I detest and wish to know absolutely nothing about.* I hope the paradoxical nature of this wish is plain. Imagine my likely ambivalent feelings for a partner who is willing to love what I hate in myself!

Whereas we often formulate the problem by saying that we hope to be loved in spite of our flaws, or, more colloquially put, warts and all, perhaps we more truly want to be loved precisely for our warts. And indeed, we must wonder if in our partners it is not so much their qualities that we love – we may admire those qualities and want to have those same qualities ourselves – but their flaws, symptoms, and unconscious.[19] Consciously we may abhor their failings, but perhaps they are what allow us to love them.

Can we, after all, love someone who seems to us to be perfect, someone who seems to us to *have* everything? Isn't it often the case that although we may be fascinated or captivated by someone who appears to have only good qualities, we only begin to love him or her from the moment we suspect that he or she is somewhat (if not deeply) unhappy, quite clueless about something, rather awkward, clumsy, or helpless? Isn't it in his or her nonmastery or incompleteness that we see a possible place for ourselves in his or her affections – that is, that we glimpse the possibility that we may be able to do something for that person, be something to that person? In this sense, we perhaps love *not* what they have, but what they do not have; moreover, we show our love by giving what we ourselves do not have.

Love as a Metaphor: The Signification of Love

The third point I would like to bring out in Lacan's reading of Plato's *Symposium* is the way in which love is structured like a metaphor. Among the Greeks, it seems that many men were far more concerned with expressing their love and desire for someone than with having their love reciprocated.[20] The positions of lover and beloved, the latter simply accepting the former's love, were well established in homosexual couples, where the lover was often an older, well-to-do man, and the beloved a handsome young man who was as yet relatively uneducated.

"The metaphor of love," as Lacan calls it, refers to the fact that, in certain cases, the beloved – that is, the person who had passively accepted his lover's attentions up until that point – suddenly became a lover himself, suddenly began to burn with passion for the man who loved him (Lacan, 2015, p. 40). Lacan says that this is when "the signification of love is produced," meaning that love is the "poetic or creative" signification produced by the substitution of the beloved for the lover.

One of the examples mentioned in Plato's *Symposium* is that of Patroclus and Achilles as described in Homer's *Iliad*. At the outset, Patroclus is the lover and Achilles is the beloved, according to Phaedrus:

$$\frac{\text{Patroclus is the lover}}{\text{Achilles is the beloved}}$$

Love is produced when the beloved in the relationship becomes a lover himself. Then the tables turn and the signification of love is produced:

$$\frac{\text{Achilles is the lover}}{\text{Patroclus is the beloved}}$$

Love here is a changing of places or a shifting of positions in a relationship. It was relatively easy for Achilles to demonstrate such a change in roles in the relationship, as Patroclus was already dead at that point, having been killed by Hector. But we see another example of this in the *Symposium*, for Alcibiades complains of Socrates that "he presents himself as your lover, and, before you know it, you're in love with him yourself" (222b). Although Alcibiades and other young men like him were reputed for their good looks, whereas Socrates was reputed for his ugliness, Socrates was clearly a master at transforming men, at bringing out the lack in them. Even as he claimed to be lacking in knowledge himself, he managed to point out the lack in others, turning them into lovers of knowledge – philosophers – lovers of knowledge that they believed he had, and this often led to them falling in love with him.[21]

We might even characterize this changing of positions as *the moral imperative of love*, along the lines of Freud's (1933/1964, p. 80) gnomic formulation "*Wo Es war, soll Ich werden*": Where the beloved object was, I must come into being as a lover. In other words, where I was content to be adored by someone else, I must come into being as a loving subject in my own right. Yet many people do not. Indeed, given the two radically different positions here – the lover and the beloved – we can imagine that love itself (apart from any possible "moral imperative of love") might well be characterized differently by people on the opposite sides of the divide:[22]

1.   For the lover, it is *loving itself* that is most important. Indeed, Freud hypothesized that the Greeks gave preference to the drive over the object, celebrating Love itself more than the beloved. This may have been true especially in Homeric times, for what seems primordial to the Greek gods in Homer's work is that they themselves love: it is their own passion and amorous intoxication that is of the utmost importance. By the time of the *Symposium* and Aristotle's discussion of friendship (some four centuries later), however, the object too is highly prized, and there are speeches that sing the praises not simply of Love itself, but of the beloved too.[23] Nevertheless, even in classical Greek times, people do not seem to have been as concerned as we are today with whether feelings were mutual between themselves and their chosen objects: it was the intensity of their own love that seems to have made them feel alive, feel they existed. (This may have been true of the courtly love tradition of the late eleventh to fourteenth centuries as well, as we shall see in Chapter 7.)

2.   On the other side, that of the beloved, love might be characterized differently; indeed, love might be characterized in the way Freud (1957c, pp. 88–9) depicted it for women, when he claimed they are like cats: they prefer to be loved than to love, they are wrapped up in their own narcissism and this is part of why others love them – their love for themselves shows the onlooker that they are worthy of love. Although Freud has been taken to task for this vast overgeneralization, many women obviously being quite interested in loving, it may have applied fairly

well to the position of the beloved in ancient Greece, where the essence of love was to be admired, worshipped, and loved by someone especially worthy. A concern with such adulation and love can be seen on a much grander scale in many celebrities of the silver screen, the political scene, and so on, who become disconsolate as soon as they feel they are no longer adored by the masses. Such adoration is so important to them that without it they feel they no longer exist.

It is, thus, only from the standpoint of those who are seeking mutual feelings, who wish to have their own love reciprocated, that the height of love is the transmogrification of the beloved into a lover.

The Greeks seemed to think that a man transitioned – albeit with separate partners – from being the beloved early in life to being a lover of boys later in life, thereby perhaps coming to love boys who are just like he was when he first became someone's beloved in his mid-teen years.

If we consider the change in positions involved in the metaphor of love from the standpoint of Lacan's (1998a) notion that love arises when there is a change of discourses,[24] we could hypothesize that the beloved who becomes a lover adopts a new discourse, insofar as he implicitly says for the first time that he is a divided subject ($) who is lacking in something and who sees the object he is missing (*a*) in the other.[25]

The Miracle of Love

> What we do not have seems better than everything else in all the world, but should we get it, we want something else.
>
> Lucretius, 1990, p. 43

The fourth point I will make here about Seminar VIII concerns what Lacan (2015) calls "the miracle of love." He formulates a sort of myth about how love comes into being: love arises, he proposes, when we reach out toward an object – the examples he gives here being a flower, fruit, or log in a fire – and another hand reaches out toward us (pp. 51–2, 179). Presumably the miracle is that our love is reciprocated, the beloved reaching almost simultaneously for us. Lacan comments that "it is always inexplicable that anything whatsoever responds to [love]" (p. 52), which is why we need a myth. In other words, we cannot explain how the miracle of love occurs, how the beloved changes positions and becomes a lover; all we can do is provide an image for it.

Note that in this image Lacan does not say that we are reaching directly for the beloved (though perhaps for an object metonymically related to the beloved?) or for the beloved's hand.[26]

Later in the seminar, Lacan indicates that the hand that extends toward the log in the fire must do so with its own warmth or heat so that the flame leaps from the object, setting the object afire, at its approach (pp. 388–9).[27] This warmth or heat is obviously the flame of desire: it is pure desirousness. This leads to one way of understanding the formula "Desire is the Other's desire" (p. 178): we begin to desire when we sense the other's desire for us. It is the other's desire for something in us, represented in the reaching out, that sets us ablaze for something in him or her, leading us to reach out in turn.[28]

This is, I believe, one of the things that allows Lacan (1998a, p. 4) to claim in Seminar XX that "love is always mutual" (which harks back to his earlier claim that "feelings are always mutual"),[29] his sense being that love does not fully emerge in one person until it has begun to emerge in the other, and that we desire in response to and as a function of the other person's desire. The Greeks might have begged to differ here. And certain obsessives might say it is just the opposite: they can fully love only when they are sure their love is impossible, when they are sure their love will be unrequited. (In such cases, it might well be desire they are feeling, however, not love.)

Lacan mentions the fear and trembling we experience, in our own times, before declaring our love when we are not sure the other is ready to respond in kind. A great deal is made of this in novels and films, where we see that each partner refuses to declare his or her love for the other until he or she is pretty sure the other in fact reciprocates, as if the worst thing imaginable were for love to be unrequited. In contemporary Hollywood films, this sometimes leads to both partners declaring their love for each other simultaneously. This may be a somewhat new obsession, and it is certainly not found in Homer's *Iliad*. It is probably related at least in part to some political-correctness sense about the equality between the sexes; one cannot be the pursuer and the other the pursued – that would be sexist. But I believe it corresponds to something else as well.

For my hope as a lover is that if I take the plunge and declare my burning love, the other's love will be aroused – just like a log that suddenly bursts into flames when I stir the fire. My fear is that I will declare my burning love and the other will be left cold and uninterested; I will have taken the risk of showing that I lack and the other will neither agree to be my beloved object nor love me in return. After all, what if Lacan is wrong and love is *not* always mutual? What if there really is such a thing as unrequited love?

To admit to my lack already wounds me narcissistically, but to then find myself unloved may call into question my very lovability. It may call into question the ideal image of myself as lovable that I carry around in my head, the ideal ego at the core of my sense of self, the ideal ego that I believe to be approved of by the Other (see Chapters 4 and 5).

The trembling of love, the anxiety and palpitations that love involves, revolve around the question whether I will be loved in return, that is, the question whether I am worthy of being loved – more worthy than someone else, more worthy than everyone else![30]

As psychoanalysts, it is not, of course, our job – even if certain therapists think that it is – to convince the analysand that he or she is worthy, to spur the reluctant analysand on to declare his or her love sooner rather than later, or to generally help improve the analysand's sense of timing in all things amorous. It is our job as analysts to get the analysand to come to grips with the *castration* that lies behind all declarations of love.

Love in the Analytic Context

The analytic cell, even if it is comfy and cozy, is nothing but a bed for lovemaking.

Lacan, 2015, p. 15

The fifth point that I will highlight in the *Transference* Seminar here concerns love in the psychoanalytic context. What appears to have been of the utmost importance to the Greek gods was that they themselves loved: it was their own passion that was primordial; they were not terribly concerned whether feelings were mutual between themselves and their chosen objects. Now isn't that true of the analyst as well? The analyst desires and loves, without hoping for any reciprocation, and is even suspicious of reciprocation, given how often love in the analytic setting is a form of resistance. It is often precisely when analysands most fervently declare their love for the analyst and the analysis that they do the least real analytic work!

As Lacan (2015, p. 193) puts it, analysis automatically places the analysand in the position of the beloved. The analysand, by speaking, demands to be found lovable, and we as analysts take the analysand as someone who is important and listen to him in a way that no one has ever listened to him before.[31] Like Socrates, we ask myriad questions of the analysand, questions to which he often has no answer or only a confused one. Like Socrates, we know almost nothing apart from the art of love – which in Plato's Greek, τὰ ἐρωτικά (*ta erotiká*) – is a play on *erôtan*, the art of asking questions. By asking the right questions, we highlight the lack in the analysand, who then comes to believe that we ourselves must have the answers since we have asked the questions. Although we cannot have the answers – we have no idea at the outset, and even for a very long time, why the analysand made the life choices he did, adopted the stance he adopted vis-à-vis his parents, teachers, fellow students, or partners – he nevertheless believes that we have the answers and are simply holding out on him. He does not find the answers in himself, for they are written in his unconscious and are as yet illegible and indecipherable, being inscribed in a language to which he does not have the key, dictionary, or Rosetta Stone. Not finding the answers in himself, he projects them onto us, and comes to love us as possessors of knowledge (much as Socrates' disciples loved him as someone whom they believed possessed knowledge that he nevertheless claimed not to have). For the analysand, we become the "subject supposed to know," as Lacan dubs it – the subject whom he assumes has the knowledge he is seeking.[32]

If the analysand becomes a lover, it is because he comes to believe that something in us corresponds to the lack in him. And like Alcibiades, he may even come to see still more in us, what Lacan calls object *a*, just as Alcibiades sees what he calls the precious, shiny *agálmata* in Socrates. Indeed, it is precisely these *agálmata* that first allow Lacan to formulate the notion of object *a* as we find it in all of his later work, the object that makes one person incommensurate with all others, nonfungible, irreplaceable.[33] Alcibiades says, "I had a glimpse of the figures (*agálmata*) Socrates keeps hidden within: they were so godlike – so bright and beautiful, so utterly amazing – that I no longer had a choice – I just had to do whatever he told me" (216e).[34] We analysts, however, realize that it is love for object *a* that we have managed to incite, not love for ourselves as living, breathing human beings with our own personalities. We do not seek to be loved "for ourselves" in analysis: we seek to set the analysand ablaze so that he will do the difficult work of analysis.

We ourselves are merely placeholders: placeholders of the knowledge inscribed in the analysand's own unconscious and/or placeholders of object *a* – that shiny, glittering, quintessentially fascinating thing Alcibiades saw in Socrates that raised the latter to a position of dignity above all other potential partners (it might be understood, in one sense, as desirousness itself).

If we are seeking to be loved by our analysands for ourselves, we end up feeling that we exist only or primarily by being loved by them. This occasionally happens to therapists who allow themselves to be paged, called, or otherwise contacted by their patients day and night, spending much of their time returning their calls. It may seem that such therapists are reassuring their patients, or even mothering them, but the therapists are the ones who are being propped up and made to feel important. It is not just "Love and the Single Analyst" that can be problematic, as it is in the film *Sex and the Single Girl* (1964); married or not, in a "committed relationship" or not, practitioners who are unhappy or feel unloved outside of the consulting room are likely to begin looking for love in all the wrong places.

Now, if "to love is to want to be loved," the analyst's true position is unique and paradoxical with respect to love, since *the analyst must love without wanting to be loved* in return. Like Socrates, the analyst must refuse to adopt the position of the beloved in the analytic setting, preferring instead to always be in the position of the lover, the gadfly who is forever provoking the analysand to produce knowledge. The analyst, like Socrates, must not succumb to the charming attentions of the handsomest of interlocutors (whether Alcibiades, Agathon, or anyone else), but must endlessly pursue discourse in the stead of intercourse, as it were. Insofar as the analysand is transformed through the metaphor of love, from beloved into lover, let him be a lover of the knowledge in the unconscious, says the analyst, and/or a lover of someone found outside of the confines of the analytic setting, not of me. The analysand's love must become the motor force of the analytic work, but the analyst does not seek to become its object. Its cause, yes, but not its object.

He must not *actively try* to make himself a desirable object, but must rather adopt the same position as Socrates, who does not trouble himself with wondering whether he is lovable or not. Like Freud, the analyst must not consider himself overly charming and must not seek to render himself worthy of love in the analysand's eyes. If he loves only in order to be loved in return, he will be nothing but a beggar. If he worries when the analysand places him on "the scale of comparison" – comparing him unflatteringly to other clinicians or his ministrations unfavorably to those of spiritual leaders, friends, or lovers – he has fallen into the trap of seeing himself as a beloved who is concerned about being dumped or exchanged for a more worthy object and has ceased to operate in the analysis as object *a*. As object *a* for the analysand, he must function in the analysis as pure desirousness (Lacan, 2015, p. 369).

Freud realized early on that the love his patients expressed for him had little if anything to do with his personal charms and pretty much everything to do with the role he played for them. As he put it, perhaps wistfully, "I am not that irresistible."[35] He was different in this regard from the person who employed the forerunner of psychoanalytic methods, Joseph Breuer. Breuer, as we saw earlier, seems to have mistaken Anna O.'s affection for the role he played with genuine affection for him as a charming, handsome man. It led to a fiasco in their work together – in our times it would have led to a malpractice suit – which is indicative of the fact that bringing out the lack in other people by asking them questions to which they have no answers, and thereby making them fall in love with you (the analytic art of love is the art of asking questions), is a risky business. It may blow up in your face, leading to embarrassing public outbursts like Alcibiades' in the *Symposium*. Such outbursts probably did not help Socrates' case later in life when he was brought to trial by the Athenians.[36]

Now, this is not to say that the analyst cannot adopt the position of beloved outside of the consulting room – he certainly need not carry his ascesis to the extreme point that Socrates is portrayed as carrying it to in the *Symposium*! Indeed, the more the analyst has found love in his private life, the less he is likely to be looking for it in the consulting room.

Soler (2003), following Lacan, refers to what the analysand finds in analysis as a new kind of love ("*un nouvel amour*"). As Lacan (1975, p. 16) himself puts it:

> Transference is based on love, a feeling that takes on such a new form in analysis that love is subverted by this form. [Transference love] is no less illusory [than the more usual forms of love] but it brings with it a partner who has a chance of responding, which is not the case in the other forms. This brings me back to the question of good fortune [that is, of having the good fortune, the incredible luck of meeting the right person], except that this [good] fortune comes from me in this case and I must furnish it.

It does not come from me, as an analyst, in the way it did from the former therapist of one of my female patients some years ago. This prior therapist prepared for her patient what was supposed to be a match made in "Freudian heaven," the therapist having fixed up two of her own patients! But the happy or lucky encounter and the miracle of love did not occur, perhaps because the therapist miscalculated, but perhaps, rather, because the unconscious conditions of love are not alone sufficient, a certain two-step dance being necessary for the spark to occur; the intervention of a third party backfired. Anyone who has ever tried to play matchmaker with friends may well have had similar experiences.

What Lacan means by "good fortune" here is, I believe, that the psychoanalyst, as the partner who responds in the transference, is not simply a partner with whom one repeats everything that one had done with one's previous partners, love essentially involving repetition prior to analysis – whether that repetition involve love for a master who was put in the place of one's own ego-ideal, anaclitic love for someone who took care of one like one's parents did, narcissistic love for someone like oneself, or some combination of these (see Chapters 4 and 5). The analyst harnesses the analysand's love in order to get her to produce knowledge of her unconscious conditions of love that determine object-choice, allowing those conditions to be transformed in the process. For often those conditions are so restrictive that no fortunate or lucky encounter can occur, no object can ever fit into the predetermined mold, or, when it does, the repetition of a painful scenario begins. Transference love works to disrupt that repetition, making something new possible where there had previously been just a repetition of the same old story.

This points to a fundamental dichotomy in positions between analyst and analysand: they do not play similar roles for each other when it comes to love, but very different roles. The analysand does not help the analyst produce knowledge of his or her unconscious conditions of love that determine object-choice or overcome his or her repetition compulsions. These things should have been accomplished, for the most part, during the analyst's own analysis. This is not to say that the analyst learns nothing from the analysand – on the contrary, in the best of cases he or she learns a great deal – but the very structure of the situation creates a polarity in which the analyst lends him- or herself to a role that is radically different from that played by the analysand: the analyst loves the analysand and asks for nothing by way of love in return. Whereas it is absolutely crucial that the analyst show love for the analysand in the form of intense listening and curiosity, it is not absolutely crucial that the analysand show love for the analyst, and demonstrations of such love can even prove problematic, creating as they often do considerable obstacles to the work of the analysis.

The contemporary notion that analyst and analysand mutually influence each other more or less identically, breaks down in at least this realm. Like Socrates, the analyst knows how to love/ask questions, but he does not crave love in return (he does not crave questions in return either, "answering" the analysand's questions with questions of his own).[37] Whereas the analysand situates object a in the analyst, the analyst does not situate object a in the analysand (Socrates, similarly, perhaps never situated object a in Alcibiades or any one else, refusing any other position for himself than that of cause of other people's desire). Instead, he willingly plays the role of object a in the consulting room, his desire being caused by something else, not by something he locates or sees in the analysand. The analyst, moreover, is far from taking expressions of the analysand's love for him at face value, does not seek out or relish the role of the beloved, and certainly does not wish to be loved for his "subjective difference." The analysand, on the contrary, expects to be loved by the analyst, and even complains bitterly when he or she feels inadequately attended to by the analyst!

An analytic colleague of mine once expressed to me his chagrin when, at the very end of a somewhat lengthy analysis, his obese patient rose from the couch and at the door remarked to him, "You've always found me repulsive, haven't you?" The patient thereby expressed her bitterness at having felt insufficiently loved by her analyst, who she felt was just going through the motions, doing the strict minimum that he felt professionally obliged to do. The analyst recognized all too late that, indeed, he had all along felt repulsed by this particular patient and was dismayed to realize that he had, in spite of himself, conveyed this to her. The analysand need not come to love the analyst – that is not a requirement or *sine qua non* of the treatment, at least certainly not in its initial stages. But if the analyst cannot find at least something to love in a particular analysand (to wit, his or her unconscious), trouble will ineluctably ensue and the analyst would do better to refer the analysand to a trusted fellow practitioner than to continue to work with the analysand him- or herself (see Chapter 7).

Note that whereas Plato, at least in the guise of Diotima, took love to be a means to an end – that end being knowledge or wisdom – in psychoanalysis love is viewed not merely as a helpmate (i.e., the motor force of the analysand's exploration of the unconscious), but as an end in itself. Indeed, Erik Erikson quoted Freud, perhaps apocryphally, as saying that analysis took it as its goal to allow the patient to "love and work," not to *know* all about himself or about anything else for that matter. In psychoanalysis, knowledge and understanding are not ends in themselves (see Fink, 2014a, 2014b). Love is.

In Chapter 8, we shall examine some of the myriad other fascinating things Lacan says about Plato's *Symposium* in Seminar VIII – for example, he points out that Socrates seems to be rolling his eyes at Diotima's infamous "ladder of love," and comes up with an explanation of Aristophanes' hiccups, which are rarely if ever elucidated by other commentators – but we shall, for the time being, turn to the imaginary and then the real facets of love.

THE IMAGINARY

IV

Freudian Preludes

Narcissism

Ce n'est pas de l'amour, c'est de la rage. (It's not love, it's fury.)
French proverb

When we turn from the symbolic to the imaginary, we leave the register of desire, strictly speaking – human desire for Lacan being a thing of language – for the register of passion, often uncontrolled and uncontrollable passion, which requires that we review and explore in depth some of Lacan's earlier work on the mirror stage. For Lacan writes that "the phenomenon of passionate love [is] determined by the image of the ideal ego" (Lacan, 2006a, p. 344), which is the image of oneself that results from the mirror stage.

First, though, we will explore some more of Freud's views so as to better grasp the backdrop to Lacan's work on the imaginary.

Narcissism and Love

Love is selfish.[1]
Love thy neighbor as thyself. (Leviticus 19:18)

In 1914, Freud takes up the subject of love largely from the perspective of narcissism. He sees love as involving a transfer of libido from the subject's own self or person (*Ich*, not yet *das Ich*, the latter being the ego as one of the three Freudian agencies) to another person, a transfer he refers to as a *Besetzung* – cathexis, interest, or investment. Such an investment can be made for a variety of reasons, as we shall see, but note first that the investment is revocable – that is, it can be taken back at certain times as need be. Note too that when such an investment is made, the subject's own self is less highly invested, or, as Freud puts it at times, his self-regard diminishes, the idea being that each subject only has a certain amount of libido at his disposal and thus, if some is transferred to an object (thereby becoming "object-libido"), less remains for the subject. (It is not terribly clear here whether Freud thinks of the object as a representation in the subject's psyche or as a real object in the "outside world"; his language would seem to suggest the latter, in which case it is not clear how the libido passes "outside" the subject.)

In the detailed discussion of love found in "On Narcissism," Freud (1914/1957c) strenuously upholds the distinction between "ego-libido" and "object-libido," even though the sum total of both of them must always remain constant in his system ("ego-libido" is libido that is invested in oneself or one's person; note that although Freud does not yet use *das Ich*, the English translation uses the term "ego" throughout this paper for *Ich*, instead of referring to "me-libido" or "self-libido"). An increase in object-libido necessarily leads to a decrease in ego-libido and vice versa; there does not seem to be any room here for the notion that both object- and ego-libido could grow simultaneously.[2]

$$EL \text{ (ego-libido)} + OL \text{ (object-libido)} = C \text{ (constant)}$$

The first form of ego-libido Freud discusses is what he terms "primary narcissism"; it is the kind of concern for itself that every animal has, insofar as it considers itself to be worthy of being alive, meaning worthy of eating and of defending itself (activities associated with the so-called ego instincts or life drives). To Freud, there is nothing mysterious about how libido becomes attached to oneself – it does so automatically and we can understand "primary narcissism" as a kind of hardwired "animal narcissism."[3] (In Lacan's view, the way in which libido becomes attached to oneself is far more elaborate, and anything but automatic.)

When one becomes attached to or makes an investment in an object, one's primary narcissism declines: some of the libido attached to one's own person flows over to the object. Should one lose that object, the libido invested in it flows back, like a fluid, to oneself, leading to what Freud calls "secondary narcissism" (strangely enough, associated by Freud with schizophrenia).[4] We might call this the "Law of Libido Conservation" (LLC).

According to Freud, libidinal situations can vary because people choose objects of two fundamentally different types:

1. If we choose someone who resembles or reminds us in some way of the person who looked after us as children and satisfied our earliest needs, we make what Freud calls an "anaclitic-type" (or "attachment-type") object-choice; love is based on or

propped up by need in this case. The new object may resemble the original (that is, the early caretaker) in several ways or in but one: name, eye color, hair color, or smile, for example. Falling in love is based here on confusion of the object with a pre-existing ideal image we have in our heads: we equate the partner with our mother, father, or some other primary caretaker.

2. If we choose as an object someone who resembles us instead of resembling some other person, we make a "narcissistic" object-choice. The resemblance here may be quite global or involve nothing more than the primary sexual characteristics, the object chosen being of the same sex as the subject. Falling in love here is based on the confusion of self with other, on the virtual identification of self with other (me = other).

These two different kinds of object-choice lead to two different situations as concerns narcissism or self-regard:

1. When we fall in love with someone who resembles one of our earliest caretakers, our ego is depleted: we are at the lowest level of ego-libido and at the "highest phase" of object-libido. The main examples Freud supplies of this are a male subject who falls in love with a female who reminds him of his mother – she does not necessarily resemble him in any way and is of the opposite sex – and a female subject who falls in love with a male who reminds her of her father: he does not necessarily resemble her in any way and is of the opposite sex.[5] In these cases, the object is felt to be everything and the subject to be nothing. (This may be what led Lacan to once say that "love is a form of suicide"; Lacan, 1988, p. 149.)

$$EL \text{ (virtually zero)} + OL \text{ (constant)} = C \text{ (constant)}$$

Naturally, however, the object does not fully coincide with the mother or father, and this will be discovered in due time, presumably leading some of the object-libido to flow back to the ego.

2. "The state of being in love" does not deplete the ego of libido, however, when the object chosen is similar to oneself, for one is essentially in love with oneself in the other or with the other in oneself (me = other).

$$EL = OL = C$$

As Lacan puts it in a play on words in Seminar XX, *"elles se mêment dans l'autre,"* "they love each other as the same" or "they love themselves in each other" (Lacan, 1998a, p. 85).

In Freud's view, men tend to love, to invest their libido in objects, whereas women need to be loved, not to love. Freud's view here leads to the following configurations for the different sexes:

Man: EL = zero, OL = C
Woman: EL = C, OL = zero

Although the association between women and cats who are stand-offish and wrapped up in themselves is a longstanding one, there are, as we saw in Chapter 3, plenty of women who feel a need to love and not simply to be loved. (Does Freud restrict women to loving either themselves or children as extensions of themselves, but not men?) In any case, Freud introduces here a curious facet of love, which would seem to apply not only to men, which is that we human beings are attracted to people (women and children, for example) and animals (cats, for example) that show little or no interest in us. Are we then interested in anything that seems narcissistically wrapped up in itself (its interest in itself pointing the way for our own interest or desire?) or are we interested in these things precisely because they seem inaccessible? Do we pursue them because they shun us and wound our own narcissism? Do we pursue them because they seem the most valuable – valuable precisely because they are so difficult to win – because we suspect that we will never win them?[6] Or do we pursue them because we identify with something about them or want to be like them?

I will leave this as an open question, and will confine myself to suggesting that Freud provides us here with something of an obsessive theory of love, allowing us to speculate about what a hysterical theory of love might look like. (Might it be giving what you do not have? After all, Freud's lover merely gives what he has – namely, libido.)[7]

A less extreme reading of what Freud thinks the usual male and female libidinal configurations are might be formulated as follows:

Man: EL (1/3C) + OL (2/3C) = C (constant)
Woman: EL (2/3C) + OL (1/3C) = C (constant)

The quotient of ego-libido the man has here (1/3C) either was never (or only provisionally) invested in the woman, or else it comes back to him from the woman as if from his mother. The quotient of ego-libido the woman has here (2/3C) either was never (or only provisionally) invested in the man, or else it comes back to her from the man as if from her father.

It might not be too unfair to suggest that *Freud's anaclitic type of object-choice is made with a view to "real satisfactions."* For even if the choice of object is fostered by one or more symbolic or imaginary traits, the emphasis here seems to be on the search to find anew the kinds of satisfaction one experienced with a caretaker as a small child. In contrast, *the narcissistic type of object-choice is made with a view to imaginary satisfactions*, so to speak, or perhaps even with a view to avoiding a decrease in primary narcissism. It involves wanting to see oneself reflected in the other, and is imaginary in that the other is thought to be the spitting image of oneself, or at least like oneself in some very important regard. In any case, the first seems to emphasize the real, the second the imaginary. (This is curious because Freud's earlier papers on love, discussed in Chapter 2, seem to emphasize the symbolic.)

Nevertheless, Freud does introduce a possible symbolic component here insofar as he indicates that narcissistic object-choice can involve the choice of someone who is like you now, someone who is like you were before (think of the older lover in Greek times who chose as his beloved a boy who was like he himself was when he was first chosen to be someone else's beloved), someone who seems to be the way you would like to be, or someone who was once part of yourself (unless he is referring to Siamese twins who become surgically separated, I would assume he is thinking of mother and child). It is especially the part about "someone who is the way you would like to be" that introduces the question of ideals – that is, the ego-ideal – which shifts things to the symbolic register.

Love for the Ego-Ideal

Difference rubs us the wrong way;
Sameness rubs us the right way.

At an intrapsychic level, Freud suggests that when the ego-ideal forms – and it forms based on our parents' ideals, their approval and disapproval, and what we think we need to do and be in order to be loved by them – libido is displaced onto it, and we become satisfied with ourselves when we live up to the ideal and dissatisfied when we do not (again, Freud's *Ich-ideal* might, at this stage of Freud's thinking, have better been rendered in English as the "me-ideal," "self-ideal," or even "ideal I hold out for myself"). He refers to the ego-ideal here as "imposed from without" (Freud, 1914/1957c, p. 100), presumably by our parents, suggesting thereby that it introduces a kind of alienation: something grafted upon us that we can perhaps never achieve or live up to, an ideal that we can only asymptotically approach.

I would argue, however, that the ego-ideal does not come into being automatically. Our parents have to care enough about us to try to instill ideals in us – or, failing all else, impose them on us – and we have to accept and indeed want to please our parents if we are to assimilate their ideals (on the coming into being of the ego-ideal for an individual, see Chapter 5). Even if we do accept our parents for the most part, we may nevertheless continue to feel their ideals to be a sort of foreign body, something grafted upon us. In other cases, we may come to love the ideal they have transmitted to us more than ourselves; we feel that we are worth nothing next to our ideal, nothing without our ideal; if we cannot realize it, if we must give it up, we are indeed nothing at all.

We feel miserable when we do not live up to it – we have low self-regard or low "self-esteem" – and can often only resolve the dilemma by finding a love object who we think embodies those ideals: we put a lover in the place of the ego-ideal and love the person in the place of that ideal. Freud suggests here that the choice of lover is often based on narcissism, for the goal is "to be [one's] own ideal once more [as one was] in childhood" (p. 100). This harks back to the "primary narcissism" theme whereby we all supposedly take ourselves to be her or his "majesty the baby" right from the outset. Here we seem to want to love someone who is like ourselves but better than ourselves. Freud refers to this as a "cure by love" (p. 101), the problem that is cured presumably being the libidinal depletion of the subject, for Freud writes, "In the last resort we must begin to love in order not to fall ill" (p. 85).

This curious claim would seem to apply in his theory to men more than to women. Note, however, that it foreshadows problems for both men and women. For men, the beloved woman is put on a pedestal: ideals are projected onto her (for example, beauty, purity, honesty, truth, and love) as the man tries to place and keep her in an idealized position. She is not chosen to satisfy his needs like his mother did here but to be his better half, be what he feels incapable of living up to. This likely impedes his sexual interest in her. Problems arise for the woman, too, should she take the bait and identify with the position she is put in by men: frigidity, for example, according to Lacan (2006a, p. 733). What if she puts him in the place of her ego-ideal? Is he loved by her then as a (more perfect) child than she was? Is he put on a pedestal while she takes herself to be worthless? Freud does not expound upon this.

Even though Freud introduces the notion of the ego-ideal here, he nevertheless seems to situate the choice of an object that embodies this ideal as a narcissistic choice (as falling, that is, within the imaginary register), perhaps simply because it is based so entirely on *one's own* ego-ideal, not on the beloved's ego-ideal; for it does not in any way take into account what ideals the beloved has for him- or herself. Here the beloved's goodness is presumably prized insofar as it can rub off on oneself, allowing one to see oneself as more valuable, worthy, and lovable.

V

Lacan's Imaginary Register

Even though Lacan is best known today for stressing the importance of language, his earliest work focuses a great deal on the imaginary. Rather than introduce the imaginary dimension by starting with the mirror stage, as is usually done, I will discuss a number of this dimension's salient features, beginning with the all-important fact that Lacan does not call it *imaginary* to emphasize the dimension of illusion, the dimension of that which does not really exist, but rather to emphasize the importance of images in the animal kingdom and for human beings as well. An excursus into the power and importance of images is necessary for us to grasp the degree to which human passion is tied to images of ourselves and others.

Animals in the Imaginary

Lacan is impressed early on in his career by the *formative role of images* in the animal kingdom. He is familiar with ethology (that is, the study of animal behavior), most notably that of the work on grasshoppers by Rémy Chauvin (1941) and on the sexual maturation of pigeons by L. Harrison Mathews (1939). Their research is discussed in Lacan's papers entitled "Some Reflections on the Ego" (1953) and "Remarks on Psychical Causality" (2006a, pp. 189–91). Lacan was also quite familiar with Konrad Lorenz's earliest work on fish, geese, and other animals (see, for example, Lacan, 2013, p. 12).[1] The emphasis in all of these ethological studies is on the importance of images for triggering significant developmental processes. For example, in the migratory locust (*Schistocerca*), a solitary individual changes into a gregarious one when it sees the characteristic shape and movements of another member of its own species. In a second example, a female pigeon matures sexually upon seeing (not simply hearing and/or smelling) another pigeon, upon seeing just a rough cut-out facsimile of a pigeon, or even upon seeing her own reflection in a mirror.

An example Lacan does not cite, as it had probably not yet been studied at the time, is that of the whydah, a kind of parasitical bird that lays its eggs in other bird species' nests, leaving the feeding and raising of its young to foster-parents. The "female whydah becomes reproductively active and ovulates only when she sees the reproductive activity of members of her particular host species" (Avital & Jablonka, 2000, p. 129). The field of ethology has found many more such examples in the 70 years since Lacan first published his work on the formative nature of images.

Images are also of crucial importance in aggressive behavior in animals. As Konrad Lorenz (1966) shows with numerous examples in his book *On Aggression*, species are generally "far more aggressive toward their own species than toward any other" (p. 15). The Darwinian explanation of intraspecies aggression is to keep a species evenly spread out over all the available territory so as not to exhaust its food supply, which would lead to extinction of the whole species. This implies that an aggressive response is often elicited when an animal sees a member of its own species on its home turf.

Seeing a member of its own species does not always lead to immediate aggression, of course. Most animals, such as dogs, adopt certain postures that announce their propensity to aggression, indicating how dominant or submissive they are (for example, dogs crouch in front of each other to show submission).[2] Such postures are signs to other members of the same species, indicating whether or not individuals are ready and willing to fight.[3]

Dominance and submission postures in varied species have been studied extensively by ethologists, owing to their importance in establishing hierarchies and pecking orders in animal groups and in the avoidance of constant conflict within such groups. De Waal and Tyack (2003, p. 278) provide images where we see one zebra demonstrating a submissive posture toward another zebra. The neck of the first is bowed compared to the more ordinary greeting posture (it is but a short step for many ethologists and psychologists from the zebra's bowed neck to stooping postures and the bowing of heads in human beings).

In the same image, the zebra seems to have a sort of pained smile on its face. It appears that a great deal of ink has been spilled in the field of animal behavior studies about the origin of so-called smiling in mammals, smiling having for many centuries apparently been considered (perhaps since Aristotle) to be an attenuated form of laughter, or a stage on the way to laughter (the latter being characteristic primarily of human beings: as Rabelais said, *le rire est le propre de l'homme*; yet some have tried to find laughter in chimps too). A number of ethologists have gone to rather great lengths to demonstrate that smiling with teeth bared derives phylogenetically from a fear response. It arises spontaneously, according to them, in many species as a demonstration to another member of the same species that one is afraid of that member and has no intention to attack it.[4]

The visual size of an adversary is often crucial in determining whether an animal will attack or retreat, both in intra- and inter-species confrontations. A lone hyena will attack animals that are smaller than it is or that seem more or less its own size, but is less likely to attack animals that seem much larger. Among sea lions, when the bulls face off to fight over territory and access to females, a sac in their heads inflates to make them look more vicious and bigger than they are. *In the imaginary, size really does matter.*

In this dimension, another member of one's own species is viewed as essentially the same as oneself, operating on the same principles. Indeed, there is nothing that would allow one to recognize the other as *qualitatively* different from oneself; there is only quantitative difference at this level: *the other is larger and stronger or smaller and weaker.* Or, if the other is about the same size as oneself, one gauges the other in terms of whether it seems more or less aggressive than oneself. The question here seems to be that of domination or submission: either the other is a threat to oneself or is not, but there is no *recognition* of the other as possibly operating on altogether different principles than one's own.

There is something fundamentally mimetic involved here, which is that one grasps another's motives only on the basis of one's own. If one is feeling attacked the other must be aggressing one;[5] if one is starving, the other must be motivated by hunger.

Among African hunting dogs, the female of the species usually has more pups in a litter than she has teats and her young pups fight for the right to nurse from the most tender of ages. This is a genuine struggle for survival, for those pups that do not nurse often remain small and far weaker than their siblings who grow larger and stronger and who eventually wrestle and fight with them until they become crippled and die. The same pups may be happy to play with and cuddle with each other when it is not feeding time, but when hungry nothing stops them from simply pushing others out of the way so that they can eat or drink their fill, even if that involves using all of their nascent strength.

The aggression shown in such situations knows no limits. It is not as if the animals said to each other, "Now it's our little brother's turn to drink: it's only fair, we've been nursing for ten minutes already." It is not as if the animals said to themselves, "That's enough horsing around, we're really starting to hurt him."[6] Just as there is no *recognition*, in the imaginary dimension, of the other as operating on principles different than one's own, there is no *recognition* of limits to what can be done to a rival.

A young lion reluctantly moves away from a freshly killed antelope only because the larger lions in the pack leave it no choice. It does not give them the place of honor out of respect or deference to its elders – there is no such notion in the animal kingdom; in other words, there is no such notion in the imaginary dimension. *For the imaginary dimension is the one that reigns supreme in the animal kingdom.*

There is nothing but its own feeling of satiety or bloatedness that stops a lion from eating, even though it may no longer be hungry and there are other hungry members of its own species around. And there is nothing that stops it from biting and hurting other animals that try to muscle in on the animal carcass it is still eating beyond all hunger except the sheer size and aggressiveness of the interlopers. The limits to its eating are thus real, not imaginary. The imaginary does not bring limits with it.

Instinct does, however: one animal will often stop harassing another animal as soon as it feels the animal is no longer a threat, because it has moved far enough from its territory or is sufficiently wounded not to be back any time soon. In the case of human beings, however, instinct does not come into play much; it does not give us much guidance.

Now, the lack of limits characteristic of the imaginary dimension can be found in the human world as well. Saint Augustine, who is occasionally quoted by Lacan (2006a, pp. 114–15), mentions a two- or three-year-old boy who became pale with envy at the sight of his foster-brother being nursed – to his mind, someone else was moving in on his territory (i.e., his primary caretaker's breasts). He had not yet developed the notion of sharing, of each having equal rights to things. And even if he had to some degree, it might not have stopped all of his venom.

Such venom can at times go as far as murderous rage, and it is far more likely to arise between members of the same species than between a child and the family dog, for example. The responses and reactions an animal has while hunting are clearly distinguished by ethologists and wildlife biologists from the anger signals and signs seen in fighting within species. A certain species of fish will allow ten members of certain other species to inhabit its territory, but not a single member of its own species. Those other species do not compete with it for the same resources. Children in a family, on the other hand, do compete for the same parental resources (Sulloway, 1996). A parent's time, care, and love are limited and children compete with each other to get them, especially at the outset. Teaching children to share is one of the most difficult tasks parents face, enduring as they do requests to take the new baby back to the hospital or even attempts, when the parents' backs are turned, to throw the baby out in the garbage or "accidentally" lose the baby in the park. Few struggles in a young child's life elicit so much hateful passion and rivalry as does the struggle with siblings. (One of my analysands shoved his baby sister into a dresser drawer when he was a young child, hoping she would be forgotten about.)

Animals in Love

Having said a bit about animal aggression and angry passion, let us turn briefly to the role of images in courting and mating behavior among animals. As Konrad Lorenz (1966) tells us, among argus pheasants the hens prefer males with very large secondary wing feathers decorated with "eye spots," so called because they look like eyes (p. 37). The number of progeny produced by a male is in direct proportion to the length of those feathers, even though they are so cumbersome as to make him less likely to be able to escape a possible predator (he can barely fly with such long feathers). Something about the eye spots themselves fascinate the hen – they are what she wants more than anything else (just as it seems that it is the male praying mantis' head that the female praying mantis wants more than anything else; Lacan, 2015, pp. 212–13).

The importance of images in courting and mating behavior in the animal kingdom can be further illustrated by the fact that in many bird species,

> a female looks for a mate with the most extravagant traits – the most colorful male, the biggest, the strongest, the one presenting the most elaborate and demanding ritual. In some polygynous [i.e., polygamous] birds, including the peacock and a variety of game birds and waders, males gather together in advertising congregations called "leks," where they show off, and females come to look them over, compare them and choose the best male. When the female preference is not innate, and discernible markers of male quality change with circumstances, inexperienced young females may face a problem: they cannot easily tell who is the superior male. In such cases, young females seem to observe the behavior of older and more experienced females,

and copy their choices. [. . .] The consequence for males is that an already successful male becomes increasingly more popular! (Avital & Jablonka, 2000, pp. 143–4)

Further on, the same authors comment that:

The peahen chooses the peacock with the largest and most colorful tail, and middle-aged males, who have proved their ability to survive, are often preferred to young, inexperienced ones. The brightness of the male's plumage reflects his health, since parasite-infested males tend to have dull plumage. [. . .] Attractiveness *per se* is also important. [. . .] A female who chooses a male considered to be attractive will probably have attractive sons. These sons will attract and mate with many females, and consequently produce many grandchildren. If attractiveness does not reduce the survival of the males too much, then in each generation the most attractive males, and the females most susceptible to their charms, will be selected. This can sometimes lead to evolutionary escalation – to exaggerated female preferences and inflated male traits that have more to do with fashion than with quality. The magnificent tail of the male peacock [which is sometimes so big and heavy that he can barely fly] and the complex and lengthy song of the nightingale are famous examples of traits that probably evolved both as extreme advertisements of genetic worth and as escalated fashions. It seems that both good sense and fashionable structures drive female preferences. (Avital & Jablonka, 2000, pp. 144–5)

The analogy between such courting and mating behaviors in animals and in humans was noticed by observers early on.

The Formative Role of Images in Human Beings

Turning now to Lacan's discussion of the role of images in the human world, let us note that in "The Mirror Stage" and "Aggressiveness in Psychoanalysis," Lacan (2006a) situates himself within a very broad tradition. He does not limit himself to psychoanalysis, but refers to experimental psychology, ethology, anthropology, and even optics.

In exploring the formative role images may play in human beings, Lacan considers a species closer to our own than those discussed in the preceding section. He notes that chimpanzees recognize their own image in a mirror and play with it or around it. Dogs and cats do not seem to pay attention to those images (although some reportedly do). Chimpanzees apparently play with the image for a while, but are not fascinated by it. There is no jubilation – they quickly exhaust what Lacan (2006a, p.93) refers to as the "uselessness [or inanity or emptiness] of the image" and move on to the next thing that attracts their attention.

Chimpanzees being among our closest neighbors in terms of evolution, it should be noted that chimpanzees are able to do a lot of things very quickly after they are born. Humans are probably the most incapable and slow-developing of all animals. They are "premature" at birth – that is, they are not good for much. A foal can stand up within a few hours and learns to walk very quickly; its nervous and motor systems are already quite functional at birth. Humans are essentially helpless and unable to do virtually anything for themselves for ages. Standing up competently takes most of us at least a year!

Freud mentions this already in his work and Lacan makes a big deal of what he calls the human infant's *prematurity at birth*. Not only are we incapable of doing most anything for ourselves at birth, but the future coordinated functioning of the human nervous and motor systems is not even a given, not something whose development occurs automatically over the course of time. An autistic or schizophrenic child may *never* move as a coordinated, unified being (see Bettelheim, 1961, 1967). Such a child may be in the process of defecating and most of the rest of its body shows absolutely no signs of it. The human body's ability to function as a unit cannot be taken for granted: its unity has to be established or constructed. This, Lacan hypothesizes in the 1930s and 1940s, cannot be brought about by internal developmental processes alone, as in the foal or chimpanzee, but only in conjunction with something that originates outside of the child: an image.

The Mirror Stage

In formulating what he calls the mirror stage, Lacan sets out to explain a fact noted by several observers to occur between the ages of six and 18 months: *the human infant's jubilant experience of seeing itself in the mirror*. The child, according to Lacan, "assumes" its mirror image in the sense in which one says "assume a responsibility": the child takes it on or takes it upon itself, and by extension here takes it in or assimilates it.

What can we say about this image? It is totalizing: it gives or reflects back to the child an image of its own body as a whole, and it is the first such "holistic" or total image the child ever has of itself. Note that we never see our whole bodies all at once except in a mirror (or a drawing, painting, photograph, or video), and even then it is just about a half of them (the front or back side). Without the help of a reflective surface, we see but a much smaller part of our bodies, never seeing our own faces, heads, or necks.

The image seen in the mirror does not resemble the still uncoordinated, ununified infant sitting or standing before the mirror, but a more unified child, complete in shape and form, who resembles the complete unified people (e.g., parents and older siblings) the child sees around it. This is why Lacan uses the term *Gestalt* here: the child sees itself or experiences itself as a whole being for the first time thanks to this image. Prior to that it experiences itself as a series of shifting states, sensations, and perceptions with no obvious core or center. This *Gestalt* is, in a sense, the first anchor for all of these fleeting experiences, giving the child some sense of unity.

Now the child's vision of itself in the mirror is deceptive, given the child's state of fragmentation and lack of motor coordination, and it also involves a reversal endemic to all mirror images: when you see yourself in the mirror, there is a right–left reversal and a front–back effect (which, when combined, make it very difficult to cut your own hair while looking in a mirror, for example). A mirror image is thus in some sense a "mirage," a "distortion," or a "fiction" – an image which does not *accurately* reflect the infant's body or state of being at the time. In a sense, it idealizes the child's body: it suggests that it is capable of things of which it is not yet capable. This image makes its body seem unified and coordinated like the bodies of the child's far more capable, powerful parents or older siblings. It is not a faithful representation or reproduction of who and what the child is at that precise point in time; rather, it smoothes out the rough edges. In this sense it is alienating: it makes the child hold out for itself an ideal that it cannot immediately attain, and which it can only "asymptotically approach" over the course of a long period of time. Lacan (2006a), in his cryptic fashion, puts this as follows:

> The important point is that this form [i.e., image] situates the agency known as the ego, prior to its social determination, in a fictional direction that will forever remain irreducible for any single individual or, rather, that will only asymptotically approach the subject's becoming, no matter how successful the dialectical syntheses by which he must resolve, as *I*, his discordance with his own reality. (p. 94)

"His own reality" is the state of uncoordination, inability to move and speak and command others like they command him. A child will never be able to fully coincide with the masterful image he sees of himself in the mirror. This is why Lacan associates this mirror image with Freud's *Ideal-Ich* or ideal ego.

This image is, Lacan suggests, the primordial form of the ego: the ego's very first mold or matrix (*matrice*). Let us equate the ego and the self here, as it may be simpler to think of this ideal image as providing the first crystallization of the self – of what one thinks of as one's "self." Freud stresses in *The Ego and the Id* (1923/1961b) that the ego is not there at birth – it is a product or construct, something that is built up over time. Animals seem generally to do without the "sense of self," "inner self," ego, or homunculus we humans create or develop. Some psychologists seem to think that the sense of self or ego is present from birth in humans,[7] but I think even they would admit that it changes over time. Lacan suggests that it "begins" or at least first crystallizes with the mirror image between six and 18 months of age. This does not mean it has not been prepared for and cannot be formed without any mirrors around. Narcissus saw himself in a lake, and still bodies of water have been around for a long time! (Parents can also be understood to function as mirrors in certain ways, as can siblings, as we shall see.)

This first *matrice* – mold, cast, or matrix – or crystallization is added onto in the course of time. It is a first identification (or so Lacan maintains here; for Freud, it may not ultimately be as "first" as all that)[8] to which successive secondary identifications are added. To call it an identification implies that it is an identification with something else – that is, something that is not initially thought to be the same as me. To establish that two objects are identical – that is, to bring about an identification of one with the other – they first have to be experienced as nonidentical. This something else with which I identify is an other. I become alienated from "myself" insofar as I bring this image in the mirror or foreign fiction into myself. Lacan cites the poet Rimbaud who says, *"Je est un autre,"* implying that what I come to call me is at least at first other, different from me, and it may forever remain other to a certain degree.

This initial matrix is added onto by secondary identifications, which are identifications with *both* parents. Lacan's theory here is thus that the ego, as Freud (1923/1961b) describes it in *The Ego and the Id*, is – and this is only one of the four definitions Freud provides of it in that text – *a sedimentation or crystallization of identifications*, and the mirror image internalized during the mirror stage constitutes the first such identification. The mirror image, once assimilated, becomes the cornerstone or foundation of the ego.

Insofar as this first identification is a fiction or a mirage, the implication is that all identification involves a modicum of illusion, mistaken identity, and alienation. There are always differences between the things that get identified (insofar as identification necessarily involves the equating of two *different* things), and those differences are lopped off, as it were. *The ego is thus essentially based on misrecognition or misunderstanding*, in other words, mistaken understanding. And it is a wishful misrecognition in the full sense of the French term *méconnaissance*, because the ideal ego is *ideal* – we would like to see ourselves in a certain way and thus ignore what does not fit. As infants, we want to believe we are unified and powerful like the people we see around us; and there is thus a true libidinal impulse to equate ourselves with the seemingly unified and powerful image we see in the mirror.[9]

The process of human "development" – unlike what we see in animal development – thus jumps from inadequacy (the-body-in-pieces, the body as fragmented, ununified, and an "original organic disarray" or jumble (*désarroi*, Lacan, 2006a, p. 116)) to anticipated wholeness: an artificial or anticipated unity prior to real unity (somewhat akin to the reunification of Germany – an artificial unity is created at a national level long before any kind of real social, cultural, or economic unity has been achieved). "The child *anticipates* at the mental level the conquest of his own body's functional unity, which is still incomplete at the level of volitional motricity at that point in time" (p. 112).

"Anticipation" is a very important concept in Lacan's work, and it should be understood here in the sense not so much of expectation, excitement, or fear regarding something that is going to happen in the future, but the realization or creation of something "before its time." The infant creates something *now*, in its mind, which has not yet been achieved in reality. The mirror image comes to serve the child as a prosthesis by which development and coordination of its motor systems can be achieved. Thanks to the mirror image, the infant for the first time imagines being coordinated and powerful like the others it sees around itself even before it is coordinated and powerful like them; and *this image of itself as coordinated and powerful assists the child in becoming coordinated and powerful*.[10]

One of the questions that might be raised at this point is why? Why does the child anticipate in this way? Why does it create something prematurely? Why does an ego precipitate out? Lacan provides two different explanations, one in the 1930s and 1940s (in "The Mirror Stage" and "Aggressiveness in Psychoanalysis") in the midst of his focus on the imaginary, and another in 1961 in Seminar VIII after he has devoted considerable attention to the symbolic. The first explanation relies on something immanent to the imaginary, as though something entirely new could be born from the imaginary alone – just as Hegel theorized that a form of transcendence could arise from man's "fruitful illness, life's happy fault," as Lacan (2006a, p. 345) puts it, or from the struggle to the death between master and slave. The second explanation takes into account the fact, which Lacan eventually comes to, that such transcendence requires something *qualitatively* different, the symbolic register – in other words, that a dialectical development cannot begin without the introduction of another dimension.

In his early work, Lacan proposes that something new, like an identification, can be precipitated when considerable tension has been generated. In his paper on "Logical Time," someone can come to identify himself as a man through a kind of competition with other men – a competition that increases tension to a breaking point, in a sense, to the point at which a decision or "jumping to a conclusion" is precipitated out (Lacan, 2006a, pp. 211–23).[11]

Where would such tension stem from for a six- to 18-month-old child? At least partly from sibling rivalry. Just like African hunting-dog puppies, the children in a family struggle with each other for precious and limited parental resources such as care, protection, and nurturance.[12] Especially when they have older siblings, they experience pressure to be as active, coordinated, and powerful as their older siblings. In Lacan's thinking in the 1930s and 1940s, it is this pressure or tension that leads to the child's precipitous conclusion that the image of a unified being that it sees in the mirror, and that resembles the images it has long perceived of its older and more capable siblings, *is* himself or herself, *is* identical to him or her. "I am a whole, accomplished being like they are," the child seems to joyfully conclude.

By 1961, Lacan no longer thinks this identification can occur without an additional element; but before turning to his later explanation of the mirror stage, let us consider the libidinal consequences of such an identification.

The ego as precipitated or formed during the mirror stage clearly seems to have a quantum of love or libido attached to it, which Lacan refers to as narcissistic libido: love or libido attached to the self. Unlike Freud, Lacan does not think that we cathect our*selves* automatically, like animals do; to cathect our*selves*, we require a totalizing image of ourselves as in some way positive and worthwhile. Lacan does not endorse the notion that, like animals, we have something akin to Freud's primary narcissism, which is there from birth. In order to invest libido in ourselves, we require something that is found outside of ourselves – an image created by a mirror.

This image is joyfully latched onto and cathected by a child. It becomes central to the image of itself that it carries around in its head thereafter, central to the particular kind of sense of self that Freud referred to as the ideal ego. Freud (1923/1961b) indicates that "the ego is first and foremost a bodily ego," and what makes the sense of self *ideal* here is, as I said earlier, that it is not fragmented or partial, but rather total and indeed totalizing. It helps a child, who had formerly been a somewhat disorganized set of disparate motor systems, to begin operating as a whole. It is by using this initially external image as a sort of prosthetic device (or homuncular child within the child) that the nonautistic, nonschizophrenic child becomes able to function more harmoniously at the motor level.

Lacan certainly does not claim that prior to the invention of mirrors children were never able to form an ideal ego, and thus were unable to ever function in a coordinated fashion – that would be absurd. There are obviously other ways in which children can form a sense of themselves as whole or unified. But in the age of mirrors and the ever greater proliferation of images of oneself provided by cameras, a unified sense of self often derives at least partially from an image that originates from elsewhere than within one's own psyche. And the ever greater importance of images in our culture may well be associated with the kind of modern subjectivity with which we are all familiar, where we each carry around a fairly well-developed image of ourselves in our minds, and very often picture ourselves as if from the outside doing things, saying things, acting in the world, and so on. I would hazard a guess that fantasies and dreams in which one sees oneself doing something – whether engaging in sexual activity or any other kind of activity – as if from some outside position (some "bird's-eye view") are far more common in our day and age than they were in Homer's time, for example. (Of course, I am not taking a very big risk in hazarding such a guess, since no one can disprove it.)

The Image We Love More Than Ourselves: The Ideal Ego

True love gives way to hatred.

Lacan, 1998a, p. 146

One of Lacan's important claims from the 1940s is that the image of another child similar in age to oneself can serve the same purpose as the mirror image (at least at the imaginary level) – in other words, I can form an image of myself as a whole person like my brother: I can see myself in him, both literally and figuratively. I can use the image of my "semblable" (someone who resembles me in many respects)[13] or fellow child as a prop for my own sense of self, as

a prosthesis originating outside of my own psyche on the basis of
which to construct what I think of as myself. Parents often unwittingly encourage this when they compare children to their siblings,
talking about how much they are alike in looks, temperament, and
ability.[14]

When Lacan returns to the theory of the mirror stage in 1961, it
is to provide a new explanation as to how this ideal image becomes
internalized. It is not automatically assimilated, for if it were, we
would never encounter (autistic or schizophrenic) individuals who
seem to never have formed any sort of clear sense of self. Nor is
competition with siblings – the tension or pressure to identify with
the mirror image owing to the Hegelian-like struggle for dominance among brothers and sisters – enough to generate or explain
internalization of the unifying image, as Lacan had previously
thought. Something else is required. In Seminar VIII, Lacan (2015)
hypothesizes – on the basis of a film showing footage of six- to
18-month-olds placed in front of a mirror as their parents stand
nearby[15] – that a child's mirror image becomes invested with libido
and internalized due to *recognition* of the child by the parent, due,
for example, to the parent's exclamation as a child looks at itself
in the mirror, "Yes, Baby, that's you!" A child – as seen in this
film – often turns its head away from the mirror image toward its
parent to see the parent looking at the child looking at itself in the
mirror, and the parent often provides a kind of confirmatory nod
or approving gesture, if not an exclamation. This leads to what
Lacan calls a certification or ratification (*entérinement*) of the mirror
image.

The "parent's nod" serves as *ein einziger Zug* (a single trait,
stroke, or characteristic), a term Freud (1921/1955e) uses in *Group
Psychology and the Analysis of the Ego*.[16] This trait concerns the
respect in which the parent approves of the child or finds the child to
be lovable. The child identifies with or brings into itself the external
point or place from which it is seen as lovable by the parent, and
thereby comes to see itself as it is seen by that parent. It begins to
see itself as if it were itself in the parent's position, viewing the child
from the outside.

This leads to the formation of what Freud calls the ego-ideal – the
point at which one is viewed as worthwhile by the Other – which is
what allows a sense of self to form. This *einziger Zug* (which Lacan
eventually translates as "unary trait," his shorthand for it being
S_1), as the core of the ego-ideal, is the anchoring point of the entire
symbolic order, leading as it does to internalization of an outside
position whereby one (at least believes that one) learns to see oneself
as others see one. The Other's approving gaze at oneself is brought

inside, as it were, and one begins to view oneself approvingly as the Other views one (the Other's disapproving gaze will, of course, come into play as well).

The parent's approval or ratification here (S_1, the core of the ego-ideal) allows, in theory, for the *internalization* of the mirror image itself – that is, of the ideal ego – there being henceforward an ideal image or set of images that structure one's sense of self. This perhaps accounts for the phenomenon with which many of us are familiar of looking in the mirror and being surprised that we do not exactly resemble the images we have of ourselves in our own minds. For even when we are able to internalize the ideal ego, we remain alienated from it insofar as we can only approach it asymptotically, as Lacan puts it; there is always a gap between the ideal image we have of ourselves and what we see in the mirror every day as adults.

The question I would raise here is whether the ideal ego is ever completely internalized, or whether it is in fact always found to some degree outside of ourselves. For Lacan (2015, p. 356) writes that "The ego-ideal is a symbolic introjection, whereas the ideal ego is the source of an imaginary projection,"[17] and, although introjection of the ego-ideal is a kind of anchoring point for the ideal ego (see Fink, 1997, pp. 87–90), perhaps the latter always remains somewhat external.[18] To examine the question, let us consider the extreme case in which no confirmatory nod or ratification is provided to the child by a parent, no witnessing or attesting to the child's mirror image occurs (Lacan, 2015, pp. 355–6), such that the ideal ego is perhaps not internalized at all.[19]

The Myth of Narcissus

I [Narcissus] am deluded and know it, but what love is not delusion? And ought not love be judged by its distance from dreary reason, the height of its flight, the depth of its madness?
Ovid, *Metamorphoses*, III.448–50

Consider the mythical case of Narcissus, as recounted by Ovid. Narcissus is not interested in girls or in guys either. A male gallant who is shunned by him prays that Narcissus will be made to feel unrequited love ("Let him know how it feels to yearn without hope"), and indeed he does feel it after Nemesis, the righteous, hears the man's vengeful prayer (Ovid, *Metamorphoses*, III.402–6). Narcissus – who is in his sixteenth year and although "no longer a boy, [is] not yet a man, [and is] truly gorgeous" (III.350–2) –

becomes enamored of his image in a pond; and, in Ovid's version, Narcissus becomes well aware that it is an image of himself, not a water-spirit.

It is the beauty of the image that fascinates him; he is captured by it as certain predators are paralyzed by the peacock's eye spots on its feathers or the rabbit is by the weasel's mesmerizing look. It *captivates* him, it hypnotizes him, and he can do nothing but gaze at it. There is a kind of mortal passion for or fatal attraction here to this image, to this reflection of himself that he sees for what is perhaps the first time ever. He becomes so enamored of this image that he can never leave the pond, "so that by degrees he lost his color, his figure, and [his] beauty. [. . .] He pined away and died" (Bulfinch, 1979, p. 121).

Perhaps the problem for Narcissus is that he is unable to take this image that he loves as himself and more than himself into himself, unable to introject it, to internalize it the way one does through the help of the parental Other in the mirror stage. In Narcissus' case, the beloved image remains exterior, outside of himself.

Sibling Rivalry

Likeness, properly speaking, is a cause of love.

Aquinas, 1952, p. 738

Let us shift now from a mythical case to certain actual cases – in this instance, cases of sibling rivalry that Freud discusses in his 1922 paper, "Some Neurotic Mechanisms in Jealousy, Paranoia and Homosexuality," a paper that Lacan himself translated into French in 1932, which is probably indicative of its importance to him. In this paper, Freud (1922/1955b) reports on several cases in which brothers who initially rivaled with each other for their mother's attention later became "the first homosexual love-objects" for each other (p. 231). Owing to the repression of sibling rivalry, love displaced from the mother to the brother with whom they rivaled.[20] Early antagonism (forced into the position below the bar that symbolizes repression here) turned into affection:

manifest love for sibling
———————————————————————————
repressed hatred for sibling

What strikes Freud here is not so much the reversal of hostility into love, which is common enough, but rather that it is precisely the opposite of what happens in paranoia where it is the person who is originally loved who later becomes the hated persecutor. Love turns to hate in paranoia, whereas hatred turns to love in such cases of intense sibling rivalry.[21]

Lacan comments on this in his paper on the Papin sisters in *Le Minotaure* 3/4 (1933–4), written a year after his translation of Freud's text was published. He says, when "the forced reduction of the early hostility between brothers occurs, an [. . .] inversion of this hostility into desire can occur," giving rise to "an affective fixation still very close to the solipsistic ego, a fixation that warrants the label 'narcissistic' and in which the object chosen is as similar as possible to the subject; this is why it takes on a homosexual character." Here it is the boy's sibling who he genuinely loves as himself, the sibling's image showing him who and what he is.

In other words, whereas Freud perhaps saw this reversal of hate into love among brothers as a nonpsychotic path to homosexuality (nonpsychotic insofar as it involves repression, which is a specifically neurotic form of negation), Lacan, at this very early stage of his work, emphasizes the importance of the "solipsistic ego" in such cases, which is no doubt a synonym here for the ideal ego that we love as and even more than ourselves.

Lacan's "Beloved": Crimes of Passion

Redoubled desire is love, but redoubled love turns into delusion.
                                    Lacan, 2015, p. 404 (endnote 50,3)

Let us consider next the detailed case of psychosis on which Lacan reported in his doctoral dissertation in 1932, the case of a woman he referred to pseudonymously as Aimée (meaning loved one or beloved). He mentions that all of her persecutors were duplicates or stand-ins for her first persecutor, her older sister, whom she dearly loved early on in life. He suggests that a reversal of love into hatred occurred in Aimée's case, leading to her dramatic assault on an actress who was one of the later stand-ins for her sister. The series of her persecutors was made up of "the doublets, triplets, and successive 'printings' of a prototype [of her older sister]. This prototype ha[d] a twofold value, both affective and representative" (1932/1980, p. 253).[22]

Here is what Lacan says about the kind of woman who could become a persecutor for Aimée:

She is the stereotypical famous woman, who is adored by the public, newly successful, and living in the lap of luxury. And although the patient attacks the lives, artifices, and corruption of such women vigorously in her writings, one must highlight the ambivalence of her attitude; for she too, as we shall see, would like to be a novelist, have a place in the footlights, lead a life of luxury, and make her mark on the world. (p. 164)

In short, the women who become Aimée's persecutors are women who live the kind of life she herself would like to lead. They are the very image of a woman worthy of love in her eyes; they are what she feels she would have to be in order to be loved by herself, to be as loved by herself as she loves others: *they are her ideal*. Regarding one of them (referred to in the case as Miss C. de la N.),[23] Lacan says:

this type of woman is exactly what Aimée herself dreams of becoming. The same image that represents her ideal is also the object of her hatred. She thus strikes in her victim [a famous actress of the time] her *externalized ideal*, just as the person who commits a crime of passion strikes the sole object of [both] his hatred and his love. (p. 253)[24]

He says that in striking this actress with a knife, Aimée "*struck herself*," and that it was at this precise moment that she felt relief, manifested in her crying, the delusion abruptly dissipating (p. 250). There is an obvious confusion in Aimée's case between inside and outside, internal and external.

Lacan suggests that:

The main persecutor [in such cases of paranoia] is always of the same sex as the subject and is identical to, or at least clearly represents, the person of the same sex to whom the subject is most profoundly attached in his affective history. (p. 273)[25]

Lacan even comments in a footnote here that although many authors have reported on cases in which this is true, few of them have realized how regularly this is the case. He mentions in his 1932 dissertation that shared delusions almost always involve mother-and-daughter pairs or father-and-son pairs (p. 284).[26]

In Aimée's case, the ideal image continues to be found in the mirror or in the rival of the same sex, but not in herself, so to speak.[27] Her ideal ego is encountered in the outside world, not in herself. The beloved image – beloved because it provides an elusive sense of unity, wholeness, and power – is found elsewhere than in herself. And it is loved more than herself.

It is something she does not carry around with her, so to speak, but rather something she finds in reality, whether in her sister's face, or in the other women who become her persecutors. She should be her own ideal, as most of us are to at least some small degree; but instead she sees her ideal out in the world, in an actress who is what she feels she herself should be. It would be inaccurate to say that she has no sense of self whatsoever (or that she has lost all sense of self, as certain schizophrenics describe the implosion they experience, often between 18 and 25 years of age); rather, it would seem that she has never been able to locate her self inside herself.

"Family Complexes"

Passion is "what one suffers" – in the final analysis, it is death.
                                        Rougemont, 1983, p. 46/44

Aimée's image of herself seems to have been inextricably bound up with her image of her sister, which is related to what Lacan referred to in *Les complexes familiaux* ("Family Complexes"), as the "intrusion complex."[28] As only a small portion of this text is available in English, and as even this small portion is not readily accessible, I will summarize a number of the points Lacan makes in it that are relevant to our discussion here.

Long before Lacan comes up with the idea that parental approval is necessary to the internalization of the ideal ego in the mirror stage and before he formulates the notion of the symbolic, he hypothesizes the existence of an initial mother–child unity that is lost at the time of weaning. It is at the moment of weaning that the child loses the "unity of himself" (Lacan, 1938/1984, p. 44) – a unity that he had apparently found in his nondifferentiation from his mother, that is, in his sense of forming a whole with her (a sense that is only constituted retroactively, of course, when it is lost), or at least with her breast ("the imago of the maternal bosom dominates all of man's life," p. 32).[29]

As he is weaned, he suddenly finds himself to be a fragmented body and experiences a "tendency [that is, an impulse of some kind] to restore his lost unity"; he attempts to restore a sense of unity by relying on the "imago of the double" (p. 44), a "foreign" image or model: the image of another person. Lacan calls this the "intrusion complex" and he proposes that it is "starting from this very stage that one first begins to recognize a rival, that is, an 'other' as an object" (p. 37) – indeed, this seems to be his first use of the term "other" as semblable.

This "intrusion complex," which is most common, according to Lacan, when there is only a very small age gap between the children in question, involves "two opposite and complementary attitudes" that children seem to be required to adopt: seducer and seduced, dominator and dominated. The small difference in age between the children involved means that the subjects are very similar to each other in size and capabilities. "The imago of the other is linked to the structure of one's own body, especially the structure of its relational functions, by a certain objective similarity" (p. 38).

Lacan does not see the positions of seducer and seduced, dominator and dominated, so much as choices, but rather as established by nature – by instinct, one might say, since these same positions are found in many other species. He suggests that they are at the origin of sadomasochism (p. 40): both parties are required to play these roles whether they like it or not and both parties relate equally to both roles, at least at the outset. The sense we have of the other at this stage is, he claims, entirely imaginary (p. 38): the other is not fundamentally different from ourselves.

The kind of identification with the other (with a lowercase *o*) that is at work here leads to a situation in which aggression toward the other is tantamount to aggression toward oneself; Lacan even refers to the role played by masochism in sadism as an "intimate lining" or "intimate doubling" [*doublure intime*] (p. 40).

Lacan characterizes the child's world at this stage as "a narcissistic world" and says that it "does not contain other people [*autrui*]" (p. 45). As long as the child simply mimics another child's gestures, faces, and emotions through a form of transitivism, "the [child-] subject is not distinguished from the image itself," that is, from "the image of the semblable" – in other words, from the image of a person very like himself. "The image merely adds the temporary intrusion of a foreign tendency" – that is, a tendency borrowed from another – to the child's pre-existing tendencies. Lacan refers to this as a "narcissistic intrusion," saying that "before the ego affirms its [separate] identity, it is confused with this image that forms (or shapes) it, but that alienates it primordially" (p. 45). (Insofar as there are not two fundamentally distinct objects present here, except from the outside observer's vantage point, it is perhaps not strictly correct to talk about "intrusion" here, intrusion requiring that there be two separate objects, one of which encroaches upon the space of the other. In other words, this can only be experienced by one party as intrusive *after* two distinct parties have come into being.)

Lacan goes on to try to explain here how this primordial confusion of self and other is overcome through jealousy, it being rivalry for a third object that triangulates the situation and introduces a pact or agreement between the two originally indistinct parties. We see another example here of Lacan's early attempt to use the Hegelian master/slave dialectic to go beyond the dyadic struggle to the death, an attempt he relinquishes once he realizes the symbolic's important contribution (the *einziger Zug* or unary trait from the parent) to the mirror stage. Whereas Lacan initially attempts to bring the symbolic pact into being out of a purely imaginary dialectic, he later gives up such an effort as futile.

The "solipsistic ego" that Lacan refers to in his discussion of the intrusion complex concerns, I would venture to propose, the ideal ego: the image of the self as a totalized whole, as a unit that seems imbued with power like the powerful adults one sees around one. The child's joyful *assumption* (owning, taking on, or assimilating) of this image is motivated by his search for a newfound unity, once the early mother–child (or mother–breast) unity has been shattered by weaning (which, like the mirror stage itself, generally occurs between six and 18 months of age in the West), and by competition with others like himself for prestige and power; but it is made possible only by the unary trait provided by the parent.

The mother now becomes constituted as an object separate from the child, and although rejecting the child's needs at the time of weaning, she is nevertheless experienced as overwhelming, due to her enigmatic desire, which comes into focus for the first time. Lacan goes on to suggest in Seminar VIII, some two decades later, that "This function, $i(a)$ [his shorthand for the ideal ego], is the core function of narcissistic investment" (2015, p. 373) and that $i(a)$ forms as a defense against a mother whose desire is now viewed by the child as potentially invasive and enveloping (such mothers can be discerned in certain depictions of Madonna and child; p. 377). The narcissistic attachment to oneself serves as a barrier, as something that stops libido from fleeing the ego and leaving it depleted when the child is exclusively attached to the mother (and possibly vice versa, stopping the mother from overly investing in her child?). Our investment in another person is blocked at a certain point: "the specular image [. . .] is a dam against the Pacific of motherly love" (p. 394). Without the internalization of the ideal ego (based on the specular or mirror image), we would be overwhelmed, Lacan proposes, by a mother who is now separate from us. She is not experienced as a worrisome ocean of attention prior to weaning; but post-weaning, the constitution of selfhood via the ideal ego is fragile and easily threatened by a mother whose desire we cannot fathom.

Transitivism

What could be finer than to have someone to whom you may speak as freely as to yourself? How could you derive true joy

from good fortune, if you did not have someone who would
rejoice in your happiness as much as you yourself do?

Cicero, 1971, p. 55

Lacan notes that very young children show no real signs of empa-
thizing with others; their relations with other children are, instead,
characterized by identification. One child identifies with another
because the latter resembles the former's own self-image. This
attachment can be characterized as one of "narcissistic identification": I identify with someone who resembles the image (i.e.,
self-image) I love; I love that person *as myself*, as in the biblical
injunction, because at some fundamental level I do not distinguish
between myself and this other person.[30]

In this context, Lacan (2006a, p. 113) provides a number of examples of what he calls "normal transitivism," whereby one child falls
down and its companion cries in its stead, or one child hits a second
but claims that the second hit him ("he hit me" instead of "I hit
him").

There is a *confusion of selves* here. Of course, the confusion of
selves that occurs in "normal transitivism" in very young human
beings does not necessarily lead always to what looks like empathy
or sympathy to observers (e.g., one child crying when a nearby child
falls down) – it can also lead to fierce rivalry and acts of aggression
that know no bounds other than the limits of the combatants' physical strength.

*Transitivism is thus clearly associated by Lacan with the imaginary
register*. Transitivism is put an end to, for the most part, by the
introjection of the parent's nod in the mirror stage as the core of the
ego-ideal and the anchoring point of the symbolic. Self and other
become far more separate and distinct at this point, and indeed
we have to work quite hard hereafter to mentally put ourselves
in another's shoes and try to imagine or anticipate how he or she
would feel if we did one thing instead of another. But transitivism
is never put an end to in cases in which the child does not get the
approving nod from the parent and in which the ego-ideal thus
never comes into being (as that which can seal off the still somewhat
amorphous ideal ego; see Fink, 2004, pp. 108–9; 2014a, pp. 30–7).[31]

How did this play out in the case of Aimée? She overcame the
early fragmentation brought on by her prematurity at birth (and/
or by weaning) by relying not on her own image in the mirror as
approved of by a parent, but on the "imago of the double" (Lacan,
1938/1984, p. 44), a "foreign" image or model: that of her sister. In
Aimée's case, "the ego is modeled" on "the primordial imago of the
double" (p. 48). Lacan goes on to argue that something similar can

be seen in other cases as well, including certain cases of homosexuality and fetishism, and in cases of paranoia where it plays a role "in the type of persecutor, whether outside or inside" (p. 48).

The Intrusion (or Fraternal) Complex and the "Solipsistic Ego"

These people love their delusion *as they love themselves.*

Freud, 1954, p. 113

In other words, at least in 1938, Lacan does not restrict the influence of the "intrusion complex" – or "fraternal complex," as he sometimes calls it – to paranoia, where it leads to "the frequency of themes of filiation, usurpation, and spoliation, [and to the] more paranoid themes of intrusion, influence, splitting, doubling, and the whole set of delusional transmutations of the body" (1938/1984, p. 49). He implies that an important role may well be played by the fraternal complex in other diagnostic categories as well.

Lacan suggests that psychoanalysis allows us to see that the "elective object of libido at the [fraternal complex] stage[32] [. . .] is homosexual" and that love and identification fuse in this elective object (pp. 38–9), leading to *passion tied to the image of someone who looks very much like oneself* (giving rise to a relation between semblables that can be abbreviated as *a-a'*).

Lacan goes on to propose that this fusion of love and identification

is refound in adults, in the passion of jealousy in love relations and it is here that one can grasp it best. One must recognize it, in effect, in the powerful interest the subject shows in his rival's image: an interest which, although it is asserted as hatred – that is, as negative – and although it is motivated by the supposed love object, [. . .] must be interpreted as the essential and positive interest of this passion. (p. 39)

In other words, the passionate interest in "the other woman" in hysteria, for example (mentioned in Chapter 1), may in certain cases be based less, Lacan would seem to be suggesting here, on a passionate attachment to the man who is supposedly the true object of her affections, than on a fascination with the rival woman as the imago or ideal ego at the core of her own being. Lacan does not emphasize this facet of things when he discusses the dream of the butcher's wife many years later, but he does mention it in a more general discussion of hysteria in 1957 (Lacan, 2006a, p. 452). It might be thought of as playing a role in Dora's fascination with Frau K., insofar as the latter represents Dora's own femininity (although there seems to be no conscious hatred expressed toward Frau K. by Dora). Indeed, women's concern with the question of femininity, of what it means to be a woman, may well be related to this fascination with the imago of another woman.[33]

The fraternal complex may also play a role in a man's attempt to fathom what it means to be a man, and in the frequency with which another man is present in men's otherwise heterosexual erotic fantasies, where it seems there has to be a struggle with another man to make it interesting: a brother-like rival or father figure.[34]

I have associated the "solipsistic ego" that Lacan (1933–4) refers to in his discussion of the fraternal complex with the highly cathected ideal ego, and his point there seems to be that anything that touches upon this ideal image generates a passionate response, whether positive or negative. When the mistress of one of my perverse analysands one day called him "trash" and acted uninterested in him, he went wild, wanted to strangle her, rape her, and possess her, as he said. He did none of those things, but it was clear that by rejecting him and striking out at his ideal ego, his mistress got an incredibly big rise out of him. He referred to the word she called him as "a piercing sword" and broke up with her promptly. Hell hath no fury like a lover scorned![35] (He nevertheless soon went back to her, nothing seeming to enflame certain men more than a woman who challenges their masculinity, strikes out at their narcissism, and makes them feel weak, inadequate, and castrated.)[36] We shall see further on how such "touchiness" regarding the ideal ego manifests itself in the analytic setting.

Lacan (2015, p. 373) refers to the ideal ego in Seminar VIII as "the core function of narcissistic investment," and argues that the formation of the ideal ego involves a massive identification, whereas the ego-ideal involves a very punctual, limited identification with a single trait (pp. 355–6). He goes on to maintain that although we are ready and willing to risk everything for desire, even life itself, we are not ready to risk $i(a)$, Lacan's shorthand or matheme for the ideal ego (p. 394).

What we perhaps see in the case of Aimée is the way in which the imaginary, functioning not under the supremacy of the symbolic, but quite independently, affects love. It makes love into an *infection*; it leads to passion for an image, an image of the other (who is oneself) which is captivating or detested by turns, leading to an imagined love affair – erotomania – or persecutory paranoia.

Regarding people who are suffering from a shared delusion, like the Papin sisters, Lacan says:

The "problem [or malady] of being two [*mal d'être deux*]" from which these patients suffer hardly frees them from Narcissus' problem. It is a mortal passion that ends up taking its own life. (1933–4, p. 28)

This expression, *mal d'être deux*, borrowed from Stéphane Mallarmé's (1842–98) poem "L'après-midi d'un faune" ("The Afternoon of a Fawn"),[37] implies that, like Aristophanes' creatures who are desperately seeking their other half, those who share a delusion want to become one, want to fuse not just imaginarily but really, and yet are unable to do so. Unlike Narcissus, there are two of them, and thus their love for each other is not unrequited the way his was. Lacan suggests, however, that their passion for what they see in each other, for that image of self/other, consumes them in the same way, destroys them just as it did Narcissus, perhaps at least in part because they are unable to become one in reality.

Love and Psychosis

What is the difference between someone who is psychotic and someone who isn't based on? It is based on the fact that a type of love relationship that abolishes him as a subject is possible for the psychotic, insofar as it allows for a radical heterogeneity of the Other. But this love is also a dead love.

Lacan, 1993, pp. 287–8

The psychotic's Eros is located where speech is absent. It is there that he finds his supreme love.

Lacan, 1993, p. 289

The beloved image (ideal ego) that is found elsewhere than in oneself perhaps explains why, when close friendships develop among psychotics, it is often between people who look somewhat alike, and who then progressively make subtle or not so subtle changes to look even more alike (for an example, see the case of "Tina" in Fink, 2014a, pp. 189–94). They become "twinsies" and indulge in "same person syndrome" without even realizing it or finding it curious. They only recognize their similar looks when other people remark upon them. Should one of them become ill and die, or meet with death through an accident or war, it is as if the other had died too (which can create thorny problems for the analyst attempting to treat the survivor).

This perhaps also explains the instantaneous and all-consuming love affairs certain psychotics have, which begin in a flash (the instant of the glance, we might say) and remain for some time at an all-consuming pitch bordering on total fusion; indeed, of all love, psychotic love most completely conforms to the theory of love professed by Aristophanes in Plato's *Symposium* to the effect that two lovers strive to become one, and to that professed by Cicero (1971, p. 80) when he says, "Man is ever in search of a companion whose heart's blood he may so mingle with his own that they become virtually one person instead of two." When the psychotic's chosen partner is not psychotic, he or she is likely to become exhausted in fairly short order; although thrilled and enchanted at the outset, he or she is likely to feel "creeped out" or "freaked out" at the exclusiveness desired by the partner. Whereas it was exciting and captivating at the outset, it becomes smothering and overwhelming.

Should the nonpsychotic partner attempt to pull away, the psychotic's response may well be rage, impassioned hatred, and/or a thirst for vengeance. The psychotic may even begin to engage in "stalking" the former partner, a practice the public mind seems to have become fascinated with in recent years, no doubt due to the flattering nature of the stalker's interest in the "stalkee." A neurotic partner rarely makes one feel so important and interesting, rarely expresses a passion for one so great that only prison can put an end to it. The hallmark of neurosis is doubt and uncertainty, particularly with regard to love; the neurotic is full of ambivalence regarding love matters, and is never certain (the way a psychotic can be) of his or her love, except perhaps after analysis, after his undecided desire has become decided.[38]

Love songs and romance novels have accustomed us to declarations of love that are so powerful that they outlive the longest war, the longest separation, overcome the greatest obstacles imaginable, defeat all foes, move mountains, and circumvent all social, economic, and familial constraints.[39]

Such omnipotent, overpowering love fascinates us; indeed, most of us have perhaps at one time or another experienced somewhat milder forms of it when falling in love, at the beginning of a new relationship, and dream of it being stronger still or lasting forever. For what we are used to, for the most part, and become more or less resigned to is often so much less overpowering – it is "underwhelming," one might say.

At some point, nevertheless, we would most likely find psychotically intense love impossible to bear: the fusion with us sought by our partner would seem reckless, suicidal, and perhaps even homicidal. It would seem to seek to utterly negate our own individuality, our own subjectivity – for, as Lacan (1938/1984) says, there is no other in this narcissistic universe, no recognition of the other as such

(p. 45); there is only one. We are flattered because we think we are being loved for our own particularity, but in fact our subjective difference from all others is being totally negated. The otherness of the other is completely denied here: there is neither $ (the barred subject) nor A (for *Autre*, i.e., the Other) here, only *a-a'*.[40]

The Dangers of Imaginary-Based Love

> Thus a man shall leave his father and his mother and cleave to
> his wife, and the two shall make but one flesh.
>
> Genesis 2:24

A question we must raise is whether this mortal passion is operative for all of us or only for psychotics. For those of us who are not paranoiacs, for those of us whose imaginaries have been largely overwritten by the symbolic, it seems that the relation to the other is still quite capable, in certain circumstances, of approaching the "solipsistic ego" or ideal ego, unleashing a kind of narcissistic passion within us. The question whether it becomes a mortal passion for neurotics as it does for paranoiacs is perhaps a question of more or less rather than all or nothing.

As Lacan (1998a) warns us in Seminar XX, insofar as love is the narcissistic aim to make one of two, to fuse two into one, it aims at the annihilation of difference (p. 6). In the attempt to find oneself or one's ideal self in the other, one tends to overlook all difference between self and other.

In neurosis, the attempt to merge two into one is an attempt to turn back the hands of time, to return to a moment before alienation and separation have occurred,[41] to a time before any transitional object or object *a* could come into being (or, in another vocabulary, before any separation/individuation has occurred). It is an attempt to reverse the loss of the object, to make it such that there is no lost object, to make good the rift between mother and child, or, in Aristophanes' terms, to rejoin the two beings sundered by Zeus' anger at the spherical beings we once were – a chimerical project at best,[42] but one that unleashes more passion in most of us than we experience at any other moment (except perhaps that of murderous rage).

In fusion is the annihilation of difference, and falling in love is perhaps the best illustration of this. Many of us have had the experience of falling in love very quickly and intensely while knowing precious little about the person with whom we have fallen in love. Having found a few points of agreement between ourselves and the other – shared musical tastes, culinary or cinematic interests, philosophical views, or what have you – we suddenly begin to feel that we have met our soul mate, that this other person is essentially another version of us in a somewhat different material package (we feel we are "twin souls," as P. G. Wodehouse so often puts it). This equation of ourselves with the other during the passionate experience of falling in love often goes so far as to ignore any signs that the other is in fact quite different from us, and to read all signs as if they corroborated our hypothesis that the other is just like us. As Lacan (2015, p. 356) says, "the ideal ego is the source of an imaginary projection" and, insofar as we are looking to find ourselves in the other, the easiest way to succeed at this is to project onto the other what we believe we ourselves are.

It would seem that some of the intensity of the experience of falling in love derives from the joyful, albeit deluded, recognition of ourselves in another. This would simultaneously explain some of the tension and hatred generated when we can no longer ignore some feature of the other that clearly does not fit into our own view of ourselves – that is, into our own self-image.

Imaginary Passion in the Analytic Setting

Love [. . .] is a passion that involves ignorance of desire.
                                                        Lacan, 1998a, p. 4

As I indicated in an earlier book (Fink, 2007), analysts – especially those trained in certain schools – have a tendency to forget that many (certainly not all) of the reproaches and criticisms addressed to them by their analysands are not really about them, but about other figures in their analysands' lives, past and present. This is why such reproaches, and the anger and tension that often accompany them, are referred to in psychoanalysis as "transferences." They are not directly caused by anything specific the analyst has said or done, but by a "false connection" made by the analysand – to which the analyst lends him- or herself – between the analyst and some other figure.

Ideally, the analyst allows such transferences to occur, as they are fruitful for the treatment, and does not take them personally; but many an analyst feels immediately defensive and/or wounded by such criticism and hastens to dispute the justice of the reproach (retorting, for example, "I am not distant and cold – I've always been warm to all my patients"; or "How can you say I'm not trying to help? I offered two new interpretations just last week").

Rather than taking such transferences up at the level of the symbolic and seeking to determine to what episode, incident, or relationship they may be attached in the patient's past or present life, certain analysts take such criticism not as transference, but as a direct attack on their own precious view of themselves as warm, helpful, trying hard, understanding, insightful, and so on. They feel that their self-image as good therapists is under siege and attempt to justify themselves or – in the worst-case scenario – counterattack (saying such things as, "*You* are the one who is being uncooperative, not me!*").

Such defensive and furious reactions are indicative that transference has been mistaken by the practitioner as a personal attack and that the entire situation is being grasped by the practitioner solely at the imaginary level. This is generally what is operative when we hear of analysts yelling at their patients, slamming doors, and refusing to ever meet with them again. Professionalism – which in the analytic setting means never forgetting that we are there to allow patients to project and transfer all kinds of things onto us in order to help them work these things through – goes out the window in such cases, and the therapist takes everything highly personally.

We should expect a *patient* to generally take criticism from people personally, even when it seems unlikely that it is personal, insofar as the patient has not yet realized the extent to which people's criticism is often far more about them (reflecting their own criticism of themselves and their behavior) than about him or her. Nevertheless, analysts often express surprise at how easily certain patients read implicit criticism into almost every question they raise or remark they make, especially in the early stages of the treatment, forgetting the degree to which patients may easily feel their idealized view of themselves (i.e., their ideal ego) to be under attack. In cases of neurosis, such "touchiness" often subsides once trust develops between analysand and analyst, but in cases of paranoia the analyst must be especially careful to say nothing that might wound the patient's fragile sense of self.

Absurdly enough, patients with such fragile senses of self have been dubbed "narcissistic" by contemporary psychiatry and psychoanalysis, clinicians failing to realize that it is precisely those who are least sure of themselves and can least easily love themselves who must constantly guard their ideal ego (or $i(a)$) against attack and prop themselves up. If they seem so obsessed with themselves, it is precisely because their own sense of self is so unsure and vacillating! What could be more logical than their blowing their tops or counterattacking when they sense their fragile selves are being challenged or attacked? The clinician's goal should obviously not be to "take them down a notch" narcissistically, but rather – among other things (see Fink, 2007, chapter 10) – to help them consolidate a sense of self that will allow them to love themselves.

THE REAL

VI

Love and the Real

The real is what does not depend on my idea of it.
Lacan, 1973–4, class given on April 23, 1974

You can't do just any old thing you want with the real.
Lacan, 1965–6, class given on January 5, 1966

Leaving behind the symbolic – related to desire as found, for example, in love triangles – and the imaginary, related to narcissism, we turn now to the facets of love that are connected to the real. The role played by the real in love can be explored from several different angles, but we will take up just a couple of them here.

Repetition Compulsion

The imitation characteristic of the first days of life is such
that we contract the passions of our parents even when those
passions poison our lives.
Stendhal, 2004, p. 258/225

The first is the real understood as the traumatic cause of repetition compulsion. A young woman, whose father abruptly left her family when she was a young girl, later in life found herself repeatedly acting in such a way as to encourage her partners to abandon her. A man, whose mother had, when he was a small child, divorced his father owing to his abusive behavior while drunk, compulsively sabotaged his relations with the women who most unreservedly expressed their love for him, unwittingly and uncontrollably repeating his father's modus operandi.

In another case, a woman seemed unable to have any amorous connection with anyone unless she got so drunk she would virtually black out; once plastered, she would have sex with almost any man she met. Although she regularly berated herself for this behavior (not simply because it generally involved unprotected sex), she could not help but repeat the pattern again and again. It turned out, not surprisingly, that, when she was a child, her father had once touched her sexually when he himself was drunk.

Something from the past that is not verbalized and worked through in analysis leads to repetition compulsion. This is perhaps the most easily visible effect of the real in the field of love, confirming in a sense Tina Turner's notion that love is "but a secondhand emotion" insofar as it involves repetition.

The Unsymbolizable

A second way of thinking about the role of the real in love involves the real as that which is not only currently unsymbolized but *unsymbolizable*. There is something about the encounter with sexual sensations and feelings that is traumatic for each of us, none of us ever being adequately prepared to feel them when we do so for the first time, some of us being unprepared even at later times as well. We sometimes undergo sexual sensations as a kind of impingement from within and attribute them to an outside source, experiencing them, like numerous authors in Antiquity experienced love itself, as something outside of our control, a kind of attack on us from the outside. The adolescent boy who finds himself having erections while sitting across from a woman he describes as an "ugly old hag" on the subway, and a woman who has an orgasm during a terrifying rape are just two of the most obvious examples of this.

In an intriguing account of love and lust in Antiquity, Christopher Faraone (1999) distinguishes between two forms of magic used in seventh-century B.C. Greece, suggesting that "eros magic" included spells designed to induce passion, whereas "philia magic" involved spells aiming to induce affection.

> In archaic and classical Greek discourse there is a clear differ-
> ence between the *invasive and dangerous onset of eros* and the
> more benign feelings of *philia*, a term that generally describes a
> reciprocal relationship based on mutual affection. Thus, from
> the earliest periods *Greeks either describe the onset of* eros *as
> an invasive, demonic attack or use a ballistic model in which
> Aphrodite is said to throw and hit someone with* eros *or* pothos
> [longing]. (p. 29; my italics)[1]

A patient of mine once told me how difficult it was for her to let her husband of many years manually bring her to orgasm during intercourse. It was, as she put it, "too stimulating," leading her to almost pull his hand away a couple of times, and she came faster than she ever had before. "I didn't see it coming," she said, and it made her feel "undone and vulnerable."

Her sexual jouissance was, in this case, a kind of attack. She told me that she usually "regulated" her excitation during intercourse by touching herself; letting her husband do it changed the experience into something entirely different and she claimed that afterward she felt she "belonged to him" for the first time ever.

Another analysand was telling me about a man he was crazy about, and mentioned that he was afraid of his intense attraction to the man. He wanted more from this man than just sex, and had gone "all the way down fantasy lane," fantasizing that this man "was powerlessly attracted to" the patient or that both of them were helplessly attracted to each other, and that there was some sort of ideal relationship like that of Tristan and Isolde between them. In discussing how powerfully and powerlessly he felt drawn to this man, he slipped and instead of saying "attraction" said, "attacktion."

For some, the way jouissance at times sneaks up on them or steals over them is disconcerting and even destabilizing, fitting into no neat categories or sets of familiar experiences.

Love at First Sight

> Love is like a fever: it comes and goes without the will having
> anything to do with it.
>
> Stendhal, 2004, p. 38/51

Love as an attack can also be seen in what in English we typically call "love at first sight," and what the French call le coup de foudre, translated in English-language versions of Stendhal's work as "the thunderbolt." (One might also say that someone is thunderstruck or hit by lightning.)

In Antiquity, Cupid (also known as Eros) was depicted as shooting arrows (out of the blue) that would pierce someone's body and heart, or as brandishing torches designed to make the beloved burn – not just figuratively – with desire. Love then was seen as a sudden and aggressive attack. A ritualistic form of this can be seen in the fact that a man could show a woman that he was interested in her by throwing an apple at her; if she picked it up after it hit her, it was a sign that his love might be reciprocated.

In ancient Greece, love was most clearly considered to be a kind of attack in instances of love at first sight, which were associated at the time primarily with male homosexuals, but also with courtesans who were considered to be like men in their way of loving. Faraone (1999) mentions an author who states that a certain woman "assumes the male initiative in courtship and [. . .] falls in love at first sight," something that Faraone characterizes as a typical "topos of pederastic infatuation" (p. 153 n. 76). In Apuleius' *Metamorphoses*, in Roman times, the protagonist Lucias is warned about the wife of his host who, like a typical male *erastés*, falls in love at first sight and uses erotic magic to have her way: "'No sooner does she catch sight of some young man of attractive appearance than she is consumed by his charm and immediately directs her eye and desire at him'" (p. 158). Contemporary research on the exact frequencies with which love at first sight occurs in the different sexes seems sparse and inconclusive; but love at first sight seems to have been considered to arise more often in men in Victorian times and has been discussed most often in women's magazines since at least the 1980s (Matthews, 2004).[2]

In our own times, we obviously come across men who fall in love instantaneously, seeming to perceive object *a* in someone in a flash. Even though the same man often falls in love instantly with a number of different women over the course of time, each occurrence is experienced by him as a kind of attack, as beyond his control.

As Colette Soler (2003, p. 252) has put it, love at first sight (*le coup de foudre*) "bypasses the Other [understood as] language, operating directly on the basis of the drives," the drives never being more than partially socialized or symbolized, according to Lacan. There seems to be a narcissistic – and hence imaginary – component to falling in love at first sight (especially when the beloved closely resembles oneself). But there is also something drive-related and hence real in the sense in which we feel unable to do anything about our attraction to this other person, who may seem to be wrong for us in so many obvious ways. We feel that we cannot help ourselves, *c'est plus fort que nous*, as the French say. It is something that comes over or overpowers us; we are swept up in it, swept away. Freud, in his typically terse way, calls it "compulsive."[3]

The persecutory nature of love or lust at first sight can be seen in the case of one of my analysands, who told me that when he was a teenager he wished he was already an old man so that he would not be bothered by lustful feelings upon seeing a beautiful girl, having heard that old men like Socrates were not so bothered by them.

It also can be seen in the case of another of my analysands, who told me that he once seriously contemplated becoming a Trappist monk so that he would be unable to see women and be tormented by his attraction to them. He wished not only to shut himself in some-where so would not see women's bodies, but also to be required to recite prayers all day long so that he would be unable to fantasize about any of the women he had been fixated on in his past. When this particular patient saw a woman with what he considered to be "a perfect butt," he immediately felt that it promised him "infinite orgasms" – or, as we might put it, infinite satisfaction of the sexual drive – and he became hopelessly obsessed with her, everything else in his life falling by the wayside.

In 1973, Lacan (1998a) went so far as to refer to "the indirect character of that attack called love" (p. 104/95).[4]

Note that not every instance of falling in love at first sight need be viewed as completely short-circuiting the symbolic and imagi-nary orders. One of my female analysands reported an instance of falling in love at first sight that seems to have had less to do with the drives than with a certain competition with other women: the man she fell in love with instantaneously was surrounded by women who appeared to be his wife and daughters. The analysand herself had several sisters and she had found it difficult as a child to get atten-tion from her father, who seemed thoroughly preoccupied with her mother. She also mentioned, in the course of her experience of the incident, that this man had a "nice body," which for her seemed simply to mean that he was thin, suggesting that there was also an imaginary or imaginary/symbolic component to her attraction.

Kierkegaard fell in love with Regina, the woman who inspired so many of his writings, at first sight, and he once commented that he believed "that he had seen her long before, that all love like all knowledge is recollection" (quoted in Lowrie, 1970, p. 202). Where might he have seen her before, if we are to take this comment seriously? Perhaps she resembled his mother or some other early caretaker of his in some significant way?[5]

The Other Jouissance

Regarding lust and the more explicitly sexual sensations and sat-isfactions people have, we find that certain kinds are generally experienced as less problematic than others. For example, despite the fact that it is sometimes followed by feelings of guilt, orgasm is often an almost thoroughly positive experience for men – so posi-tive, indeed, that men often resort to having sex or masturbating to relieve tension, lessen anxiety, or induce sleep.

Although someone long ago came up with the idea that *post coitum omne animal triste est*,[6] and even though this was repeated by various authors right up until Freud's time, Lacan remarks in Seminar XIII that, at least since the advent of psychoanalysis, the male animal does not seem to be terribly sad after orgasm, even if the French do still occasionally talk about *la petite mort*, the little death (Lacan, 1965–6, class given on April 20, 1966).

There seems to be something reassuring for men about the highly localized pleasure they derive from the penis as a physical organ, something that allows them to become or remain centered, in some sense. There was a joke back in the 1970s that asked why sex was so popular, the answer being that it is "centrally located." But the fact is that the jouissance we derive from sex is not nearly so centrally located for many women as it is for men. Organ pleasure, as Freud puts it, which corresponds to what Lacan calls phallic jouissance, *is* centrally located and often serves to help a man consolidate a sense of self or ego that has been threatened by competition with others or anxiety.

This organ pleasure is localized, of finite duration, and comes in discreet units that are easily countable. And, indeed, many men are fond of bragging about the number of times they can have sex in a single night, and fond of adding up their conquests (putting notches on their belts or totals in their little black books). The higher the number, the more positive their sense of self, and this connection between number and sexual satisfaction clearly shows the link between phallic jouissance and language, for without language there would likely be no such thing as number.

Women too can, of course, have organ pleasure – the kind of pleasure that Lacan refers to as phallic jouissance – and they too can count their multiple orgasms and conquests. But this seems to be not nearly as common in women as it is in men. For in the case of women – for those who, regardless of anatomy and genetics, Lacan considers to be characterized by feminine structure – we must often reckon with a kind of jouissance that is not so discreet in duration or so very localizable. Not being so centrally located, it is not necessarily terribly centering for the subject who experiences it – indeed, it may well be decentering.

Although women may rarely have been said in earlier times to be sad after coitus (*post coitum omne animal triste est sive gallus et mulier*), in our own times they have come to be sad if they do not reach orgasm; Lacan made this observation already in the mid-sixties (1965–6, class given on April 20, 1966), and it is no doubt truer still today. But certain women are, nevertheless, sad some of the time after sex especially when they *do* reach orgasm, owing perhaps to what they encounter that leads to decentering. Many women report sobbing and crying hot tears after orgasm, whether there is or is not a partner present.

The decentering a woman experiences can be understood in a number of different ways. If it occurs after intercourse, it may be due to the fact that her position as cause of her partner's desire is at least momentarily suspended or disrupted, and this may lead to a feeling of missing that prized position, and a loss of a sense of who and what she is: "If I am not desired, I am nothing." This may account, at least in certain cases, for the hysteric's wish to be the cause of the partner's desire but not the object with which the partner *satisfies* that desire and obtains jouissance. Especially when faced with a sexual partner who leaves her immediately after intercourse, the hysteric learns that her very being is likely to be called into question after the sexual act, there apparently being nothing more that her partner wants from her.

This is not the whole story, however, for it cannot explain the sense of destabilization certain women feel from masturbation, intercourse, religious transport, or other experiences that may be hard to characterize: a sense of having completely lost track of time while being out in one's garden or sitting on the beach, for example. Some women refer to these as "ecstasies," saying that they come when they are alone and find themselves transported outside themselves. One might think here of Dora's rapt contemplation of the Sistine Madonna at the art gallery in Dresden that apparently lasted two hours (Freud, 1905/1953a, p. 96).

A female analysand I worked with mentioned periods of "ecstasy" that she likened to "flowers exploding" and to "fireworks, but without the percussion." She reported having had similar episodes as a child when she would go out into the mountains, and complained that even in her fifties she could not shut the feeling off when she wanted to and could not go to sleep without taking medication. The feeling often came to her when she had been in a good mood all day and found herself alone in the evening.

She complained that such periods were "not productive," and proffered that she would like to be able to turn them off at will so she could go to sleep and be refreshed for work the next morning. She clearly seemed to experience these ecstasies as outside the phallic order of productivity and, indeed, in conflict with it. On another occasion, she characterized such moments as "vibrating at too high a pitch." She said that she would find herself "reverberating," "trembling" ("not out of fear"), and having trouble slowing down. She referred to it as "this wrong vibration."

Lacan hypothesizes that at such moments women experience another kind of jouissance, a jouissance that differs radically from the discreet, localizable, countable jouissance associated with language and its relatively precise designation of the erogenous zones, the zones that one is prohibited to touch as a child and that become all the more exciting to touch as a result of that verbalized prohibition. The prohibited kind of jouissance is closely tied to the symbolic order, according to Lacan, insofar as the parts of the body involved have been subjected to requests and demands made (and perhaps punishments meted out) by one's parents. By calling it phallic jouissance, Lacan is saying that it is a form of enjoyment that includes parental injunctions even as it contravenes them, that it is a socialized form of enjoyment, an enjoyment subject to the symbolic order.

Lacan theorizes that what certain women experience during moments of transport or ecstasy is a radically different kind of jouissance, which he calls the Other jouissance. It is radically Other in the sense that it stands outside the symbolic order, having no designated tie to it or name within it, no pre-established erogenous zone associated with it. The literal meaning of ecstasy (ex stasis) is standing outside, or standing apart from something. Not all women experience this Other jouissance, and even among those who do, not all of them experience it on a regular basis. But insofar as it stands outside of the symbolic order, it may be profoundly unsettling and decentering, having no obvious or direct connection with either the woman's ego or unconscious.[7] (Lacan associates the Other jouissance with "ex-sistence," not existence.)

It is only love, Lacan hypothesizes, that can forge a link between that foreign experience of absence from herself (that experience of being transported outside of anything she associates with her self) and her partner who has, in most cases, remained firmly anchored in the symbolic. In this sense, love creates a link between that which is profoundly inassimilable in a woman, inassimilable even to herself or by herself (she is Other to herself in this respect),[8] and another person who is associated by her with the symbolic – whether that other person be a man or a woman.

Love Is Real?

It is clear that I went into medicine because I suspected that
relations between man and woman played a decisive role in
the symptoms of human beings. [. . .] The ultimate truth is that
things do not work between man and woman.

Lacan, 1976, p. 16

Insofar as the Other jouissance would clearly be characterized by Lacan as real, as opposed to imaginary or symbolic, we might wonder whether the love that establishes a link between the Other jouissance and the phallus, between the Other jouissance and the symbolic order, is itself real. If it is, we might be led to endorse the folksinger Carol King's view that "only love is real," although we might quibble with its exclusivity.

In Seminar XXI, however, Lacan (1973–4) situates love as symbolic in religion, where *l'amour divin* (divine love or God's love) is, he hypothesizes, the symbolic link between the body as imaginary and death as real. And he situates love as imaginary in both the courtly love tradition and in psychoanalysis where love serves as the imaginary link between knowledge – knowledge as that which props up jouissance – and death. He even goes so far as to say that "when love truly becomes the means by which death is tied to [*s'unit à*] jouissance, man to woman, and being to knowledge, love can no longer be defined as *ratage*" (*ratage* means failure, botching something up, a slip-up, screw-up, or making a mess of things). When love unites these things, it can no longer be defined as botching something up but rather as *nouage*, knotting things together, tying disparate things together.

Perhaps this can help us understand Lacan's (2004) cryptic comment in Seminar X that "Only love allows jouissance to condescend to desire" (p. 209).[9] Love is the third term that establishes the two or couple of the One and the Other – desire and jouissance, man and woman – forming a Borromean knot (see Lacan, 1973–4, class given on March 12, 1974).

Love and the Drives

Insofar as the drives always come back to the same place – always revolving around the same thing, always seeking the same satisfaction again and again – they fit Lacan's (1973a, p. 49/49) definition of the real. Just as little children want to be read the same story over and over again so that they can refind the same enjoyment they took in it again and again, once the drives have managed to find an outlet to satisfaction, they tend to flow repeatedly in the same pathways, riverbeds, or streams. We might even go so far as to say that the drives involve a sort of metaphor of love, insofar as object *a* brings the metonymic slippage of desire to a halt, fixating the subject on an object *a* around which the drive revolves (p. 153/168).

At the risk of being overly schematic here, at the end of our discussion of love in the symbolic, imaginary, and real registers, we might propose that there are at least three components to love, as shown in Table 6.1.

Table 6.1

Register	Aspect of love	Rhetorical trope
Imaginary	*Passion* as a projection of perfection onto the beloved as a reflection of oneself (as one would like to see oneself) – narcissism	Isology or isomorphic parallelism
Symbolic	*Desire* as by its very nature desire for something else	Metonymy: slippage from a' to a'' to a'''
Real	*Drive* which always returns to the same place, being of its very nature compulsive	Metaphor: I come to love the object a I find in my partner

Love as a Link

However we formulate love, as imaginary, symbolic, or real, it seems clear that love can be understood as constituting a very important social link or bond that is not easily provided by anything else. As Soler (2003) points out, capitalism has progressively destroyed the many earlier ties we in the West had to places, and has broken up and scattered our previously extended families. Love – not for the Fuhrer or for a leader who establishes links between all those who put him in the place of their ego-ideal – but rather love as a link between the same and the other, between the symbolic and the real, between the phallic One and the Other sex, might be thought of as the foundation for the minimal social link we have left: the bond between two people, that bond being at the core of the smallest social unit, the household reduced to its barest bones, so to speak.

Following Soler here, love is perhaps one of the few forces we still have that can undergird a social bond that does not exclude the Other as such, the Other sex and the Other jouissance.[10]

In order for love to serve this purpose, it cannot be the love of fusion, the attempt to make one of two, which is ultimately love for the One with a capital O. Not surprisingly, we find love formulated as a making of one from two in many a text by men, whether by Aristophanes, Cicero, or Abelard. The latter, in the recently redis-covered early love letters between Abelard and Heloise (see Mews, 2001), claims that through their love he and Heloise have become one; she retorts that they are not One, and that their love still has a long way to go, seeming to sustain the importance of love between *different* people (they are not *indifferenter*, without difference, to her way of thinking).

If love is to forge a link between the One and the Other, it must involve a two that remains two – a two that does not collapse the Other into the One. This is very rare indeed!

GENERAL CONSIDERATIONS ON LOVE

VII

Languages and Cultures of Love

Stepping back from the categories of the symbolic, imaginary, and real, let us now consider just how broad a field of human experience love covers. Some of the experiences often associated with it include:

- Dependency (or so-called natural love)
- Attachment
- Friendship
- Agape (or Christian love)
- Hatred
- Attraction
- Fixation on the human form (beauty)
- Physical love, sexual desire, lust, concupiscence, sex drive
- *Fin'amor* (or courtly love)
- Romantic love
- Falling in love.

One could argue that love partakes of all of these, and we must be careful not to create overly sharp and inevitably artificial or spurious distinctions among them. When we try to grasp the meaning of a term, almost regardless of what that term is, we try to determine something about its semantic space, so to speak – that is, its various possible usages and the way in which it is distinguished from the other terms around it that hem it in, in a manner of speaking,

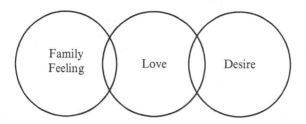

that overlap it in certain respects, and that contrast with it or are considered to be its opposite.

As Saussure (1959, pp. 114–15) tells us, the value of a sign (a sign, for him, being the relationship between a signifier and its signified) is nothing but its difference from all other related signs. Each language covers the whole of the conceptual space of the people who speak the language, even if we are astonished, at times, that certain teenagers can get by with vocabularies of no more than 300 words (the way they are used, stressed, and combined being enough to cover the whole field of what they have to say).[1] Now, the similarities and contrasts among signs change over time, and thus so do relations among signs: one term comes to the fore and begins to take up more semantic or conceptual space than it had previously, effectively pushing other related signs aside.

Even just 50 years ago, the English expression to "make love" signified the activity of courting or wooing someone. Today, the signification of the expression is almost completely different, implying sexual intercourse, though at least with more love involved than in the expression to "have sex." "Wooing" and "courting" have almost completely disappeared, having been elbowed aside first by terms like dating and going steady, and more recently by terms like "hanging out," "hanging" *tout court*, and "hooking up." (A larger sociological question that might be raised is whether the activity of courting itself has actually disappeared or whether it is simply that the words to talk about it have changed.)

Just as the relations among signs change in one and the same language over the course of time, there is no one-to-one correspondence between signs in different languages. French, for example, does not have two different verbs corresponding to such importantly opposed notions in English as liking and loving, and thus relies on qualifiers and context to distinguish between them. The verb *aimer* in French, when applied to things, can be used to simply express fairly ordinary liking in English; when it comes to people, however, it requires the addition of *bien* (*je l'aime bien*) to specify that it is liking and not loving, or *beaucoup*, to specify that it is liking very much, not loving. *J'adore* implies that one does more than merely love, but loves extremely, whereas in English one may, I believe, adore someone without it necessarily being stronger than love. (You could say it to a person who does you a big favor: "You're adorable" or "I adore you.")

As we shall see further on, what Aristotle, Aquinas, and others understand by love may differ significantly from what we understand by love today, especially insofar as they did not write in

English and used vocabulary that we still struggle to translate. In Greek, we find such overlapping and/or interconnected terms as "Eros," *philia*, and *agape* (Reeve, 2006, p. xvi), to which Latin adds *dilectio* ("dilection"). Over the course of time, the Greek term *agape*, for example, gradually replaced *philia* in a great many written texts (Faraone, 1999).[2]

I will explore here a number of terms and notions that hover around the general vicinity of love, that border at times on love, but that we may want to distinguish from it at other times.

Dependency (or so-called Natural Love)

Love and cupidity cannot coexist in one and the same person.
If love does not stem from a purely gratuitous sentiment, if it is
granted only in expectation of something in return, it is not love,
but a mere simulacrum thereof that profanes and falsifies it.

Chapelain, 2004, p. 20

Dependency might be associated with what Saint Thomas Aquinas (1952, p. 312) called "natural love," which according to him is "found in all things, even those lacking reason," including animals. It is the kind of love found in the animal kingdom between a cub and its mother, for example, and is clearly related to what Freud called "anaclisis"; as we saw in Chapter 2, anaclisis literally means leaning up against or propped up by, and anaclitic love is propped up by or is based on the self-preservative or life drives – namely, the drives for nourishment, warmth, and care. A baby animal has this natural sort of love for its mother (or parents, in cases where both parents participate in raising it) owing to the care it receives from her.

Although in the human world love and dependency are not complete strangers to each other, and dependency at times gives way or paves the way to love, we are aware that a mother might complain of her children that they are happy to have her cook for them and wash their clothes but do not really love her. Here a simple form of dependency is sharply contrasted with some other, perhaps more exacting, notion of love.

Attachment

As there are some minds whose affections [. . .] are solely placed
on one single person [i.e., themselves], whose interest and

indulgence alone they consider on every occasion, regarding the good and ill of all others as merely indifferent [. . .], so there is a different temper of mind which borrows a degree of virtue even from self-love. Such can never receive any kind of satisfaction from another without loving the creature to whom that satisfaction is owing, and without making its well-being in some sort necessary to their own ease.

Fielding, Tom Jones, IV. 6, pp. 117–18

Similarly, we might talk about certain forms of attachment as related to love. But they might also be characterized as mere liking that has grown out of habit, out of being thrown together, or out of feeling familiar or comfortable together owing to long proximity. Some might wish to contrast that with love. You may feel attached to your neighborhood, your school, your home, and even your fellow classmates or neighbors without loving them per se, and you may not even miss them terribly much once you have left them.

We can wonder, for example, whether a bear cub – which has clearly been attached to its mother for about two years of its life, having played with her, depended completely on her, nuzzled and napped with her – experiences the effects of separation from a loved one the way human beings do. Although young bears often resist being chased away by their mothers at around age two, we do not know if they pine away for her afterwards, mourn her loss, experience separation anxiety, or call her memory to mind with fond, regretful feelings and an intense sense of desolation (whether in dreams or daydreams). Fond, regretful feelings and/or desolation – leading to mourning which may last years, if not a lifetime – are often, however, associated by authors with separation from a loved one in human beings.

If we are not to call what the bear experiences "love," are we then claiming that love requires the kind of memory that only human beings have, the kind of memory that is linguistically structured for the most part, allowing us to conjure up thoughts and images and feelings related to the beloved simply by repeating his or her name? Is what we are calling love, then, characteristic of human beings alone? Or do we want to have a conception of love that includes the attachments and affections that animals clearly have for one another, whether they be cats and dogs that – against all odds – become best friends, or horses that stand alongside each other head to tail in pastures, each swishing the flies off the other's face with its tail?

I am mentioning "attachment" in particular here because

"attachment theory" has become one of the major thrusts of contemporary psychological and psychoanalytic research, and one of the explicit tenets of attachment theory is that love between human mothers and human children can be understood at least in large part by studying the interactions of primate mothers and their young. In attachment theory there seems to be no threshold or jump required to differentiate between animal love and human love.[3]

Note that in a good deal of British literature in the nineteenth century – when courting was something that often took place over the course of quite a long period of time, and it was not unusual for engagements to last several years, often for financial reasons, as it was thought that couples should not marry before the man was able to earn (or otherwise receive, from rents, for example) a certain amount per year, but not always for financial reasons – one of the commonly used terms for relationships was "attachment." Jane Austen, for example, very often speaks of one person being "attached" to another, and it appears in certain instances that nothing like what we would call romantic love or passion is involved – indeed, attachment is often contrasted with intense romantic love in Austen's books (for example, Marianne's very slow-to-develop attachment to Colonel Brandon in *Sense and Sensibility*, as opposed to her lightning-fast, head-over-heels love for Willoughby).

We might imagine that, in the best of cases, people whose marriages have been arranged for them by their families eventually grow to feel quite attached to each other. In the play *Fiddler on the Roof*, the question is raised in the song "Do You Love Me?" whether it is merely attachment or whether it deserves to be called love. Our literary tradition is such, I believe, that this kind of gradually forming attachment-based love is rarely written about, not giving rise to the kinds of passions we expect to encounter in novels. Indeed, I think I would not be making a vast overgeneralization to say that what is celebrated for the most part in novels and movies is the primarily romantic period of people's lives, and that 99 percent of love stories that are not tragic end with the marriage of the individuals involved, not bothering to delve into the evolution of their love during their subsequent lives together. Novelists perhaps believe that in the course of marriage love disappears; or at least that its passionate phase ceases and is at best replaced by the friendship, companionship, and attachment that grow out of proximity and familiarity. In this they are seconded by certain psychologists who distinguish between what they call "passionate love" at the outset of a relationship and "companionate love" later in a relationship, and who note that certain people seem to be unable to (or refuse to) make the transition from the one to the other.[4]

We should not, of course, lose sight of the fact that for many centuries (and even now in certain parts of the world) few people actually chose their own husbands or wives, most marriages being arranged by the parents with little or no input from the future bridegroom or bride, and little or no knowledge by the future spouses of their betrothed. In such cases, the character of the potential love object was rather random.

Even when it was not totally random, the future spouses often knew each other only very superficially, if at all. According to legend, for example, Protis – the Phoenician chief who founded the city of Marseille – was chosen by Gyptis, the daughter of the Ligurian King Nann, to be her husband at the end of her wedding feast. It was apparently the tradition at the time that no one would know who the husband was to be until the festivities were over! Protis had arrived just recently in Gaul from Greece and out of hospitality King Nann invited him to the banquet. All the king's daughter Gyptis knew of him was what he looked like and that he came from elsewhere: he was not one of the local suitors from Gaul with whom she was already somewhat familiar. Such was the nature of her choice at the end of the nuptial feast – she picked an unknown quantity with whom she was probably unable to even converse, as they spoke different languages.[5] Whether the story is entirely true or not is of less importance than the fact that couples often married who had precious little previous knowledge of each other. And that people are far more interested in her instantaneous attraction to this stranger than in knowing whether they grew to love each other over time.

Indeed, novelists generally seem to feel that marital felicity does not involve love per se, or at least not the kind that lends itself to gripping narratives, whereas passionate love – which is by turns deliriously happy and suicidally unhappy – inspires genuine page turners.[6]

Friendship

Friendship grows from similarity.

Plato, *Phaedrus*, 240c

The notion of friendship may be closely associated with that of love in certain cases, but the two do not entirely overlap, as, for example, when someone you are passionately in love with tells you, "Why can't we just be friends?" In the literature of Antiquity, there was much discussion of famous pairs of friends, such as Achilles and

Patroclus, but we should note that they were also lovers (at least according to Phaedrus). In our times, we seem not to celebrate pairs of friends so much; Thelma and Louise constitute one of the few well-known current, yet fictional, examples.[7] Novelists and playwrights – our contemporary storytellers – appear to feel there is not enough passion in friendship to make for a good story. Freud (1929/1961a, pp. 102–3), on the other hand, views friendship as a passion – that is, as sensual love that has simply been inhibited in its aim.

Aristotle distinguishes between love and friendship, not in terms of the degree of passion involved, but as follows: "it looks as if love were a feeling, friendship a state of character" (*Ethics*, 1057b). His discussion of love centers primarily on an in-depth exploration of *philia*, generally translated into English as "friendship."[8] Friendship (*philia*) is where each party wishes the good of the other. "To love is," as Aristotle puts it in the *Rhetoric*, "to wish someone well" (1380b35), a formulation that strikes us today as quite awkward, distant, and even perhaps as a kiss-off (akin to "Well, good luck with that!"), whereas Aristotle clearly means that *philia* means wanting what is best for one's friend, wanting what (you believe) would be for his own good, or – as Jane Austen (2000, p. 191) put it in *Pride and Prejudice* – feeling "a real interest in [someone's] welfare," that is, being genuinely concerned for the other's welfare.

Passionate love, it seems to me, quite transparently goes beyond that, wanting to possess the beloved whether it is in the beloved's best interest or not, or even in the lover's best interest! Aristotle holds the belief, naïve from a psychoanalytic perspective, that "each man wishes himself what is good" (*Ethics*, 1166a) – that is, that each man is a friend to himself and loves himself. Further on, he adds that a man "is his own best friend" (1168b). But, as Freud teaches us, we often wish ourselves ill; indeed, we harm ourselves and engage in self-defeating acts. Self-love is not always something to be taken for granted. Indeed, a man is sometimes "his own worst enemy."

All of this is further complicated by the fact that the very notion of the Sovereign Good has been largely critiqued and/or jettisoned in our thinking about ethics, for we realize that there is little agreement among us as to what the Good is; indeed, we question – even in psychoanalysis (see Fink, 2007, Chapter 9) – whether there is anything that is good for everyone and even if we can know what would be good for any one person. This distinguishes psychoanalysis from numerous other forms of therapy – dialectical behavior therapy, for example – where the therapist believes he truly knows what would be good for his patients and works toward it, whether his patients accept it as their own good or not!

Lacanians take it for granted that we do *not* know the Good in any absolute sense. We believe, perhaps, that we know what we feel is good for us – whatever it may be – but we realize that what seems good for us may not be good for someone who is quite differently constituted from us (symptomatically, diagnostically, or temperamentally) and who has been raised in a very different cultural or religious context (an Amish teenager, for example). Even as supposedly "neutral" a goal as "symptom reduction" – which has been welcomed with open arms by the "evidence-based" movement as a goal or "good" everyone can endorse (especially since it can purportedly be measured and quantified) – makes no sense in many cases where someone's symptom is the only thing that keeps her going or gives her the will to go on living.

Add to this the fact that (1) people's motives for doing "good deeds" or "charitable deeds" are often quite hypocritical (the will to do good often involves condescension and self-aggrandizement) and that (2) the attempt to do good often backfires, doing harm instead (see Balzac's *L'Envers de l'histoire contemporaine* or *The Wrong Side of Paris*), and you can see why analysts do best to limit themselves to simply trying *not to do harm* (*primum non nocere*).

It is often said that "the road to hell is paved with good intentions," for we often fail in our attempts to do good and, indeed, we often manage to convince ourselves we are acting in someone's best interest (our child's, our neighbor's, our student's, our partner's) when we are actually doing what suits us best, fits best into our own view of things, schedule, life goals, and so on. A parent who is unsupportive to his child often rationalizes his behavior by telling himself that it is best for a child to be raised – like the parent believes he himself was – in the "school of hard knocks": "No one helped me and I turned out all the better for it." Such reasoning often simply covers over the fact that he has little or no interest in or love for his child and secretly hopes his child will not surpass him in affection, happiness, or worldly success. Consciously he tells himself he does wish all of those things for his child, but unconsciously the story is quite different. It is all too easy to turn the so-called Good to one's own purposes, convincing oneself one is doing what is for the other's own good when one is merely doing what one (at some level, perhaps unconscious) pleases.[9]

Analysts cannot skirt the problem by simply adopting as goals what each patient thinks is his own good, for in many cases what he thinks is good for him is self-sacrifice, self-mortification, self-destruction, power over all and sundry, or world domination! Practitioners cannot assume that, just because someone wants these things, they are actually good for him or would truly fulfill him.

In Seminar VII, Lacan (1992) says we might go so far as to characterize the analyst's desire as a "non-desire to cure" (p. 258/219), which differs considerably from Ferenczi's passion to cure patients, stigmatized by Freud (1912/1958, p. 119) as "therapeutic ambition" and by Lacan (2006a, p. 324) as a *furor sanandi*. Instead of striving to do what we think is for the patient's own good, Lacan (2015) suggests in Seminar VIII that we try to foster the patient's Eros, "the realm of Eros [being one that] goes infinitely beyond any field the Good can cover" (p. 9). As he puts it, "I am not there, in the final analysis, for a person's own good, but in order that he love" (p. 15).[10] This is a fundamental ethical position that distinguishes one group of therapies quite radically from another. In psychoanalysis, we do not aim at befriending our patients in Aristotle's or anyone else's sense, except at times in our work with psychotics (see Fink, 2007, p. 250).

As for the more narcissistic (as opposed to supposedly altruistic) components of friendship, Aristotle proffers that "a friend is a second self" (in another translation, "one's friend is another self"), and thus "devoted attachment to someone else comes to resemble love for oneself" (*Ethics*, 1166a–b). Yet, if I do not love myself and wish to hurt myself, a friend whom I treat as I treat myself had better watch out!

Agape (or Christian Love)

Thus he puts the other, as it were, in the place of himself, and regards the good done to him as done to himself.

Aquinas, 1952, p. 121

Whereas Aristotle emphasized *philia* (friendship), Saint Thomas Aquinas emphasized agape, often rendered as "Christian love," "altruism," "brotherly love," "dilection," or "pious love." According to Webster's (1986), agape is "spontaneous self-giving love expressed freely without calculation of cost or gain to the giver or merit on the part of the receiver."

Kierkegaard – in whose work Socrates and the theme of love are very much present right from the beginning (he wrote a whole section on Plato's *Symposium* in his doctoral dissertation, published as *The Concept of Irony* [1841/1965, pp. 78–89], and presented his own version of Plato's *Symposium* called "In Vino Veritas" or "The Banquet" in Part I of *Stages on Life's Way* [1845/1988]) – developed the notion of Christian love extensively in his sprawling *Works of Love* (1847/1995). Unlike many other authors, he does not speak of love as a state of being, feeling, or passion, but about "works of love." Since at least Freud's time, most of us have realized that actions that are ostensibly taken out of love may well be performed for all sorts of reasons other than loving ones – they may be performed for narcissistic reasons (people wishing to see themselves as morally superior to those they supposedly assist), calculated reasons, to acquire a certain reputation, and so on. Kierkegaard is not unaware of this – "We can be deceived by appearances, but we certainly are also deceived by the sagacious appearance, by the flattering conceit that considers itself absolutely secure against being deceived" (p. 5) – but devotes considerable attention to the psychological and spiritual attitudes that must underpin such actions or works if they are to count as Christian love.

Unlike Aristotle, who juxtaposes Eros and *philia*, Kierkegaard lumps both of those together as based solely on an individual's own passions and personal preferences; after all, friends are people we associate with because they suit *us* in at least some way, and thus even if we are generally concerned with their welfare, our interest in them still speaks volumes about us, their welfare affecting us quite directly. Kierkegaard distinguishes instead between everyday "erotic love" (*Elskov* or Eros) and "friendship," on the one hand, and the vastly superior Christian love (*Kjerlighed*, p. 46), on the other hand, which involves self-denial (p. 52). Christian love is, he says, eternal – "it has within itself eternity's truth" (p. 8). All other forms of love blossom and eventually fade. But in Christian love, "a human being's love originates mysteriously in God's love," and this true form "of love is recognizable by its fruits" (p. 10). Its fruits may not be visible to all, for true Christian love is secretive (like true faith), and does not seek public, ostentatious display (p. 28)

Kierkegaard is quite critical of poets who profess to celebrate loving another person "more than oneself" (p. 18), saying that "what perhaps escapes the poets [is] that the love they celebrate is secretly self-love," it remaining self-centered, being determined by one's own tastes, preferences, and pleasures. "Erotic love is still not the eternal; it is the beautiful dizziness of infinity" (p. 19).

With the help of poets, lovers swear by their love to remain in love forever (pp. 30–1),[11] but Kierkegaard claims one can only swear to do so by appealing to something higher – like God or eternity – that is, to a law that is not created by any human heart (pp. 24–5), to the law that thou shalt love thy neighbor as thyself. Love seeks to eternalize itself, but cannot promise any such thing unless it appeals to God and the everlasting law. Yet if it does so appeal, then it is commanded and poets, Kierkegaard argues, cannot bear constraint of any kind. Freud (1930/1961a, pp. 109–12) claims that no human heart can obey the commandment to love thy neighbor as thyself, proffering that it is not simply difficult, but impossible (p. 143).[12] Kierkegaard takes the inhuman nature of this law as proof that it is divine or divinely inspired, not the product of any human heart; and although he would agree that it is a difficult law to obey, it must not, in his view, be impossible.

Many believe that love needs freedom, that people cannot love out of duty, and that love cannot be compelled, constrained, or forced. A poster from the 1970s read: "If you love something, set it free [or: let it go]. If it comes back to you, it is yours forever. If it doesn't, then it was never meant to be." As true as this may be of what Kierkegaard calls erotic love and friendship, Christian love *must somehow be* compatible with constraint and law. (Poets do admit to a kind of compulsion in love, when they declare "I cannot but love her!" But this has to do with the drives, and feels like exquisite freedom to them, not constraint.)

Like many lovers, Kierkegaard was obsessed with the everlastingness of love. With the love of his life, Regina – whom he had successfully wooed, having loved her for four years after falling in love with her at first sight – he broke off their brief engagement, being unable to sustain the relationship (for many very complex reasons); but he was devastated two years later when he heard that Regina had gotten engaged to another man, at least in part because she had vowed, when she finally agreed to break it off with Kierkegaard, that she would never get over him and would renounce the world and "become a governess." He swiftly concluded that all women were unfaithful (Lowrie, 1970, p. 193). He had apparently thought throughout the writing of *Fear and Trembling* and *Repetition* that there might still be a chance somehow for the two of them to get back together or to at least be engaged in some sort of perpetual spiritual union, even if unmarried. According to Lowrie, Hirsch claims that Kierkegaard's "deepest religious conversion" occurred after he learned of Regina's new engagement, and his fascination with eternity perhaps developed at that very moment (see Kierkegaard, 1954, p. 18).

Although ordinary love has eternity within itself, it can nevertheless wane over time (Kierkegaard, 1995, p. 31). But a change in the form of love can occur: "when love has undergone the change of eternity by having become a duty, it has gained enduring continuance, and it is self-evident that it exists." "Only when it is a duty to love, only then is love eternally secured." "This security of eternity casts out all anxiety and makes love perfect, perfectly secured" (p. 32). Kierkegaard's biggest concern seems to have been that his beloved might become fickle and jilt him; yet we might suspect, in a more psychoanalytic vein, that *this worry about his beloved actually grew out of the vacillating, uncertain state of his own love for her.*

"It is the same love that loves and hates" (p. 34), he writes, indicating that he is aware, long before Freud, of the flip-flopping of the one into the other and of their common libidinal source. Eternal love is, however, unchangeable, he argues. "Never has any greater security been found, and never will the peace of eternity be found in anything other than in this [commandment: thou *shalt* love]" (p. 34). It seems that he will never rest easy unless he is absolutely sure that his beloved will not stop loving him, and that he will never stop loving her (yet it seems he stopped, or foresaw the end of their relationship, almost right from the beginning).[13] If they are both *obliged* to love, he can relax.

Kierkegaard dwells (rather obsessively, one might say) on the "inconstancy" of love. Like myriad other philosophers and theologians – who have attempted to reconcile their own personal experience of love as unstable, unfair, unforgiving, and unpleasurable with the oft-repeated notion of love as perfect or of the perfect love God has for his flock – Kierkegaard contrasts the imperfections of man's earthly, carnal, corporeal love with God's spiritual love. Love that is perfect is inhuman, in the sense that it is divine.

"The love that has undergone the change of eternity by becoming duty does not know jealousy; it does not love only as it is loved, but it loves" (p. 35).[14] In other words, it transcends the tit-for-tat imaginary relationship in which one only loves as much as one is loved; indeed, it transcends the desire to be loved in return. Kierkegaard clearly foreshadows Freud's notion that ordinary love for our beloved often involves a good deal of narcissism (which he calls "self-love") and selfishness (which Kierkegaard equates with sensuousness, or "the flesh," in Church doctrine; for him, the flesh is not the body per se, but rather selfishness and self-centeredness). He views paganism – by which he means the Greek and Roman moralists and philosophers – as ostensibly disparaging self-love but nevertheless exalting erotic love and friendship as real love. For Christianity, however, erotic love and friendship are forms of "passionate preferential love" (p. 53) and are thus just as self-centered as self-love: in loving in this way, giving preference to one person over another because of one's own likes and dislikes, one's own personal preferences regarding looks and personality, one simply wants to be loved and admired in return (pp. 54–5).[15]

The command to love your neighbor goes much further than this: it is not a command to love only those neighbors whom you happen to like, owing to your own tastes and distastes, and whose company you find enjoyable, interesting, or otherwise rewarding. "It is very unrewarding to love the neighbor" (p. 69), Kierkegaard writes; indeed, "*the neighbor* is the *ugly*" (p. 424). The neighbor is precisely he who is repulsive to us, or that which in another is repulsive to us, that which it is supremely difficult if not virtually impossible to love! Whereas Plato seems to celebrate the love of beauty, Kierkegaard celebrates love of the ugly – love of those who are ugly or of that which is ugly in our fellow beings.

As much as Freud may have found the commandment to love thy neighbor impossible to obey, it is nevertheless fairly obvious that analysts must find something to love in patients, who are not always physically or spiritually beautiful by any stretch of the imagination, if they are to work effectively with them. A patient requesting treatment could be viewed as one of the analyst's neighbors, and there is often a good deal of ugliness that analysts see in their patients – it may be only skin-deep or superficial (as in the case of the colleague I mentioned in Chapter 3, whose obese patient told him at the end of their last session together, "You've always found me repulsive, haven't you?"), or it may concern traits that the analyst finds morally or interpersonally objectionable in the patient (whether concerning the patient's job, pastimes, sexual practices, dissimulation, treatment of other people, politics, social style, snobbism, or what have you). Granted, analysts may not be able to love such perceived moral ugliness, perhaps hoping to eliminate it through analysis, but if they are unable to find *something* to love in each patient, the analysis will almost certainly fail. And the less they can find to love in a patient, the better they would do to refer the patient to another analyst who might not find so ugly what they find ugly.[16] (Like beauty, ugliness is in the eye of the beholder.) They need not be able to love all and sundry, but must be aware of dislikes on their part that go so far as to impede the work.

Lacan suggests that what we often most object to or cannot bear in our partner is what our partner enjoys or gets off on, and this is clearly something that the analyst has to be able to bear in an analysis if it is to achieve anything. Thus as "impossible" as the Bible's commandment may be (reminding us of Freud's three impossible professions: governing, educating, and psychoanalyzing), there is undoubtedly something to be gleaned here regarding the analyst's training and practice.

In supervising other analysts and therapists, I often detect a lack of understanding of and indeed a scorn for what makes other people tick – that is, their thinking and enjoyment, which are inextricably bound together. I have heard many a therapist snicker at his patients' supposed irrationality, illogicality, stupidity, foolishness, or sickness. This is not merely useless but actually dangerous on the practitioner's part. Therapists tend to have very little appreciation for the fact that other people function in radically different ways from themselves, even when both patient and therapist are neurotic! And when patient and therapist are not in the same clinical category, the misunderstanding is often far greater still.

Christian love for the neighbor or "divine love" seems to require that we find something divine, or some spark of the divine, in everyone, or that we love everyone via the divine ("All true love is grounded in this, that one loves another in a third"; Kierkegaard, 1995, p. 395). Yet, one would think that if there is something divine in everyone it must be terribly abstract or generic: something like humanity, life itself, or the soul. One might wonder at how essential the concept of the soul has been in virtually all discussion of love for millennia, as if love could not be conceptualized without such a notion.

Riffing on Lacan's (1998a) notion of "soul-love," I might be inclined to propose that the analyst needs to love the soul *qua* unconscious – the analyst must be enamored of what is unconscious in each patient who comes his or her way, as different as it will be on each occasion. As Lacan (1973–4) puts it in the title of Seminar XXI, *Les non dupes errent*, those (analysts) who do not allow themselves to be led around by the nose by the unconscious go astray. And as he puts it in Seminar XX, "knowledge [. . .] is closely related to love. All love is based on a certain relationship between two unconscious knowledges" (Lacan, 1998a, p. 144). This might be taken to imply that the unconscious is always at work in love and that there must be some connection and indeed knowledge of the other's unconscious for love to exist. One must recognize that one's partner is affected by the knowledge in his or her unconscious.

And insofar as the unconscious can be understood as real (Soler, 2009), it has to do with sexual difference as real (as we shall see shortly), "soul" coming from the ancient Greek *psuche* or psyche, which, as Faraone (1999, p. 50 n. 48) tells us, was also a slang term for the female genitalia. Analysts must be fascinated by, indeed lovers of, the difference between the sexes. Those who are not – those who would prefer to know nothing about it – need not apply.

The love the analyst has for or gives to the patient cannot but be dissatisfying to the patient, insofar as it stems from a certain kind of analytic duty or discipline. Who, after all, would want to receive love that is given solely out of duty, not given freely? Would anyone want such love from his or her beloved? Isn't it tainted for us, in a sense, when we feel that others do things for us out of duty? For example, we wonder about the care given by foster-parents who are paid for their services, and the attention granted by therapists who are compensated for their time.

For in such cases, we feel they are doing something for us merely out of a sense of professional obligation, not out of love (most of us find love and duty intuitively incompatible, unlike Kierkegaard); worse still, they are getting something from us, some tangible material benefit (like money), instead of giving freely of their time. We might even go so far as to imagine that such people, despite their professional duty, actually have no pecuniary interest in helping us resolve our problems and become independent, preferring to benefit indefinitely from our neurosis – just like certain of our family members before them have, though perhaps not quite so obviously or directly. (I would suspect that, at least in psychoanalysis, this is most often a projection on the analysand's part, analysts' boredom and feelings of impotence to help tending to override the material benefits they receive after a certain number of years of work with an analysand; but there may well be exceptions.) In still more extreme cases, we may feel that the analyst is getting a kick out of our discourse, enjoying our predicament, and getting off on the account we give of our trials and tribulations. Although we are perhaps primarily imagining this, we may get the sense that the analyst is getting off on us in a way that is incompatible with loving us, that his or her jouissance in the analysis is getting in the way of the kind of love and attention we expect and demand.

One of my analysands believed that I was playing him for a sucker (one of whom was, as his father had often repeated to him, "born every minute") and that, although I endeavored to hide it, I must be getting a big kick out of laughing at him. This is, perhaps, a not entirely uncommon belief among patients (who are perverse, diagnostically speaking) who see themselves not as the cause of the Other's desire but as the cause of the Other's jouissance; what suggested to me that this patient's belief said considerably more about him than it did about me was that whenever he claimed I was laughing (he could not see my face at such times) I was doing nothing of the sort. There are, of course, times when – like most if not all clinicians – I find the stories patients tell amusing, if not hilarious, as do many audiences when stand-up comedians parade and make fun of their own neuroses onstage. But I rarely found this particular patient's tales or predicament funny, and never at the moments at which he thought I did.

Whether factually based or not (or a little of both), such accusations make it clear that the analyst's role is to love but not to get off on the analysand.[17] Even if the analyst receives payment for the work and is educated in many ways by the analysand (learning how to practice more effectively, learning more about *la bête humaine*, as Zola put it, or "human animal," as Desmond Morris put it, and even occasionally being struck by certain conclusions the analysand comes to that apply to the analyst too),[18] the analyst must be inhabited by a desire that goes beyond the mere wish to earn a living or to learn some useful techniques, inhabited by a desire that is stronger than one's other desires, one's more or less solid sense of duty, and one's variable inclinations to give into erotic or aggressive enjoyments: a desire to encounter the unconscious in its myriad manifestations.

If analysts love in their patients only the fact that they allow analysts to see themselves as they wish to see themselves – that is, as helpers or good, caring people – trouble will ensue. (Similarly, teachers who love their students only insofar as the students reflect back a flattering image of them as intelligent, inspiring people, run into trouble as soon as their students reflect back something else.) What is the "stronger desire" analysts must be imbued with that Lacan (2015, p. 185) mentions in Seminar VIII?

> If the analyst achieves apathy [i.e., something other than lust or aggression] it is to the extent that he is possessed by a desire that is stronger than the other desires that may be involved – for example, the desire to get down to it with his patient: to take him in his arms or throw him out the window. [. . .] The analyst says, "I am possessed by a stronger desire." He is grounded in saying so as an analyst, insofar as a change has occurred in the economy of his desire.

What sort of change in the economy of desire is involved here? Freud (1930/1961a, pp. 109–15) seems unable to fathom the libidinal configuration of someone who, like a saint, can love his neighbor as himself (much less love his enemies!). The saint seems to have harmonized what Freud would characterize as the superego command to love thy neighbor as thyself, the id's aggressive and lustful impulses toward others, and the ego's struggle with both the id and the superego, on the one hand, and external reality, on the other. In Freud's model, there is always a remainder of superego or id motivation that threatens to outstrip or overshadow any principle of conduct adopted by the ego, whereas we might imagine the saint as having completely harmonized all internal conflict (even if accounts of Mother Teresa's life, for example, suggest that no such complete harmonization perhaps ever occurs). I have met a great many analysts and do not believe I have ever encountered any in whom such complete harmonization obtained. Lacan's point, I would argue, is that total harmony is not necessary as long as an overriding *desire* has come to the fore in the course of the analyst's own analysis. The analyst need not be entirely free of erotic feeling or aggression in his or her relations with analysands, but must not give free rein to them because his or her paramount concern lies elsewhere.

Perhaps saints, too, feel a wide variety of things, but are "possessed by a stronger desire." If that "stronger desire" is nothing more than a powerful superego injunction telling them they must act in a certain way (obey their duty to love their neighbor, for example), Freud's conundrum will supervene wherein ethics and Eros, ethics and libido, are inextricably intertwined, and aggressive outbursts will sooner or later occur.

To Freud's way of thinking, it is not enough to say that we are going to adopt a certain ethical principle regarding psychoanalytic treatment. The questions are (1) what libidinal energy holds it in place and supports it; and (2) what stops one from sliding with respect to it when other forces (e.g., countervailing forces like anger and lust) impel one to? People excel, as we know, at adopting a principle and then rationalizing their every deviation from that principle. Is it only the severest of superego commands that can thwart that? Or can there be something like "the analyst's desire" that supersedes this?

The State of Pennsylvania, for example (where I have lived and practiced for many a year), does not profess to tell mental health practitioners *how* to obey the State guidelines regarding conduct befitting a clinician: it just says you have to. The ten commandments, the Bible, and the U.S. Constitution do not tell us how to configure ourselves psychologically so that we *can* obey the law – they just tell us to obey.

Jane Austen's Mr. Knightley (perhaps echoing Kant) says, "There is one thing, Emma, which a man can always do, if he chooses, and that is, his duty" (Austen, 2004, p. 137). Freud seems to retort: "It isn't that easy." Why would we make such an arduous choice? And even if we did, how could we do our duty properly, since we are but flesh and blood? Freud concludes that we cannot love our neighbors as ourselves: it is too hard. Even if it were desirable, the libidinal conditions for it do not exist. The biblical Law assumes that you can, because you must. Freud seems to conclude that because you cannot, it is not a divinely inspired Law, as Kierkegaard would have it, but, rather, a foolish law.

What then can the public expect of an analyst who works in close proximity for years at a time to analysands who may be attractive, charming, and vulnerable or unattractive, repulsive, and belligerent? As a nation, we demand that there be a "neutralization of the body" in the analytic setting, that analysts work with their minds and not with their hands, yet the "father" of psychoanalysis finds it impossible to love our neighbor – is it that, to him, the analysand is not our neighbor? Who, then, would the analysand be in his view?

Lacan provides, perhaps, at least a first sketch of an alternative view, the details of which would need to be fleshed out: in the course of the analyst's training, "a change has occurred in the economy of his desire" such that he can love and hate as passionately or violently as anyone else, but he is – at least in the best of cases, in other words, he should be – imbued with a stronger desire, a desire to get at the unconscious and follow it wherever it may lead. This is what an analyst is, strictly speaking, in Lacan's view; an analyst is not someone who has completed an official, accredited training program.[19] He is someone who is imbued *not* with a superego injunction like "Thou shalt not get erotically or aggressively involved with patients," a duty that is perilously close to an ideal (see my discussion of the dangers of ideals further on in this chapter), but who is imbued instead with a living, breathing desire. This is what makes him different from professionals in many fields (law, medicine, and so on) who are told not to get involved with their clients, but for whom this professional duty is but one impetus among others and all too easily overridden.

Perhaps it would thus be more accurate to say not that the analyst must *love* his or her analysands but that he or she must desire something in relation to them that supersedes all of the analyst's other desires, impulses, and wishes. Would that then be the same or different from true "love for the neighbor"? Some might be inclined to associate it with what is occasionally called "tough love," but I will leave it as an open question here.

Hatred

The opposite of love is not hate, but indifference.

There is no such thing as love insurance, because that would be hate insurance too.

Lacan, 1973b, p. 32

The whole day may be sometimes too short for hatred, as well as for love.

Henry Fielding, *Tom Jones*, II. 7, p. 61

It is helpful when exploring the semantic space of a word like "love" to consider its purported antonyms. Hatred is often thought to be the opposite of love, but Freud, for example, suggests that the two go hand in hand to some degree. Lacan (2015) goes so far as to coin a word, *hainamoration*, which combines *haine*, hate or hatred, and *énamourer*, to become enamored, and claims that he "wouldn't expect much from [an analyst] who has never felt [. . .] the desire to get down to it with his patient: to take him in his arms or throw him out the window" (p. 185). He who cannot hate cannot love; and the more he can love, the more he can hate when relations with the other sour. It is, after all, those we love the most who can anger us the most.

The connection between love and anger had already been glimpsed in Antiquity. As Faraone (1999) tells us, "at the base of the two Greek word groups used to describe anger [*thumos* and *orge*] we see an intrinsic connection with a man swollen with anger and one swollen with sexual desire" (p. 123). This might be likened to the proximity in psychoanalytic thinking between lustful and destructive feelings, which are linked by the word "passion."

Attraction

> The pleasure of the eye is the beginning of love.
>
> Aristotle, Ethics, 1167a

Attraction is often thought to constitute a first step on the way to love. We can be aware of our attraction to someone, or somewhat unaware of it. Recent researchers in biology even suggest that attraction can go on at levels completely outside of consciousness; virtually everyone has heard about studies on pheromones, even though it is unclear whether humans can sense them, as we do not have a specialized pheromone detector, or vomeronasal organ, between our nose and mouth like certain animals do. Nevertheless, biologists like Sarah Woodley (2009) suggest that we might be able to sense pheromones with our nose and that such chemicals might incline people to choose mates for reasons unseen by and unknown to either party.[20]

Pheromones purportedly explain some curious research on the importance of symmetry to attraction. Marcus du Sautoy (2008), a professor of mathematics at Oxford University, writes:

> Studies indicate that the more symmetrical among us are more likely to start having sex at an earlier age. Even the smell men emit seems to be more appealing to women when the male has

more symmetry. In one study, sweaty T-shirts that had been
worn by men were offered to a selection of women, and those
who were ovulating were drawn to the T-shirts worn by the
men with the most symmetrical bodies. It seems, though, that
men are not programmed to pick up the scent of a symmetrical
woman. (p. 12)

Pheromones are obviously only a part of the story (assuming they
play any role in human attraction at all) because plenty of people
are attracted to someone long before they get close enough to smell
that person or even could potentially smell him or her, seeing him or
her only from afar, on a stage, in a picture, or on a screen, or sometimes merely hearing others talk about him or her. Just as sight has,
it is said, taken precedence over smell ever since we humans began
to stand upright instead of going around on all fours like our distant
ancestors, the vision or sight of a potential partner is, for most of
us, far more important – at least initially – than his or her odor in
determining object-choice.

Fixation on the Human Form (Beauty)

Did my heart love till now? Forswear it, sight!
For I ne'er saw true beauty till this night.
Shakespeare, Romeo and Juliet, I. v. 52–3

Young men's love then lies
Not truly in their hearts, but in their eyes.
Shakespeare, Romeo and Juliet, II. iii. 67–8

What beauty is and what makes someone visually attractive has been
a matter of debate for at least some 25 centuries, and it seems likely
that varied criteria of beauty have prevailed at different historical
periods and in different cultures. Contemporary psychologists and
"scientists" have attempted to find *universal* criteria of beauty for
the human face (involving symmetry of features, spacing between
the eyes, eye size, cheekbone structure and placement, etc.), since
they would like to find a firm genetic footing for human standards
of beauty. But one could argue that the models chosen by sculptors,
painters, and other artists over the millennia – insofar as they can
be assumed to have embodied those artists' own notions of beauty
or attractiveness – vary markedly, soft facial features being preferred by some and more angular features by others, ample (indeed
voluptuous) bodies taking precedence in certain periods (Greek,

Roman, Renaissance, and 1950s), while slim (if not anorexic) or well-toned bodies take precedence in others (parts of the eighteenth, nineteenth, and twentieth centuries). Such variation can hardly, it seems to me, be chalked up simply to the greater reliability of the food supply in many countries in recent centuries, such that it is no longer unadvisable or a sign of ill-health to be slim, for fuller figures are still preferred in certain cultures and subcultures even today where adequate nutrition can be taken for granted. In short, at least certain facets of what is considered to constitute beauty are, in all likelihood, subject to cultural development and change.

Being in the presence of beauty seems, however, to give rise to different kinds of reactions, at least two of which are (1) sexual arousal and (2) fixation or paralysis. Seeing a beautiful face and body may get us all hot and bothered or may captivate us in a kind of rapt contemplation. In the first case we may seek to satisfy the sex drive awoken in us by the sight of that person by accosting him or her (adopting an approach likely to win over or seduce, whether that be delicate, diplomatic, sensitive, direct, or lewd, or stumbling clumsily, if not brutally, into his or her presence), whereas in the second beauty is not something that appears along the road to sexual satisfaction but that freezes one, that remains primarily at the level of an aesthetic experience. Greek love would seem to follow the first path, whereas Narcissus and André Gide in his love for his wife, Madeleine, would seem to follow the second.

Although many men sing the praises of beauty (male or female) and the jouissance it brings them, for the likes of Hesiod, Pandora, the "lovely curse," is a "hopeless trap, deadly to men" (Hesiod, 1973, p. 42); she was created as a curse by Zeus to make men pay for having stolen fire from the gods, and makes men burn with lust and marry beautiful women who turn out to be shrews. (He even claims that Athena helped Zeus create Pandora in order to punish men; p. 61). Foreshadowing Freud's work, Socrates claims:

> Enjoyment of physical beauty is accompanied by some sort of disgust; what we feel about food when we are full, we necessarily feel also with respect to pretty boys [after sex]. (Xenophon, *Symposium*, 8.15)

Such is the complaint of a man who has no trouble making conquests.[21] Other men curse beauty for making them lust after women they will never be able to possess, driving them to distraction and despair.

As we shall see when we turn to Lacan's discussion of André Gide further on, for those to whom fixation on beauty remains primarily at the level of an aesthetic experience, beauty seems closely tied to a kind of living death.

Lacan on Beauty

Tristan didn't love Isolde for herself but only for *the love of Love* of which her beauty gave him an image.

Rougemont, 1983, p. 244/223

Lacan discusses "the function of beauty" at some length in Seminar VII, *The Ethics of Psychoanalysis*. Whereas sociobiologists or evolutionary psychologists would be quick to claim that the function of beauty is obviously to attract mates, the most beautiful among us attracting the fittest or most "suitable" mates – they perhaps limit their purview to prehistoric times so as not to have to account for the utter unsuitability of so many of the mates attracted by good-looking movie stars and models – Lacan takes up beauty's functions at a very different level.

He remarks first that truth is not pretty to look at, and that beauty covers over or disguises truth (Lacan, 1992, p. 256/216–17). What sort of truth is he referring to in that context? Had he stated this in the 1970s, it would have been the absence of a sexual relationship between the sexes. The truth here, however, is somewhat different: it is the materiality of sexual difference itself. Just as Socrates yields the floor to Diotima, Lacan lets a courtly love poet, Arnaud Daniel, speak about the truth of Woman in his stead. The poet recounts a potential sexual service that a Lady's servant could provide, involving cunnilingus or anal licking (it is not altogether clear which); and the upshot appears to be that a woman is not a lofty, pure, spiritual thing, but rather something quite material and, indeed, scatological, smelly, and disgusting.

Such is the "truth" of woman in Arnaud Daniel's poem, and Lacan seems to take this to be the truth that is covered over by the focus on feminine beauty (p. 192/162); he puts the following words in a woman's mouth: "I am nothing but the void to be found in my own internal cesspit [. . .]. Blow in that for a bit to see – to see if your sublimation still holds up" (p. 254/215). Lacan seems to agree with Freud that the majority of men have at least an initial reaction of horror, disgust, or shock at the absence of a penis in a woman, and that most cannot handle female anatomy. The focus on beauty is a way of denying or overlooking the materiality and enigma of the female genitalia, a sight overwhelming to many men (and to certain women, too). Such men are led to focus on the aesthetic dimension of women's outer form or shape rather than reckon with their inner materiality or substance. This leads Lacan to suggest that beauty is more closely linked to the Thing (*das Ding*, in Freud's work), or the real (the reality of sexual difference), than it is to the Good; it is closer to evil than it is to the Good (p. 256/217). He refers to beauty as the "final barrier," the last barrier or mask before death, the death drive, or the female genitalia.

He goes on to say that beauty suspends desire, that it disarms, intimidates, decreases, and even puts a stop to desire (p. 279/238).[22] Why does it do so? Beauty, he argues, makes us come to a screeching halt on the path to our desire because the truth behind it is anything but pretty. Were we to pursue our sexual desire freely and directly, we would soon encounter the disgusting truth. So although the popular mind is inclined to think that beauty increases sexual desire, that the more beautiful the object is the more our desire is heightened (as we saw earlier), in fact it is quite the opposite: beauty paralyzes desire – beauty mesmerizes us and makes us incapable of pursuing sexual desire.[23]

Lacan's notion here is perhaps that we feel that our sexual desire would sully or soil such beauty. We have a certain kind of respect for beauty that makes us shy away from doing anything to it that might compromise it or imply that it is not as valuable as it seems. Hence beautiful forms and features inspire love and respect but put a damper on sexual urges. This seems to amount to the fairly classic division between beauty as form and perfection versus sex as material and base. This perhaps applies far more to a certain ethereal notion of innocent, angelic beauty, involving exquisitely fine, delicate, and perhaps girlish features, than to mature womanly beauty.[24] And it is perhaps above all the beauty of faces that freezes desire, the beauty of bodies heightening it.

Lacan on Gide

> Vision, of course, is the sharpest of our bodily senses, although it does not see wisdom.
>
> Plato, *Phaedrus*, 250d

The classic division between beauty as form and perfection versus sex as material and base may not apply to all men, but we certainly see it in André Gide's life, as Lacan (2006a) discusses it in his 1958 article, "The Youth of Gide, or the Letter and Desire." Gide's choice of his cousin Madeleine as his ideal love object occurs precisely at the moment when Gide's desire for Madeleine's sultry aunt is at its height, even though he is bothered and disturbed by this aunt. Gide goes to Madeleine's house to see this aunt of uncertain morals, an aunt who has already put her hands in his clothes in an attempt to get him to loosen up a bit and to mess with his mind; there he stumbles upon Madeleine weeping because of the aunt's improprieties and makes a momentous decision to protect Madeleine against this adult, this aunt who no doubt has passions not so unlike his own. Hence it is not clear whether he is protecting Madeleine from her aunt, protecting Madeleine from the aunt in himself, or protecting himself from what he saw in her aunt. No doubt, all three of the above are at play to at least some degree.

Lacan comments that "Desire left nothing here but its negative impact, giving form to the ideal of an angel that impure contact cannot touch" (p. 754), Madeleine being forced thereafter by Gide into the role of an angel who must not be sullied or touched by anything impure. "This love [is] 'embalmed so as not to suffer the ravages of time'"; it is an ideal love, and Gide characterizes himself as a "Uranist" (p. 754). The term "uranism" was introduced in 1860 in a novel written by a magistrate under the pseudonym Numa Numantis; it refers to the goddess of pure love, uranian (heavenly) Aphrodite (mentioned, naturally, in the *Symposium*), and signifies a pure, spiritual form of love.[25] Lacan comments as follows:

> As [Jean] Delay rightly emphasizes [in his *Youth of Gide*], everything here is supported by a very old tradition, justifying his mention of the mystical bonds of courtly love. Gide himself was not afraid to relate his union, despite its bourgeois trappings, to Dante's mystical union with Beatrice. And if psychoanalysts were capable of understanding what their master said about the death instinct, they would be able to recognize that self-realization can become bound up with the wish to end one's life.
>
> In fact, Gide's feeling for his cousin was truly the height of love, if love means giving what one does not have and if he gave her immortality. (pp. 754–5)

In turning Madeleine into a Lady worthy of the courtly love tradition, Gide does not fail to see the terrible Thing behind her, referring to her as "Morella" at one point, a woman from Edgar Allan Poe's 1850 story entitled "Morella." Lacan characterizes Poe's Morella as follows:

> Woman of the beyond, disowned in her daughter, who dies when Poe calls her by her name which should never have

been pronounced. [. . .] The cryptogram of the position of the beloved object in relation to desire is there, in the duplication reapplied to itself. The second mother, the desiring mother, is lethal and this explains the ease with which the ingrate form of the first, the loving mother, manages to replace her, in order to superimpose herself – without the spell being broken – on the form of the ideal woman.

The ideal woman is a loving, self-sacrificing mother figure (mom$_1$), not a desiring female (mom$_2$). A man puts a woman on a pedestal, making her into a Lady or goddess, so as not to reckon with a desiring female, so as to hide her materiality, which is different from man's in ways that tend to scare him, with its various flows . . . The result, as we see it in Gide's case, is quite sinister: Madeleine is frozen into a kind of living death in Gide's attempt to flee from the real, the real here taking the form of sexual difference and women's jouissance.

We find much the same thing in Stendhal's 1822 book on *Love*, where he argues that a woman must be innocent, pure, ethereal, chaste, and never exude sexuality. She must be an *"âme sublime"* (Stendhal, 2004, p. 50/60): a sublime soul, someone who is immaterial and, indeed, anorexic, sickly, pale, and not of this world, someone above vulgar pleasures. His aesthetic criterion freezes a woman into a sort of dead image: she must be more dead than alive.

Beauty and Fantasy

What is beauty? It is a new aptitude to give you pleasure. [This] explains why what is beautiful to one individual is ugly to another.

Stendhal, 2004, pp. 48–9/59

Returning further on in Seminar VII to the topic of beauty, Lacan (1992) indicates that desire and beauty can, at certain moments, come together. At what sorts of moments? When we go beyond certain limits, when we cross certain invisible lines (p. 279/238). He does not provide any examples in this context, but we might suspect he has Antigone in mind.[26]

He sees beauty as being correlated with a destructive drive. Unlike the good, it is not a lure; on the contrary, beauty awakens us and makes us focus on desire insofar as desire itself is linked to the luring or deceptive structure known as fantasy. Desire is propped up by fantasy, and Lacan suggests that fantasy involves a certain "*beau-n'y-touchez-pas*": It is beautiful – don't touch it! Don't touch that beauty (p. 280/239). In other words, desire and beauty become mutually bound up in fantasy, but desire remains captivated by beauty and fixated on it rather than pursuing satisfaction. *This is an aesthetic form of desire, not sexual desire that lurches toward satisfaction.*

This is one of the reasons why Lacan formulates, in his 1964 paper "On Freud's 'Trieb' and the Psychoanalyst's Desire," that desire impedes satisfaction of the drives: desire gets caught up in the pursuit and preservation of a beautiful ideal, an ideal that would be tarnished by attaining sexual gratification with the beautiful, ideal object. Desire that is fixated on an ideal is radically separated here from the "sexual drives" which simply seek satisfaction. "Desire is desire for desire" (2006a, p. 852), not for jouissance; and beauty can be seen as but one form of ideal that is latched onto by this kind of aestheticized desire. People can fixate on all sorts of other ideals, with little or no concern for their attainment, whether they are political ideals, ecological ideals, artistic or musical ideals, or ideals about love itself. Indeed we often encounter patients whose fascination with particular political ideals (whether anarchism, communism, or other) – not to mention literary, artistic, and musical ideals – is so all-consuming and uncompromising that everything in real life that might lead to their at least partial realization counts for naught. With ideals, it is all or nothing!

Sealing the divide between (aesthetic) desire and (drive) satisfaction, Lacan writes, "Desire comes from the Other, and jouissance is located on the side of the Thing" (p. 853). This is the precise split we saw in Gide: Madeleine is associated with the ethereal, symbolic Other, her aunt with the oh-so-material Thing. Desire is associated here with the mortification brought on by the signifier.

Fantasy thus seems to be the only way in which desire (understood as strictly equivalent to the Other's desire or desire for the Other) and beauty can come together, and it is a way which obviates satisfaction of desire. Beauty is maintained as an ideal and the sexual drives cannot possibly be given free rein.

This is perhaps what allows Lacan to suggest that the form of the human body – the image – represents "man's relation to the second death, the signifier of his desire, his visible desire." We see here the "central mirage, which both indicates the place of desire insofar as it is desire for nothing – the relation of man to his want-to-be – and stops us from seeing [the place of desire]" (Lacan, 1992, p. 345/298).

This fixation of desire upon beauty in fantasy leads to a kind of living death or, as Lacan calls it, a "zone of encroachment of death upon life" (p. 331/285). This is perhaps "the place of desire insofar as it is a desire for nothing" (p. 345/298).

"Is it this same shadow, represented by the shape of the body, that forms a barrier to the Other-thing that is beyond?" – the Thing in all its horror (p. 345/298)? Although fantasy involves a kind of living death, it nevertheless preserves us from an encounter with the Thing or the real.[27] Fantasy forms to block the encounter with the real; the same could be said of dreams which only occasionally give way to nightmares.

The symbolic introduces death here: it allows for the pursuit of love, of the feeling of being passionately in love with the feeling of being in love, a state which uses the other person as a mere prop or pretext and ignores his or her difference from oneself – that is, his or her particularity. This is a passion that consumes us and leads to death (as we shall see further on when we discuss Denis de Rougemont). It is the Greek tradition that perhaps first celebrates such passion. Does Christian love celebrate instead the otherness of the other? Freud (1905/1953b, p. 149 n) claims that in our times we glorify the object that we love, whereas the Greeks glorified the instinct or drive itself.

Let me raise a question here before closing this section: is the beauty we seek in our beloved a reflection upon ourselves? Are we looking to feel more beautiful or valuable ourselves by associating with people we consider to be beautiful? Sir Walter Elliot, an admittedly odd character in Jane Austen's *Persuasion*, wishes to be seen in public only with men and women who are at least as fine-looking as himself, thinking perhaps that it will show him off to still better advantage, making him appear even more handsome than he might otherwise appear. More commonly, perhaps, men seek a "trophy wife" – usually a beautiful young woman – to somehow make up for their own perceived status as past their prime and no longer desirable. In other words, there is perhaps also a narcissistic component to the search for beauty, not just a barrier to the real . . .

Beauty and Death

Come what sorrow can,
It cannot countervail the exchange of joy
That one short minute gives me in her sight.
Shakespeare, *Romeo and Juliet*, II. vi. 3–5

Why is *beauty* the starting point of Diotima's ladder of love? Physical beauty is obviously responsible for a good deal of our attraction to others, especially men's attraction to women. As Aristotle says, "the pleasure of the eye is the beginning of love. For no one loves if he has not first been delighted by the form of the beloved" (*Ethics*, 1167a). Like Plato, Aristotle privileges visual beauty above virtually all else in its ability to inspire love and desire.

Now Lacan comments that our fixation on physical beauty is a lure, illusion, or mirage, insofar as it turns our eyes away from death. We seek some sort of immortality in the perfection of the human form. Our fascination with or fixation on beauty is thus related to or motivated by our nonacceptance of death. There is a flight from aging and a preoccupation with youth. Beauty helps us come to grips with death by hiding our desire for death, and leads us on toward immortality (Lacan, 2015, pp. 125–7) – hence the connection between beauty and death. Tragedy as an art form evokes and broaches our death wish, which explains part of its allure and frightfulness.

Recall that Socrates is widely reputed to have been quite ugly. To be with Socrates was thus perhaps to be reminded always of one's impending death . . .

Physical Love, Sexual Desire, Lust, Concupiscence, Sex Drive

> Now, as everyone plainly knows, love is some kind of desire.
> Plato, *Phaedrus*, 237d

> When one loves, it has nothing to do with sex.
> Lacan, 1998a, p. 25

Although universally recognized as usually present alongside love, "physical love" or lust is sometimes viewed as morally acceptable only when a "purer" form of love is simultaneously present; only when such pure love is present can the "disgust" or "revulsion" many feel after the sexual act – despite some five decades of "sexual revolution" – with its accompanying devaluation of the sexual partner, be avoided or overcome.[28] As we shall see momentarily, certain authors and traditions recommend the prolonged or constant deferral of sexual desire, so as to give rise to ever more frenetic states of amorous intoxication (the *Kama Sutra* provides examples of this, which Freud might have dubbed "overvaluation of the object"); to strengthen and embolden the lover to perform deeds of chivalrous valor for the beloved; or, in Socrates' case, to urge the lover on to higher intellectual and spiritual pursuits (in Freud's terms, this would encourage "sublimation" of the sex drive). Indeed, in the *Phaedrus*

(253c–254d) and the *Republic*, Plato has Socrates suggest that the human soul is divided into three parts: the white horse, the black horse, and the driver or charioteer. The black horse is associated with lust and must be suppressed through a struggle within oneself.

Lacan (2015), commenting on a remark Agathon makes in the *Symposium*, provides an amusing (and oh-so-French) contrasting viewpoint here when he says that it is (pure) love that interferes with men's sexual performance:

> [Agathon says,] πελάγει δὲ γαλήνην (*peláge de galénen*), which means that everything has stopped, a flat sea [no waves or wind]. We must keep in mind what a flat sea meant in Antiquity – it meant that nothing was going right, that the ships were blocked at Aulis, and when that happened in the middle of the deep blue sea, people were bothered by it, almost as bothered as when that happened to them in bed. To evoke *peláge de galénen* concerning love makes it quite clear that a bit of fun is being had here. Love is what makes you break down, it's what leads to a fiasco. (p. 106)

In other words, the tables are turned here: it is not lust that interferes with love but, rather, excessive aesthetic or spiritual love for a partner that gets in the way of one's sexual prowess, leading to so-called erectile dysfunction.[29] Lust gets a man up, while love (for an ideal or idealized figure) is what brings him down.

Certain patients seem to feel that the only way they can deal with and finally love others is by giving up, once and for all (as if such were possible), all desire and lust. They believe that without such a sacrifice, they will never truly love. Kierkegaard seems to endorse this notion with his concept of "infinite resignation" (see below), which Lacan (1998a, p. 77) associates with Kierkegaard's attempt to find a love beyond desire for object *a*, by giving up object *a* altogether. This may be the only solution possible in certain cases of perversion, but in our psychoanalytic work with neurotics, we certainly do not aim at anything like "infinite resignation" or renunciation. Indeed, we encourage analysands *not* to give up on their desire, for this is generally what they have been doing all along, and this is how they got into the mess in which they find themselves in the first place. We do not ask people to give up all of their sensual desire but seek instead a different compromise between love, desire, and the drives. As Lacan (2004, p. 209) puts it, "Only love allows jouissance to condescend to desire," suggesting that love can – in the best of cases, perhaps after an analysis – stop desire and the drives from being so often at odds.[30]

Fin'Amor (Courtly Love)

What is courtly love? It is a highly refined way of making up for the absence of the sexual relationship, by feigning that we are the ones who erect an obstacle thereto.

Lacan, 1998a, p. 69

Love *is* courtly love.

Lacan, 1973–4, class given on January 8, 1974

One obvious facet of courtly love – the astonishing approach to love that arose in what is now the south of France in the eleventh and twelfth centuries and then spread to northern France, Germany, and England – that Lacan emphasizes is the seemingly deliberate placing of obstacles in the way of satisfaction of the sexual drives, which would lead to a heightening of passion, a heightening of the feeling of being in love.[31] Lacan mentions this characteristic of courtly love in Seminars VII and XX. It resulted from the fact that the object of a knight's affection was a woman who was usually of higher social station than himself and who was married (generally to the knight's own Lord or at least to a highly possessive or jealous man). The Lady owed her husband fidelity, and no matter how neglected or mistreated she appeared to be by her own husband, there were often multiple obstacles to the consummation of her relationship with the knight who courted her: it would involve adultery on the part of the Lady, infidelity to his Lord on the part of the knight, and an inequality of status between the potential partners.

There has been a veritable revolution in historical research on the Middle Ages in France and elsewhere in the last 40 years, and knowledge about courtly love has grown by leaps and bounds since Lacan spoke about it in the late 1950s and early 1970s. Many poems and texts have been rediscovered and translated from Provençal into French, and a number of hypotheses about the origins and practices of courtly love have been overturned. I will begin with Lacan's discussion of the tradition, and then turn to some more recent perspectives.

Lacan says that women at that time were traditionally nothing but symbolic objects of exchange, à la Lévi-Strauss' (1969) *Elementary Structures of Kinship*. Women were taken not as human beings but as objects of desire, as signifiers (Lacan, 1992, pp. 253–4/214–15); they had power only as a function of their position in society. He recounts the tale of the Countess of Comminges, a noblewoman who was to inherit a large region of southern France, who was treated very badly by Peter of Aragon, a Castilian Lord to the south who wanted to annex her territory. He orchestrated her repudiation by her husband, married her himself as soon as she came into her inheritance, and proceeded to mistreat her to the point that she fled to Rome to seek protection from the Pope himself (p. 176/147). These kinds of things certainly happened, but that does not mean that women had no other influence or power whatsoever in society (one need but read biographies of Eleanor of Aquitaine) – such a portrait is a bit overly simplistic. Nevertheless, Lacan's basic view of relations between the sexes at the time is that they were characterized by lust (sexual desire) and possession: a man legally owned his wife, just as he owned his children; he could kill a daughter who ran off with a man not approved of by him, for example, or lock his wife in his castle's keep for 15 years without much explanation to anyone, if he claimed to suspect her of infidelity.

According to Lacan, and he finds this quite curious, it is the very men who treated women as mere objects of exchange who rather suddenly began to sing their praises in courtly love poetry: kings, dukes, and counts (pp. 176–7/147–8). In other words, it was not the men who did not have the power to treat women as pawns – that is, men lower on the feudal totem pole – who became their primary supporters, as one might suspect, imagining such lesser knights to be men rebelling against the established way of treating women, perhaps simply in order to attract those women to themselves. It was, Lacan claims, the very men who treated them as material possessions who led the way to this elevation of the Lady.[32]

Why might they have done such a thing? No one really knows for sure, but Lacan speculates that "Man asks to be deprived of something real"; courtly love is "essentially linked to the early symbolization altogether bound up in the signification of the *gift of love*" (p. 179/150). In other words, these men were, in Lacan's view, asking to be deprived of immediate sexual satisfaction so as to attain something else, so as to focus on something else – namely, love and what one gives and receives in love.[33] This is why he dwells on the literal meaning of the phrase *faire l'amour*, to make love or *create* love: we have here a creative process, the bringing into being of a love relationship that was not about a man simply taking whatever he wanted, thereby procuring real satisfactions for himself whenever he wanted them, but about taking things to a new and different level: that of a man wanting to be wanted by a woman, and thus of the creative activity of getting her to want to be taken. The shift here is from the real (the satisfaction of the sexual drives) to the symbolic, where desire is the Other's desire, where one desires to be desired by the Other, or wants to be loved.

Courtly love is, according to Lacan, "the work of sublimation in its purest form" (p. 151/126). The Lady takes on the "value of representing the Thing." It involves a scholastics of unhappy love, a "mourning unto death" (p. 175/146). In it, the woman is inaccessible, and often referred to in the masculine as *Mi Dom*, My Lord or Master (p. 178/149), apparently taking the place in the knight's affections of his own feudal master, if not of God Himself.[34]

Lacan postulates that it was in order to deprive themselves (not necessarily consciously) of something that courtly lovers became enamored of women who were unattainable – unattainable insofar as they were already married and were, by virtue of their social and political positions, inaccessible. They went about courting women who could not succumb to their solicitations, and seemingly contented themselves with the smallest sign that the ladies acknowledged their love and devotion and perhaps loved them in return.

At the same time, knights often construed their Ladies as sadistic slave drivers, as demanding almost impossible services as homage to them, and as providing only the most meager compensations in the form of signs of esteem and love. A knight's Lady was viewed as an inhuman partner, who was terribly arbitrary in the proofs of love that she demanded (p. 180/150).

Courtly love became a signifying artifice, a construction, a detour away from physical satisfaction toward what Lacan calls "another satisfaction." Certain love techniques seem to have been developed: holding back, *amor interruptus*, sustaining the pleasure of desiring, or, as Lacan puts it, "the pleasure of experiencing displeasure" (p. 182/152). Georges Duby, one of the best-known medieval historians in France in recent decades, believes he is disputing Lacan's position when he claims there is evidence that Ladies and their courtly servants *did* occasionally have sex (Duby, 1992, pp. 257–8). Rather than disputing this point, Lacan suggests that even when they did have sex, it was not taken all the way, so to speak, for the point was to keep desire alive. A question then arises about the meaning of the term *le don de merci* ("the gift of mercy"). Did it refer to a sign of love from the Lady that relieved the knight of the torturous question, "Does she love me?" or might it have referred to ejaculation?[35]

In Seminar XX, Lacan (1998a) asserts that "Courtly love is, for man – in relation to whom the lady is entirely, and in the most servile sense of the word, a subject – the only way to elegantly pull off the absence of the sexual relationship" (p. 65/69). The satisfactions provided by physical relations prior to that time seemed, no doubt, inadequate to hide the fact that, although a relationship of some kind can exist between two human beings, there can be no relationship between a man qua man and a woman qua woman (on this intricate point, see Fink, 1995a, Chapter 8). Dissatisfaction with real satisfactions and whatever other satisfactions went with them seems to have led to an attempt to sublimate relations between the sexes.

In any case, one might suggest that at a time when marriages among nobles were dictated largely by political and economic considerations, and relations between husbands and wives revolved primarily around physical satisfactions and the production of heirs to the family name and fortune, courtly love introduced the kind of question that surrounds love relations: "Does she love me as I love her?" Perhaps not surprisingly, this question arose outside of marriage, not within the political and economic constraints placed on the institution of marriage, which continued to remain intact at that time. In some sense, courtly love might be understood as a form of hystericization: can I find or bring out a lack in another to which I myself correspond? Can I be the cause of another's desire and come into being as a desiring subject myself?

Such questions were not germane to decisions at the time regarding whom to marry; nor are they even today in certain European cultures, especially in the upper socioeconomic strata, where love is often found primarily in the margins of the institution of marriage in the form of extramarital affairs. In modern-day America, marriage is rarely a transparently political and/or economic arrangement, love usually being considered the most important ingredient of marriage. Love and marriage are supposed to go together like horse and carriage in the United States (see further on), and this configuration is a relatively new one in the history of the West. It is certainly not found in a medieval tale like that of *Tristan and Isolde*, where love is virtually unthinkable within the bounds or chains of marriage. Nor was it often found in Antiquity in certain Greek city states, romantic love and passion generally being sought by men outside of marriage or at least alongside marriage. Women were expected to be faithful to their husbands but men were not always expected to be faithful to their wives, and passionate homosexual relations were very common among men, alongside their heterosexual marriages.

Whence Courtly Love?

Why, we might ask, did things shift from a situation in which adolescent boys were celebrated as magnificent love objects and women were rarely put on a pedestal, to one in which a total glorification of women occurred – a glorification so extreme that women, rather than seeming to be people different from men but equal in value to them, became like masters and gods? How and why did they become so elevated as to be completely inaccessible, and worshipped not as individuals with their own characteristics and personalities, but as Woman with a capital W?

Women's beauty had, of course, been celebrated by sculptors over the millennia, but it seems that feminine beauty was appreciated primarily insofar as it brought on carnal desire and led to material passions and satisfactions. And motherhood had, of course, also been celebrated for millennia, emphasizing a particular aspect of women, their reproductive and nurturing functions. In both cases, what was glorified revolved around the body, so much so that early Church thinkers debated whether or not women could even be said to have souls! How then could a woman be one's soul mate or heart's companion (*compagne de coeur*)?

Something changed in the late eleventh century in what is now southern France, but it was not a movement that encouraged men to appreciate women as individuals like themselves in certain ways and unlike themselves in other ways – that is, as friends in the Aristotelian sense or as Cicero might have wanted it. Instead, a quantum leap occurs and women are catapulted into the stratosphere. Given their change in status, men must put aside all their material passions and expectations of satisfaction, for Woman becomes worshipped as a deity. This newfound fascination with Woman misses or overlooks individual women with their own personalities and quirks, and becomes a passion for passion itself, love for love's sake, and indeed a glorification of dying for love, dying owing to one's love for a Lady who is, in fact, accessory, certain authors (Rougemont, 1983, p. 106/98; Lacan, 1992, pp. 179–80/149–50) pointing out that everyone's Lady is described in virtually identical terms.

Whereas women had been admired and desired as bodies, suddenly they become adored and worshipped as ethereal, angelic, spiritualized beings who are barely human. We have here the origins of the nineteenth-century themes of woman as pure, ethereal, sublime, immaterial, anorexic, sickly, pale, and not of this world, many of which we have already highlighted in Stendhal's and Gide's work.

How and why did this quantum shift occur? There are a number of different hypotheses.

First Hypothesis

Certain historians point to the shift in historical and material circumstances attendant upon what is referred to as the "great transformation of the year 1000" (*mutation de l'an 1000*). The

Carolingian (Charlemagne's) empire began to break down owing, at least in part, to the then current laws of inheritance whereby property and power were distributed equally among all of a couple's sons. This led to fragmentation of the empire and bitter infighting among the sons, culminating in certain cases in fratricide and spoliation of one brother by another. Charlemagne's governors had been able to maintain stability in the former Roman Empire that he had largely reconquered, but his sons, who spent the better part of their time fighting amongst themselves and killing each other, were unable to stave off the waves of barbarians (Vikings, Visigoths, etc.), and the former stability gave way to considerable chaos.

As new power lords emerged – this is the origin of what we now refer to as feudalism (complete with the hierarchy of lords and the lesser nobles who owed allegiance to their lords) – they began to try to extend and consolidate their property holdings by arranging marriages designed to bring adjoining lands under their own control, and their neighbors' daughters became a currency in this more or less legalized land grab. Once property to be inherited by a daughter was secured through marriage to her husband, his bride might be jettisoned or quietly murdered. Women seem to have undergone a particularly bad debasement during this period, and it has been hypothesized that the younger men at the Lord's castle may, in their rivalry and competition with the Lord to whom they owed fidelity and loyalty, have pitied the Lord's wife and taken her side, promising to uphold and defend this forsaken, mistreated Lady. Far from being mere chattel to them, she suddenly began to embody Love itself, disguised as Woman (a real woman being in some sense accessory here) who could transport a man beyond his narrow, mortal carcass. In other words, some historians see the earliest seeds of the courtly love tradition not among those who had the lion's share of power at the time, as Lacan suggests, but rather among those in the next tier down. Once the movement gathered steam, the most powerful lords, like William VII, Duke of Aquitaine, the father of Eleanor of Aquitaine, also got caught up in the fervor.

Certain demographic studies have even suggested that there were far more young men congregating around the courts of the time than there were women, and that many of these young men were not in a position to marry because of the new laws governing inheritance known as primogeniture. Primogeniture (which is still practiced, to some degree, in England today) is the system of inheritance whereby property is not equally divided among all the children in a family (as has been required in France since the revolution), but whereby the first son in a family inherits all of the family's property, leaving nothing for the other children, apart from small dowries that might be set aside for the daughters (though when there was little or no money or property for a dowry, a daughter might be sent to a nunnery).

In the Middle Ages, later-born sons had few other ways to make a living than to enter the Church or to offer their military services to a Lord. This meant that there were often dozens if not hundreds of young men gravitating around a Lord and his Lady. These men were generally not so stupid or brazen as to jeopardize their positions vis-à-vis the Lord to whom they had sworn allegiance, and thus rarely if ever tried to obtain physical contact with the Lady they secretly courted, contenting themselves instead with a kiss on the forehead or mouth (*baiser de la paix*), a favor (which in the period of jousts designated a handkerchief that a lady would wrap around the upper arm of her favored knight), or a ring signifying a secret pact.

This first hypothesis as to the origins of courtly love includes a mixture of historical, economic, social, and psychological factors, suggesting a quasi-Oedipal rivalry over a woman between the younger, second-tier nobles and their older, more powerful Lord. Note that this is the exact configuration we find in the relationship between Tristan and King Mark in *Tristan and Isolde*.[36]

Second Hypothesis

The second explanation for this radical transformation in the status of women is that it parallels the rise in importance of the Virgin Mary in Catholicism, more or less between the seventh and tenth centuries A.D. A pagan mother goddess was worshipped in Gaul (and by the Celts) long before Catholicism spread there, and some suggest that the Virgin Mary was granted ever greater importance by the Church so she would take the place of this pagan goddess, bringing pagans into the Church through the back door, as it were.

If one takes a special guided tour at the famous cathedral in Chartres, France, one can penetrate deep beneath the current structure where one finds a shrine, which is a well that was dedicated to the pagan mother goddess. The shrine was still functioning as late as the seventh century, and the first church on the site was built right over the shrine and, not surprisingly, dedicated to the mother of God, the Virgin Mary. Over the centuries, new structures were built over and around it, leading eventually to one of the biggest cathedrals in the world dedicated to the Virgin Mary. Some argue that the importance of the Virgin was increasingly stressed in Catholicism in order to co-opt the strength of the pagans' belief in and worship of the mother goddess in Gaul and elsewhere.

According to this hypothesis, women thus gained in status and importance insofar as they resembled the Virgin Mary in chastity and spirituality. Men came, then, to love them insofar as they were pure and holy. Knights sought to serve them, and not to desecrate them with their unholy material desires.

Third Hypothesis

The third explanation, as outlined in Book 2 of Denis de Rougemont's (1940/1983) *Love in the Western World*, is that the supposed exaltation of Woman in the songs of the courtly love poets is actually a symbolic reference to the Cathar Church as their Lady, and a fairly sneaky reference at that. It was sneaky because, even though in Catholicism the Church itself was sometimes referred to as the bride of Christ, and therefore in the feminine, the Cathars (a break-away sect, also referred to as the Albigeois) very specifically described their Church as a "she" (the "true Church," as they discretely said to distinguish theirs from the Catholic Church). I will not go into the origins and development of Catharism here; for our purposes, suffice it to indicate that it was considered by the Pope to be a heretical variation on Christianity, so heretical that in the thirteenth century a crusade was directed against the Cathars in the southwest of France and they were virtually wiped off the face of the earth by the French army (whole towns and cities – men, women, and children – were run through with the sword or burnt at the stake).

According to Rougemont, courtly love poetry may have been deliberately designed to be open to several different interpretations so that if the troubadours were ever accused of being Cathars (which they largely were), they could claim that they were simply talking about the Catholic Church or, alternatively, about a specific woman. Rougemont (1983, p. 103/95–6) argues that the troubadours allowed a good deal of uncertainty of signification to hover around their poetry. The Lady they sang the praises of could thus be understood in several ways (the Virgin Mary by Catholics, the Cathar Church by Cathars, a real woman by feudal society at large, or an imaginary/fantasy woman by romantics of all ilks). Their fellow Cathars might understand the "esoteric" meaning, the meaning not visible to the masses; Catholics might believe in the conventional religious meaning, which might actually have been nothing more than a smokescreen; and lovers might dwell on the more profane meaning. There was a little something for everyone in the ambiguous way in which the courtly love poets expressed themselves, and no one could pin down exactly what it meant.[37]

It is even argued that, far from glorifying women, courtly love poetry may well have been at the outset nothing more than a continuation of the mystical tradition describing people's passionate love for God. The glorification of women that it led to afterward may possibly have been an unintended consequence of the troubadours' symbolic poetry. It may have been an unforeseen side effect of ecstatic religious fervor. Ecstatic love of God thus became, almost accidentally according to Rougemont, ecstatic love of women. In a reversal of the received view, courtly love here is not an idealization or sublimation of carnal love (p. 105/96), but rather a bringing down to earth of spiritual love for God.

Fourth Hypothesis

The fourth explanation for the appearance of courtly love looks to other nearby literary traditions such as Arab mystical poetry, which entered the southwest region of France through Spain. Arab influence had been strong in a good deal of Spain for many centuries and courtly love poetry in Occitan may have developed out of contact with that literary tradition, which may also have very much influenced the development of Catharism. One of the key figures here is the Andalusian poet Ibn Hazm, whose work *The Dove's Neck-Ring* was written around 1022; but there were many other philosophers writing at the time who seem to have been inspired at least in part by the notion of "Platonic love."[38]

In Love with . . . What?

True love [. . .] rejects any and every object in order that it
may launch into the infinite [. . . It is] a desire for something
altogether unknown, the existence of which is disclosed solely by
the need for it, by a discomfort, and by a void that is in search of
whatever will fill it.
                    Fichte (cited in Rougemont, 1983, p. 240/220)

Regardless of the origins of the courtly love tradition, what is clear is that a form or practice of love arose in the Middle Ages that seemed quite new (and perhaps, indeed, out of place). Ostensibly, women were being praised and worshipped, poetry and songs being written about them; yet, since the Lady praised in each poem was virtually identical (or at least she was praised in practically identical terms), it appears to be some new notion of Woman that was being worshipped – or perhaps Love itself that was being celebrated, the specific woman being less important than the sentiments she gave rise to, whether joyous or lamentable. The ecstasy of *being in love* burst onto the Western medieval scene (or came back after having disappeared in much earlier times, for we find traces of it at least in Plato's *Symposium*, the Greek gods in particular perhaps valuing love itself more highly than the beloved), and we can ask, "Being in love with what?"

It seems it was less a matter of being in love with a specific woman, with her own characteristics and particularities, and perhaps even of being in love with a woman of lofty social status and irreproachable morals, than of *being in love with being in love*. The troubadours competed with each other to see who could most creatively describe the ecstatic joys of being in love and the tormenting pains of being parted from one's beloved, being uncertain of one's beloved's affections, and being cruelly tried by her exactions and demands. This kind of love was anything but boring – one's passions were always inflamed, always raw and ready to ignite. (Anyone who spoke deprecatingly of the Lady of one's thoughts or impugned her honor had to be prepared to be drawn on immediately and run through.) This was in stark contrast to the lowly status of love between spouses in prior times; such love was sometimes mentioned by Greek and Roman authors (like Homer in the *Odyssey*), though rarely made into the main topic. Ovid might be considered a notable exception here, although his work on love concerns seduction far more than marital felicity.

Being in Love with Being in Love

> Sublimation is the effort to permit love to be realized with the woman, [. . .] to make it seem as if it were happening with the woman.
>
> Lacan, 2006b, p. 243

Being in love with being in love is but one form of something of very great importance to many people, which is being in love with an idea or ideal. As we saw in the case of beauty, ideals are often latched onto by a form of aestheticized desire, leading to a kind of absolutism, utopianism, and/or fanaticism. This can, depending on the ideal, give rise to the most extreme, catastrophic results whereby life itself (one's own or that of others) is reckoned by the fanatic of little value next to the ideal itself. Marianne in Austen's *Sense and Sensibility* would sooner cry than sleep, and sooner waste away out of Love for Willoughby, when he leaves her for what she expects to be but a fortnight, than fail to incarnate the perfect romantic heroine who dies of unhappy separation from her beloved. Love, in her view, demands this of her.

> Marianne would have thought herself very inexcusable had she been able to sleep at all the first night after parting from Willoughby. She would have been ashamed to look her family in the face the next morning, had she not risen from her bed in more need of repose than when she lay down in it. But the feelings which made such composure a disgrace, left her in no danger of incurring it. She was awake the whole night, and she wept the greatest part of it. She got up with a headache, was unable to talk, and unwilling to take any nourishment; giving pain every moment to her mother and sisters, and forbidding all attempt at consolation from either. (Austen, 1970, p. 71)

In this literary example, the subject primarily harms herself, though her family and friends secondarily. In a fictionalized account of a lover written by Kierkegaard, that seems closely related to his own real-life experience with Regina, the love of his life, he writes:

> He was in love, deeply and sincerely, that was clear, and yet right away, on one of the first days, he was capable of recollecting his love. At bottom he was through with the whole relationship. At the very moment of beginning he took such a tremendous stride that he has leapt clear over the whole of life. Though the girl were to die to-morrow, it will not make any essential difference, he will again throw himself down, his eye will again fill with a tear. (cited in Lowrie, 1970, p. 212)

Just as Willoughby perhaps counted less for Marianne than her romantic ideal of Love did, Regina here counts for little compared to the fixation on a certain ideal, that of a tragic, aesthetic notion of love. Kierkegaard prefers to think of himself as *having lived* in a certain way, rather than actually living in that way; like the obsessive, he is living for some kind of ideal or eternity and not for today; indeed, he might be said to be dead to life already. In *Fear and Trembling* (1843/1954, pp. 52–8), he introduces the concept of "infinite resignation," which in Freudian terms amounts to renunciation and seems tied to his giving up of Regina once he had successfully wooed her. The real flesh-and-blood girl is given up by him supposedly in order for him to attain something at a "higher level"; might he have called it love of God?

In other examples, thousands if not millions of lives are counted as nothing compared to an ideal, whether it be the "purity" of a certain doctrine (like that upheld by the Catholic Church against the Cathars in the thirteenth century or the Protestant Reformation in the sixteenth century), the "superiority" of the Aryan race, or orthodoxies of all ilks (Stalinism, communism, democracy, etc.). In such fanatical devotion to a certain ideal, human beings disappear from the inhuman equation. The fanatic's own life counts for nought, his or her health and welfare being sacrificed for an abstract ideal; others barely exist to him – hence their expendability. This is not to say that one must never die for an ideal – whether freedom, justice, or one's right to practice one's own faith – but in many cases, and this was undoubtedly true of the Cathars themselves, fanatically embraced ideals turn life itself into a form of death, into a kind of living death.

To say this is to surreptitiously slip in an ideal of my own (in the guise of a counter-ideal), which is that of life – however life be defined – against death.[39] Single-minded attachment to ideals might be associated with Freud's death drive, and in psychoanalysis we ally with the patient's life drive against the death drive in all its forms. The death drive is inextricably linked to the values and ideals conveyed by and, indeed, endemic to the symbolic order. Human desire, insofar as it is bound up with symbols and signifiers, inevitably tends toward giving deadly fixation priority over real satisfactions in this life. Desire makes us live for something other-worldly, mortifying ourselves – our flesh and our spirit – for the sake of something supposedly loftier . . .

Didn't I seem to suggest in Chapter 3 that psychoanalysis requires a certain kind of mortification on the part of the analyst, who must love without asking for love in return, embodying thereby a certain kind of ideal? Although undoubtedly striving to embody a certain ideal in the consulting room, the psychoanalyst – unlike the saint – is in no wise constrained to strive to embody that ideal in everyday life, which puts rather a different face on things.

Being in love with an ideal, specifically with the ideal of Love itself, is hardly a twenty-first-century invention. In the fourth century A.D., Saint Augustine confessed, in speaking of his youth:

> I was not yet in love, but I was in love with love, and from the very depths of my need hated myself for not more keenly feeling the need. I sought some object to love, since I was thus in love with loving. (Augustine, 1961, p. 36)[40]

In the twelfth century, Capellanus – in his bizarre book in which he devotes 150 pages to telling us what love is, how best to go about winning love, and how to keep it alive, only to argue in the last 20 pages that we would do better not to get involved in love relationships[41] – celebrates the (sometimes painful) joys of being in love, saying:

> He who loves is bound to a painful slavery, he is afraid that any-thing or almost anything can hurt his love, his mind is violently overwhelmed by the slightest suspicion and his heart is touched to the quick. The lover fears every conversation his beloved has with a stranger, every walk taken or unusual lateness, because of jealousy. Because "love is something full of worried fear" [a quote from Ovid's *Heroides* I.12], he dares not do anything or think anything that contradicts in any way his beloved's will, for the lover fears always that the will of and confidence of his beloved will change and neither waking nor sleeping can rid him of this thought. (Chapelain, 2004, pp. 99–100/190)

Capellanus asserts that we feel alive when in love (even if this passage comes in the part of the book where he is trying to dissuade us from pursuing love), and it seems quite clear that the beloved is of less importance to us than the passion we feel. The same goes for Stendhal who tells us that it is far sweeter and more fulfilling to dream and daydream of one's beloved and of one's love for her than it is to actually be with her. He endlessly indulges in imagining all kinds of perfections in her – such that she is a goddess and no longer a living, breathing human being – and adores being in love with being in love. He taxes schoolchildren for being *amoureux de l'amour*, "in love with love," but he is clearly like those he criticizes (Stendhal, 2004, p. 117/110).

An Antidote to the Disappearance of the Beloved in Love?

In Book 7 of *Love in the Western World*, Rougemont proposes what he believes to be a solution to the problem that passion ends up shunting aside or overlooking the other (one's supposed beloved), celebrating Love itself instead. Eros, he argues, has to be kept within bounds or kept under control by agape (Christian love); associating agape with marriage, he defines marriage as an "institution that constrains (or restrains or hems in) [*contient*] passion – not by morality – but by love" (1983, p. 341/315). Left to its own devices and in the absence of a religious or mystical goal, passion leads people to pure self-destruction; for those who are married, it leads to rapid dissatisfaction and a search for new opportunities to fall in love. By its very nature, Eros seeks to aggrandize and deify itself, not the other person; it accepts no other before it. It is fundamentally a narcissistic passion, knowing no God above it, nor any equal. Passion boils down to a wish to be one's own God: "the sole Goal of infinite love can only be the divine: God, our ideal of God, or the deified Self" (pp. 307/285 and 323/299).

Rougemont's proposed "solution" to the problem posed by passion is that Christian love must be adopted as an antidote. Agape (1) restricts one's freedom to pursue the endlessly shifting play of Eros (by finding new partners with whom to experience anew the passion one no longer finds in one's marriage), and (2) limits the importance to the individual of passion in general (although the individual's passion could well appear in other contexts: art, politics, work, war, etc.).

He says that it is only through agape that one can genuinely concern oneself with another human being (not a god or goddess), have a true "encounter with an other" (p. 350/322), "accepting a being in itself as limited and real, not as a pretext for exalting it or contemplating it, but as an incomparable and autonomous existence at one's side" (pp. 309–10/286).

As laudable as this may sound, his notion of how and why agape can be privileged by an individual over Eros seems rather problematic: to his mind, it has to become privileged on the basis of a pure, somewhat arbitrary decision – a decision that goes beyond the weighing of the pros and cons of the potential spouse, and of the potential for there being a good match between spouses. It is a decision that obviously can make no promises as to what one's sentiments will be down the road – one cannot promise to remain in love for any given period of time – but it promises to engage in acts of love, to act for the other person's good, come what may. We cannot, he admits, commit to feeling in love at some future date, but we can commit to active love, loyalty, and raising children (pp. 335–6/310).[42] This decision is in some sense arbitrary, he argues, absurd even. One's reasons for the decision are always inconclusive and irrelevant. One decides simply for the sake of deciding – we seem to end up here with something that sounds a lot like *love for the sake of love*. Rougemont goes so far as to equate the absurd with faith (p. 348/321–2), and so to make an absurd decision is to make a decision based on faith alone, which cannot be explained or argued for.

Rougemont waxes lyrical about such an arbitrary decision based on faith alone, in a certain way reintroducing passion into a situation in which it seemed he had tried to eliminate it or at least curtail it. There appears to be something ecstatic about this self-imposed limitation or castration, the author seeming to believe that it might compensate the person who makes it with love and perhaps even passion further down the road. We see here, it seems to me, a kind of *passion to restrict one's own passion* on the basis of a decision that is described as based on faith alone, without any rhyme or reason. This is a form of love for love's sake, or art for art's sake, love being an art pursued for no good reason, thumbing its nose at life itself as life becomes "artified."

We are told here that we should make an irrevocable decision, come hell or high water, to stay with someone, not for the happiness or satisfactions it will bring, but *just because* (pp. 332–3/308). To Rougemont, there is grandeur in making an absurd choice, a choice with no why or wherefore. He gets so caught up in it and carried away with it that it becomes an absurd *passion for non-passion!* His passion for faithfulness seems to become more important than his wife herself. Rather than a celebration of the other as Other, it becomes a celebration of one's "fidelity" to the abstract ideal of fidelity! This seems to constitute a sort of obsessive solution to the problem as he has figured it.

Ideals appear to return here through the back door, as it were, love apparently being an easy terrain for ideals to invade and conquer (but perhaps this is true of all human passions?). Here it seems that fidelity and loyalty become more important than the person to whom one is faithful or loyal![43]

It seems that it is incredibly easy to end up on the slippery slope where *something about ourselves,* our faithfulness in this case, *becomes more important than our partner.* The Otherness of the other again drops out of the picture, and we wind up dealing with the One (an idea, ideal, or signifier), not the Other. Libido becomes inextricably bound up with the symbolic, steering clear of the real. It seems quite patent that animals cannot fall in love with love, or with any other sort of ideal, not having the same kind of access to or subservience to language as we do; other individuals remain what they are for them, rather than being taken up in and sublimated or abstracted into something beyond themselves.

Love Courts and Courting

> The lover must also always voluntarily offer his services to all
> ladies and obey them; it is fitting that he be humble, having
> totally ripped pride out of himself by the roots.
> > Chapelain, 2004, p. 33/152

Courtly love was, fortunately, not always taken to the extremes it was taken to at the time of the Cathars, and in the twelfth to fifteenth centuries it brought a certain refined sensibility to relations between the sexes in northern France, Germany, and England. Apparently initiated by the Countess of Champagne in the Champagne region of France, and quickly spreading elsewhere, a practice arose known as "love courts," which attempted to dictate and/or regulate what was expected and considered elegant in the realm of love.

In such courts, a woman who felt that her extramarital suitor had made unreasonable demands upon her – whether they were simply more than she was willing to do, period, or whether they were made too quickly – would air her grievances in front of a distinguished assembly of noblemen and noblewomen at the Countess' court and the assembly would give its verdict, through the Lady who presided over it, regarding who was at fault and who was not. The idea here seems to have been that there was an unwritten code of what was acceptable and what was unacceptable, of what was good form and what was not, in matters of love – that there were indeed proper stages of love. These things could be decided and legislated by a group of people educated in courtly love and their sentences were optional – in other words, one was apparently free to follow their advice or not.[44] If one did not, however, one might not be so successful in one's next suit; indeed, one's advances toward a new partner might be rejected out of hand.

As Franck Lemonde (in Chapelain, 2004) puts it:

> love courts should be compared to seventeenth-century salons rather than to our courts of law. People went to them more for amusement and entertainment than to exercise power. Various conflicts regarding love were exposed to all present for playful study and then a verdict was handed down by a *domina* (Lady ["*dame*"]), who decreed whether the union in question was legitimate or not, in other words, whether it was in accord with the code of love. (pp. 24–5)

Although their purpose was to explore and regulate love relationships, not marriage, these love courts were perhaps not so different from certain books written in our own times professing to spell out the rules of good behavior in love, above all those that a woman must follow in relationships if she is to convince a man to lead her to the altar. The idea is that there is a code of what is done and what is not done at a given stage of a relationship, and of what should and should not be expected of those who are dating.[45] Capellanus (Chapelain, 2004, p. 64/170) tells us that at a certain love court, a countess judged "dishonest" a woman who wanted to be loved but refused to give her love to her lover. A couple of other examples mentioned by him are provided below.

A man who had lost an eye or some other part of his body while fighting courageously in a battle was rejected by his lover as unworthy and painful to look at. Ermengarde de Narbonne, who presided over the love court where he presented his complaint against his lover, declared:

> This woman is decreed unworthy of any and all honor because she preferred to deprive her lover of her love when he had been mutilated due to the usual dangers of war, as are suffered always by those who fight courageously. In general, the courage of men excites women's love and strongly feeds their desire to love. Why, then, should the mutilation of members, which derives naturally and inevitably from courage, affect the lover with a loss of her love? (pp. 71–2/174)

In another case, a man used another man as his go-between in his love affair with a woman, and the go-between ended up seducing the woman himself. The Countess of Champagne, who had convoked 60 Ladies to her love court, handed down the following verdict when the shy man complained of this before them:

> Let this underhanded lover [the go-between], who found a woman worthy of his merit, since she was not ashamed to go along with such an exploit, enjoy this love acquired through evil means, if he wishes, and let her enjoy this friend of whom she showed herself so worthy. But the two must remain forever separated from the love of anyone else, and neither one should be invited to an assembly of ladies or to a court of knights, since he failed to live up to the order of knights and she to the honor of ladies. (pp. 72–3/174)

What such love courts highlight (and what even our contemporary primers of proper amorous behavior underscore as well) is that love between human beings is not a simple, automatic, biologically determined sentiment or activity, but rather a highly codified activity involving man- or woman-made conventions, rules, stipulations, stages, and telos.[46] The biologically determined goal of male–female relationships in the animal kingdom is clearly the reproduction of the species. Many of the rules and conventions concocted to regulate human love in different historical periods and cultures have little or nothing to do with reproduction, especially in the period of courtly love where sexual relations themselves were largely ruled out and producing children out of wedlock was anything but an explicit goal.

Courting – the "civilized" process by which men do not simply go out and club their chosen partners over the head and drag them back to their caves but rather woo them – is thus a product of culture, a kind of aesthetic or poetic invention. In Seminar XX, Lacan refers to the older term for courting – "making love" (which both in French, *faire l'amour*, and English has come to mean almost exclusively having sexual intercourse) – and emphasizes that the *making* should be understood in the sense of creating or fabricating. Love is thus a poetic creation, a product of human aesthetic activity. Love perhaps begins with or finds its original impetus in the kind of attachment human beings share with animals, but it is surrounded by and indeed overwritten by certain codes and rituals that have generally turned it into something quite different.

Although one finds myriad courting rituals among animals, they do not seem to change much from one group, say, of cardinals to another group of cardinals and perhaps have not changed much over the course of the last millennia. Courting rituals among human beings, however, seem to vary significantly from country to country and from one historical era to another.

Romantic Love

Good marriages exist, but there are no delicious ones.
La Rochefoucauld, 1967, Maxim 113

Romantic love has been described in the most laudatory and the most derogatory of terms by different authors. According to Shulamith Firestone (1970), in *The Dialectic of Sex*, romantic love is tantamount to a capitalist or patriarchal plot designed to keep women in their place and to keep couples from revolting against the economic and/or political system. Philip Slater (1970) argues much the same in *The Pursuit of Loneliness*, whereas Aldous Huxley (1932), in *Brave New World*, and perhaps even Walter Benjamin, think of romantic love as a potentially revolutionary force, which leads one to combat totalitarian systems. Marriage has been similarly celebrated and vilified, at times being viewed as that which best preserves love and at others as involving a kind of slavery that kills every vestige of love.

Marriage has sometimes been described as an institution that developed, not to foster the blossoming of love, but rather out of concern for property transfer from one generation to the next. Since property was traditionally conveyed from father to son in patriarchies, the father wanted to ensure that the boys who would inherit from him were actually his own. (Property relations were often more complex than this and, to the best of my knowledge, even in early Roman times boys and girls inherited property equally, and until around the twelfth or thirteenth century women could independently possess and manage property they had inherited from their own families even after they married, passing it on to whomsoever they liked.) Marriage was designed, at least in part, to ensure wives' fidelity to their husbands so that the husbands could be sure their lawful heirs were indeed their own offspring.

Certain sociobiologists have argued, on the other hand, that marriage is an institution that was obviously created by women, owing to a genetic dissymmetry between the sexes: males are biologically programmed, they believe, to try to impregnate as many females as possible, whereas females are wired in such a way as to be concerned with finding a good provider and protector for their young (in certain bird species, a female will test a potential male partner by seeing how well he feeds her during their courting period, presumably to see how he will later feed her offspring). Certain researchers have studied cheating behavior in women and tried to show that around the time of ovulation, married women often have multiple sexual partners, as if to improve their chances of getting pregnant and seeking out the best genetic material (see Baker & Bellis, 1995), while ostensibly remaining faithful to the future offspring's male provider and protector.

However, and for whatever reasons it originated, marriage as an institution exists in every culture I have ever heard of. If we examine the attitude of the Catholic Church toward marriage, we see that, while initially opposed to marriage, preferring that its members enter monasteries and convents, the Catholic Church eventually came around to sanctioning marriage – allowing, for example, marriage ceremonies to be performed inside of churches, and not simply on their doorsteps as it had for many centuries – and endorsing the more Old Testament view of love and marriage as going hand in hand (prior to that, love was for God, marriage for the corrupt body). Many religious traditions today foster the association of love and marriage, and mainstream American culture throws its full force behind this association of ideas.

As we have seen, the courtly love tradition did not. Capellanus asserts that:

> It is obvious that love cannot claim to occupy a place in marriage. It is no doubt possible for spouses to be attached to each other by a powerful, unlimited feeling, but this feeling cannot

be identified with love because that is not its definition. What indeed is love if not an unchecked desire to passionately relish furtive and hidden embraces? How can embraces be furtive and hidden between spouses who are constrained to belong to each other mutually and may satisfy each other's desires however they please? (Chapelain, 2004, p. 17/100)

For Capellanus, love is impossible without transgression of the laws governing marital fidelity, and "The bonds of marriage, when they supervene, make love flee violently" (p. 42/156). Love between courtly love couples, one or both of whom were already married, was apparently heightened by the very impossibility of any kind of legally or religiously sanctioned union between them, and would very much fit the description of what we refer to today as "romantic love." (Note that the term "romantic," which is *romanesque* in French, comes from *roman*, meaning narrative fiction in French verse, and then novel; romantic love is thus defined right from the outset as the kind of love one reads about in fictional accounts.) It was often difficult, if not impossible, for such couples to spend a great deal of time together (much less consummate their relationship), and the entire focus of the relationship was intense, passionate, romantic love, accompanied by writing poetry, singing songs, and performing deeds of derring-do for one's beloved.

Courtly love involved a total fascination with the beloved, an almost morbid obsession bordering on the pathological (the kind found among stalkers?), including a high degree of idealization. In Cervantes' *Don Quixote*, our infamously misguided knight is head over heels in love with Dulcinea, who is a simple peasant whom he takes for a princess, about whom he knows virtually nothing, and yet whom he endows with the most extravagant virtues:

> her rank must at least be that of a princess, since she is my queen and lady; and her beauty is more than human, for in her one sees realized all the impossible, fantastical characteristics of beauty assigned to their ladies by the poets. Her hair is golden, her forehead an Elysian Field, her eyebrows heavenly arches, her eyes suns, her cheeks roses, her lips coral, pearls for her teeth, her neck alabaster, her breast marble, her hands ivory, her complexion like snow, and all of her that modesty conceals from human sight is, as I think and believe, such that a sensible mind can only praise, not compare. (Cervantes, 1995, p. 64)

Note how stereotypical the traits are that he assigns to her – she could be almost any woman celebrated in courtly love poetry.[47]

In medieval times, marriage was a religious, social, economic, and political institution and few apparently expected to be happy in their marriage per se, looking for love primarily outside of marriage. Some authors seem to believe that the courtly love poets invented love as we know it today, but even a cursory reading of texts from ancient Greek and Roman times suggests that it was primarily the *form* of courting that was invented at that time, not love itself.

In the eighteenth century Mary Wollstonecraft Shelley explicitly formulated, in her book *Vindication of the Rights of Woman* (1792), a belief that marriage was a superfluous ceremony, and that love and marriage were somewhat incompatible (she went on to marry William Godwin, a well-known anarchist, although they never cohabited). Even earlier than Wollstonecraft, in the seventeenth century, Madeleine de Scudéry professed no belief in marriage. In her novel, *The Story of Sapho*, Prince Tisander falls in love with Sapho when she says she will never agree to marry, because a husband is a master or a tyrant (Scudéry, 2003, p. 20).[48]

The French aristocracy were well known to have cultivated love relationships outside of marriage for centuries, and there is a specific term for this kind of marriage even today: "the bourgeois marriage." It is essentially a social facade in which children are produced and raised by parents who are of the same socioeconomic class, while either or both of the parents may seek love elsewhere. In the 1980s, French President François Mitterrand was known by one and all to have a mistress (at least one mistress, Anne Pingeot), and official police guards were stationed outside of her apartment building throughout his presidency. She was virtually never mentioned in the French press, a French politician's private life being considered to be his or her own business for the most part. And his wife did not appear to take umbrage at this, perhaps taking it as a matter of course.

Dominique Strauss-Kahn was widely considered to be in the running to be France's next president, until accused of rape in New York City in 2011. Many French people were quite unconcerned about his constant infidelity to his wife, and even his well-known involvement with prostitutes and violent sexual behaviors toward women, believing that a man's sex life need have little to do with his marriage or politics. It is perhaps not surprising that it was a Frenchman, Denis de Rougemont, who championed a rigorous incompatibility between marriage and romantic or passionate love in his book *Love in the Western World*.

Even if few American politicians appear, upon close inspection, to have found enduring love with their spouses, often seeking love and sex with partners outside of the marital bonds, this is nevertheless viewed in American culture primarily as a personal failing and not as a philosophical problem – not something that results from a theoretical incompatibility between love and the institution of marriage.

Kierkegaard's approach to this is quite unique: he proposes that the kind of love that withers in the sacred circumstances of marriage is simply the wrong kind of love, not Christian love as he calls it, not the kind of love that is based on duty. It is not marriage that is the problem, but rather the kind of love people have for each other that is the problem.

Some argue that it is the very attempt to institutionalize love that destroys it. The more love is rendered obligatory, a duty, whether religious, moral, or otherwise, the more it shrivels up and dies like a plant cultivated under the wrong conditions. "If we really love each other, why do we need a stupid piece of paper?" they ask.

Certain supporters of arranged marriages might argue instead that it is not marriage itself that is to blame for the withering of love, but the absurd emphasis placed in our times on romance and passion as opposed to friendship, companionate love, or affectionate love between spouses – that is, a kind of love that is far more enduring than "being in love" or lust. They would point out that by emphasizing romance and being in love to the exclusion of virtually all else, our culture is rendering its children incapable of enduring relationships, ever searching as they are for intense passion. This makes them unable to negotiate the virtually inevitable waning of intense romantic love as a relationship develops over time (assuming the partners actually see each other with some regularity), through a gradual transformation of "romantic love" into "affectionate love" – this is what certain psychologists believe occurs in the course of an ordinary love relationship. Instead of being able to transition from romantic love to affectionate love, they move on to a new relationship as soon as the passion dwindles. They may marry each of their partners in passion in turn, as movie stars often do, and divorce them as soon as the romance has subsided. In this way, they never experience (and are perhaps incapable of experiencing) deep, long-term companionate love.[49]

There is probably no hard and fast rule here: some are able to find a long-lasting form of love within the confines of marriage; others are not. What seems clear is that intense romantic love or passion rarely lasts for very long. It may revive at certain times in the course of a relationship – especially when a new potential rival for the spouse's affections appears on the scene, or during fights – but the intensity of the very first days and weeks of falling in love is rarely achieved later.

Falling in Love (à la Stendhal)

Love is the strongest of the passions [even stronger than power].
In the other passions, desires must take into account cold
realities; here, it is the realities that model themselves on one's
desires.

Stendhal, 2004, p. 50/59–60

Emma: "This sensation of listlessness, weariness, stupidity, this
disinclination to sit down and employ myself, this feeling of
every thing being dull and insipid about the house! – I must be in
love."

Austen, 2004, pp. 246–7

In his book on *Love*, Stendhal (2004) attempts to systematically describe the stages of falling in love by delineating two different "crystallizations."[50] In the course of the "first crystallization," a man adorns with a thousand perfections a woman of whose love he is sure (p. 30/45); why he has to be sure of her love is unclear in Stendhal's account, but in any case he certainly exaggerates the qualities of his beloved.[51] "Pleasures increase with the perfections of the beloved object and the idea: she is mine" (p. 31/46). We could comment that imagining that someone is perfect, although no one is, involves delusion; and that asserting "she is mine" smacks of a kind of psychotic certainty!

The "second crystallization" revolves around the constant question or doubt in the lover's mind whether she truly loves him in return – Stendhal refers to the alternatives as "rending and delicious" (p. 33/47). Indeed, he seems to believe that the uncertainty of reciprocal love is what ignites the most passion – it keeps the lover constantly on his toes, on the edge of his chair, uncertain, and "deliciously" preoccupied. *It is the precise opposite of boredom.*

One might say that, for Stendhal, it is the uncertainty of the metaphor of love – of whether the beloved will become in her turn a lover – that keeps the lover interested. If he becomes certain of her love for him, he might well become blasé. Without doubt, without constant vacillation and uncertainty orchestrated by the woman's sudden moods and fits of bad temper, the lover would become complacent and lose his passion. Hence the importance of a woman's willingness to play a certain kind of society game involving resistance to his advances on most occasions with only occasional succumbing. She must evade his grasp in order to keep his desire alive; indeed, Stendhal credits women for doing so, feeling that "this folly named love, this madness [. . .] gives men *the greatest pleasures ever tasted by beings of his species on earth"* (p. 35 n/49 n. 1). Are these, we might wonder, the same doubts as the gambler's whose fortunes wax and wane, who trembles over every throw of the dice? Crystallization also occurs in gambling, says Stendhal (p. 39/52).

"What ensures the duration of love is the second crystallization in which one sees at every moment that *it is a question of being loved or of dying"* (p. 34/48). The reciprocal nature of love is so important that one is ready to die or will die if one does not have it, and yet at the same time it must never be sure! "This second crystallization is almost always missing in love inspired by women who give them-selves to their lovers too quickly" (p. 35/48).

For Stendhal, there is thus a first crystallization upon the birth of love (when one feels sure of the other's love), but what he seems to cherish most is the second crystallization, which is based entirely on doubt (p. 37/50). The first crystallization, which attributes every possible perfection to the beloved prior to knowing much about her and involves certainty that she reciprocates one's love, is quasi-delusional in nature, whereas the second crystallization involves doubt and might be considered a more neurotic sort. The first crystallization seems to involve a sort of "psychotic moment" in the experience of falling in love, which might be associated with the imaginary in Lacanian terms, involving, as it does, mere fantasiz-ing or imagining of perfections the other must, one believes, have, instead of knowledge of the beloved gained by experience.

If we are to lend any credence to Stendhal's depiction of the experience of falling in love – and leaving aside the initial conviction (which is rare in my view) that the beloved "is mine" – I believe we can view the first crystallization as one of the imaginary facets of love. The ecstatic investment of libido in the ideal image of ourselves that is made at the time of the mirror stage is mirrored, reflected, or paralleled by the ecstatic investment of libido in the ideal image of our beloved that occurs during this first moment of falling in love. Indeed, there is very often a will to see the beloved as exactly like oneself in this early stage of crystallization: one wants to find and attribute to the other the very same perfections one would like to believe one has oneself. Indeed, there is quite often a confusion of self and other at this stage.

This imaginary component of love stands in stark contrast to the symbolic component of love highlighted in Plato's *Symposium*, where desire is said to be based on lack and essentially wanting to go on desiring. To speak systematically, we might say that whereas *passion always wants the same thing* – to find oneself as perfect as seen via the other – *desire always wants something else*, something new, something different. Desire is based on metonymy, and keeps flitting from one thing to the next, from one object to the next – until, that is, its course is stopped by object *a*. This is perhaps why, in Plato's *Symposium*, only Alcibiades, who perceives the *agálmata* in Socrates, actually celebrates his beloved instead of Eros, the god of love – that is, instead of celebrating desire itself, like all the others present did before him. His praise of Socrates seems qualitatively different from Stendhal's adorning of his largely unknown beloved with a thousand perfections, perhaps because Alcibiades is moved, not by *i(a)* but by object *a* itself.

On a less clinical note, Stendhal makes a singular claim that historians and cultural critics might well dispute: crystallization is impossible in the United States, because people there are too reasonable (pp. 184/164 and 257/225). "In Europe desire is enflamed by constraint, in America it is dulled by freedom" (p. 263/229). Stendhal, who exalts the game of love, criticizes countries like the United States where he believes such maneuvering in the realm of love is bypassed. He also criticizes countries like Germany where he believes that girls too readily sleep with and satisfy male suitors. This is overly "natural" to him and does not allow for the crystallization of passionate love as he understands it. In his view, passion achieves its apex in countries where women are taught to resist, play games, torture suitors, and hide their feelings, and where men learn to feign indifference.

Stendhal also indicates the degree to which we fall in love because we want to feel what others we hear about feel ("love is the Other's love," we might quip, or "passion is the Other's passion"): "In Geneva and in France [. . .] one makes love at sixteen in order to live as though one were in a novel, and one asks oneself at each moment and with each tear: 'Aren't I like Julie d'Etanges?'" (p. 261/227), Julie d'Etanges being a character in Rousseau's 1761 novel entitled *Julie, or the New Heloise*, arguably the bestselling novel and biggest tearjerker of the eighteenth century. Here we see the overriding importance of imitation in love, seen also in La Rochefoucauld's (1967, p. 36/57) formulation: "There are people who would never have been in love had they not heard others speak of love."

Other Languages and Cultures of Love

Why should you fail when a new romance means new pleasure?
Things that are not rightfully ours please us more than our own.
Other men's fields produce a crop that's better than ours;
Aren't the udders of our neighbor's cow always fuller?

Ovid, *The Art of Love*, I.347–50

To lose yourself, as if you no longer existed, to cease completely to experience yourself, to reduce yourself to nothing is not a human sentiment but a divine experience.

Saint Bernard of Clairvaux, 1995, p. 29

In this chapter I have highlighted a number of terms related to love that grow out of a variety of traditions, but there are many others that stem from other traditions. "Ecstatic love" is given a great deal of weight in certain religious and mystical traditions, as is "surrender" ("abandon" or "sweet surrender") in a number of religious and romantic and/or sexual contexts, being arguably akin to the Amish notion of *Gelassenheit* (see Kraybill, 2001, especially pp. 29–43). The notion of "sweet surrender" seems to be of great importance to the Amish in all facets of life, whether it involves giving in to the demands of the *Ordnung* (their local unit of community organization), deferring to their elders and parents, or bearing the taunts and jibes of non-Amish people regarding their dress and lifestyle. Bowing to the will of God, giving up their own individual wishes in their families and communities, is for the Amish a way of life which presumably brings strife, at least for a time, but also its own satisfactions with it.

In the sexual realm this might be compared with allowing ourselves to be "swept away," as we say, giving ourselves over to another, which in a sense leads to losing ourselves in the other. The appeal of losing oneself in the other is felt by many, though to varying extents. Lying in our lover's arms, we may feel that time stops, that the endless drone of boring thoughts or stupid worries that plague us cease, that we forget about our incessant striving for *x*, *y*, or *z*, and that we forget ourselves or fall into a kind of sweet oblivion.

The seventeenth-century author Honoré d'Urfé (1935, p. 23) proffered that to love

is to die in oneself to be reborn in the other person, it is to love oneself only to the extent that one pleases one's beloved, and in short is a will to transform oneself, if possible, entirely into the beloved.

Surrender is presumably a certain kind of giving up of striving, and it may be related to the concept of Grace in Catholic theology, Grace being something which, if I understand it correctly, simply comes to us; it is something which, like Nirvana in a Buddhist context, one cannot strive for.

I have not broached Eastern traditions regarding love here owing to my own ignorance on the topic. I will not attempt to fill that enormous lacuna here, but will simply indicate that I have heard that the Japanese have a special word for familial love, *ninjo*, that refers to the more tender human feelings such as mercy and compassion. In Nipponese tragedies, *ninjo* is often depicted as conflicting with *giri* (some translate the latter as "passion"), this conflict resulting in the death of the hero. *Ninjo* is perhaps akin to what we call "brotherly love," "sisterly love," or "family feeling," but it may go well beyond anything we currently have a term for in Western culture.

VIII

Reading Plato with Lacan

Further Commentary on Plato's Symposium

Returning now to Lacan's reading of the *Symposium*, note that Lacan's working assumption is that Plato was rather astute and probably had a pretty good idea how he wanted this dialogue to unfold. Some readers in recent centuries have considered everything in the *Symposium* after Alcibiades' arrival to be an aberration on Plato's part or an add-on by a later scribe. And many have taken certain of the speeches very seriously, whereas Plato seems to have intended them to be quite ludicrous, at least to his most discerning readers. Irony is quite difficult to detect when one is a reader from such a different era and in no wise fluent in ancient Greek, but it is well known that Plato's texts often present a surface (or exoteric) meaning that contrasts sharply with their hidden (or esoteric) meaning. Lacan considers a great many of the things said by Pausanias and Agathon, for example, to be quite ridiculous, and believes that Plato wishes perspicacious readers to realize this.

The Relationship between Form and Content in the *Symposium*

One of the things I think we can safely conclude from Lacan's discussion of the *Symposium* (which I hope the reader will now have fresh in his or her mind) is that the progression, paradoxes, and transitions of the dialogue are intimately related to the progression, paradoxes, and transitions of love itself. If the dialogue is difficult to follow, if the transitions are perplexing at times, if we are not sure where Plato is leading us, when he is being ironic and when he is being serious, these difficulties, perplexing questions, and aporias are all characteristic of love itself. We certainly do not always know where we are heading in a love relationship, whether it is progressing toward something meaningful or is destined to fall flat on its face.

As I indicated in Chapter 3, Lacan (2006a, p. 620) proposes

that, when Freud complained in a letter to Fliess about the indirect way in which he felt compelled to proceed in composing *The Interpretation of Dreams*, the twists and turns Freud felt obliged to make in his exposition were actually dictated by the nature of the subject matter: the unconscious. In other words, it was the very difficult task of getting at the unconscious that forced Freud to adopt a roundabout approach. Lacan even goes so far as to suggest that *the unconscious is those very twists and turns*.

And we can perhaps say the same of Plato's *Symposium*: love is the very twists and turns of the dialogue. In attempting to say something that holds water about the nature of love, Plato is led to deploy silly and then serious and then more silly speeches; after that he stages Socrates, who purportedly knows something about love – indeed, love is supposedly the only thing he claims to know about (but see how he actually articulates it in the *Lysis* where he says that what he knows is how to detect when someone is in love and with whom: "I may not be much good at anything else, but I have this god-given ability to tell pretty quickly when someone is in love, and with whom he is in love" (204b–c))[1] – letting someone else (Diotima) speak in his stead, someone who at first adopts Socrates' own approach of questioning, then shifts to myth, and then resorts to wild speculation to which Socrates barely assents; and Plato then adds two boisterous interruptions that completely change the tone and tenor of the banquet!

It would seem that the form of the discussion of love in the dialogue is intimately connected with the substance of love. To call the dialogue performative would be to say too little. Perhaps we could say that *love consists in the very transitions and paradoxes* in the dialogue. This would allow us to conclude something that is perhaps not that surprising: that love cannot be defined with some sort of catchy phrase like "love is never having to say you're sorry" or even "love is giving what you don't have." Instead, love is a process, an unfolding, a movement, a winding road that doubles back on itself and takes you places you had no intention of going. Love might thus be an activity of sorts . . .

Form and substance are no doubt intimately related when it comes to many topics, due to the very nature of language and the signifying system with which we discuss those topics: something about a topic of deep human interest resists symbolization and forces us to broach it in an indirect, circuitous manner. We must wonder whether Plato wants us to come away from this dialogue feeling we have grasped some particular theory of love, or simply wants to subject us to the experience of the banquet itself, to the profusion of sometimes profound, sometimes inane speeches, and then the incredible scene that Alcibiades throws by coming in drunk, granting himself the place of honor next to Agathon, usurping the right to preside over the agenda at the banquet, and then going bananas and throwing a hissy fit when he discovers that Socrates is sitting by his side.

The effect might be likened to that of an analyst listening to a series of sessions with a particularly creative analysand who waxes eloquent about love in successive sessions, always picking up the thread at a different point in each new session, but who eventually bursts into the consulting room while another of the analyst's patients is present and makes a scene, telling the patient on the couch how much the analyst drove him crazy, hurt him, treated him unfairly, and never gave him what he wanted. The analyst might plausibly ask himself, "What is this analysand trying to say? What is he trying to convey to me?" To take it up strictly at the propositional level – as if the analysand were trying to say one specific thing as opposed to having a certain effect – would seem to be a mistake or at least a vast oversimplification.

Lacan (2015) goes even further, saying:

What Plato shows – at least this is what I maintain, and it is not especially audacious to do so – in a way that is never revealed or brought to light, is that the contour traced out by this difficulty indicates to us the point at which lies the fundamental topology which stops us from saying anything about love that holds water. (p. 43)

Lacan seems to be suggesting here that there is something that stops us from saying anything worthwhile about love, even if it does not stop us from trying!

This should tell us something about Lacan's approach to reading texts, whether psychoanalytic, literary, or philosophical, which he exemplifies in a great many of his seminars. His return to Freud was such that he did detailed readings of Freud's texts in Seminars I through VII, and in many of his later seminars as well; Seminar VIII is one of the few early seminars that does not begin with the explicitly announced intention of reading a specific text by Freud. Although Lacan pays very close attention to the particular theory being adumbrated, insofar as there is one, in a text, he is nevertheless extremely attentive both to the letter of a text – as we shall see shortly – and to the general trajectory and at least apparent breaks in the trajectory of the text.

One could try to explicitly guess at Plato's intentions, and conclude that he thinks each of the speeches in the dialogue captures some facet of love – that, for example, Aristophanes' speech captures the initial, intense attempt to merge with the other at the beginning of a relationship; Phaedrus', the metaphor of love and the beloved's transformation; Eryximachus', the carnal versus spiritual struggle in love; Agathon's, the quiet, less tumultuous phase of a relationship; and so on. Lacan does not go that route: he does not say that love is a little of this and a little of that, or that it proceeds by stages of some kind.

Homosexual Love as a Simplified Model

Lacan suggests in Seminar VIII that examining homosexual love will allow us to examine love on a simplified scale or model, because sexual difference will be left out of the equation, and sexual difference complicates matters considerably. "Greek love" allows us to put aside the problem of the nonexistence of a relationship between the sexes (to introduce a problematic from his later work) and to examine the nature of love without the multitude of complications that arise from sexual difference for human beings. In other words, it is as if we can study love in isolation from sexual difference.

Certain people might argue, alternatively, that the kind of love we find in a study of homosexuality will not be of exactly the same nature as the love between partners of different sexes. But Lacan does not seem to endorse that perspective: love is love, and we can presumably add sexual difference back into the equation at some later point in time to articulate the specificity (if there is one) of heterosexual love.[2] As Lacan (2015) puts it:

> We know that the *Symposium* dates back to the time of Greek love and that this love was, so to speak, "schoolish," in other words, love of pupils. For technical reasons – for reasons of simplification, exemplification, and use as a model – this love allows us to understand a connection that is always elided in what is overly complicated in love involving women. It is in this respect that this love for school[boys] [*amour de l'école*] can legitimately provide us and everyone with schooling in love [*d'école de l'amour*]. (p. 32)

Let us turn now to the individual speeches given at the banquet in praise of the god Eros, Love.

Phaedrus: Love and Theology

Phaedrus, in his concern to situate Love as one of the oldest and greatest gods, prefigures the Christian tradition in which to speak of love is to speak of theology (Lacan, 2015, pp. 44–5), which is no doubt why much of the discussion of love from Roman times on is by theologians. In ancient Greek times, the idea is at least in part that, like anger and other emotions, love is not caused by something inside us – for example, by the repetition of earlier attachments, as psychoanalysis would have it – but is sent by the gods. If it turns out well, the gods have favored us; if not, it was not meant to be or we have angered the gods in some way.

When Lacan tells us that the gods belong to the real and are a mode of revelation of the real (pp. 44 and 82), he is clearly referring to the multiplicity of gods associated with different facets of nature – immanent in nature and in natural events like storms, lightning, thunder, and wind – that are independent of our will and do with us as they please. The Greeks looked to reality, in a manner of speaking, to foretell the future. The flight of a bird was taken to be an omen or predictor of what was to happen, and the particular appearance of the entrails of an animal that was killed could, they felt, be interpreted in such a way as to foretell future events. Every natural occurrence was taken to be a sign that the gods either favored our endeavors or did not. If we set sail and the seas were rough, Poseidon was angry or frankly hostile to our purpose. Some people are still like this today – every event is taken as a sign. If the phone rings just before they leave the house, they feel they must not be supposed to leave. We tend to think of that as superstitious thinking today, but in ancient Greece the gods were part and parcel of the fabric of the world, coextensive with it, and involved in every facet of it.

Lacan suggests that this all changed with Christianity:

> The mechanism of Christian revelation is indisputably situated along the path that leads to the reduction and, in the final analysis, abolition of the notion [of god as the height of revelation]. Indeed, it tends to displace the God of Christian revelation – and the same is true of dogma – onto the Word, Logos. Stated differently, it is situated on a path parallel to that trodden by the philosopher, insofar as he is destined to deny the gods.
>
> Man will thus seek in Logos, in other words, at the level of signifying articulation, the revelations he encountered up until then in the real. (p. 44)

Truth is no longer sought in material signs, or at least confirmation of a particular notion is no longer sought in the flight of a bird, but in speech itself, in the self-consistency of concepts, in the internal coherence of the signifier (i.e., the signifying system as a whole). We, of course, have not completely transcended the stage of seeking confirmation of our love in reality: we pick flowers, and as we rip off each petal we say, "he loves me, he loves me not . . . ," seeking there some sort of real or objective confirmation of what we wish. The French are more nuanced about this insofar as, when removing one petal after another, they say, "*il m'aime, un peu, beaucoup, passion-nément, à la folie, pas du tout*," giving reality at least five options to choose from instead of just two.

Pausanias: The Psychology of the Rich

Castration is the altogether new mainspring Freud introduced
into desire, giving desire's lack the meaning that remained
enigmatic in Socrates' dialectic, although it was preserved in the
recounting of the *Symposium*.

Lacan, 2006a, p. 853

Pausanias introduces us, perhaps unwittingly, to the idea that love involves a kind of investment; this investment, he argues, should only be made in partners who have a certain value (Lacan, 2015, pp. 55–7). To translate his discourse into Freudian terms, each of us only has a certain amount of libido available to us and we want to be sure to invest it wisely so that we will get it back with interest. If we are mistaken and it turns out that the person we invested our libido in was not as valuable, virtuous, or worthwhile as we thought, we cannot be reproached for it since we were nevertheless *aiming* at value, virtue, and worth. One might have thought that such a relational calculus originated with capitalism, leading to the ever more widespread insistence upon prenuptial agreements in our own times, but it dates back much further, to at least the fifth century B.C.!

To exemplify the way in which value and worth can enter into someone's thinking about relationships, Lacan recounts the story of a rich man who knocks a poor girl over in the street with his gigantic car (pp. 57–8). He offers to indemnify her for her pains (she is not seriously hurt and simply shakes it off) but she refuses. He offers more insistently and she refuses more persistently. The more she refuses to have anything to do with him or his money, the more valuable she seems to him and he does everything possible to court and marry her. It seems to be an example of a relationship that is situated outside of dollars and cents (or monetary sense?), since she, for one, cannot be bought. For a rich man, things are only more or less valuable since he can afford them all; he can buy whatever he wants. But this woman becomes supremely valuable to him precisely because she refuses his money and acts completely uninterested in him. In this way, she perhaps locates herself off the scale of comparison (whereby one asks oneself, "Is this object better than that one? Better than all others?"), becoming an object to end all objects – that is, an object *a* – for him. She becomes valuable in a different register, a register where money – that quintessential phallic object of culture – is scorned, spit on, and considered to be of no value whatsoever. Whereas money – as the universal signifier allowing us to equate or at least compare everything in terms of its dollar value – places all objects on the same scale as more or less valuable in monetary terms, she situates herself off the scale, that is, outside of the signifying system that allows for such comparisons.

The rich, especially the extremely rich, are often depicted as incredibly bored, their only interest being in momentary sources of entertainment and ever-more-difficult-to-obtain highs from drugs, alcohol, or extreme experiences (such as paying huge sums for a short flight in space, or to take a stroll with a tiger). What the young woman manages to do in Lacan's story is incite a desire in the rich man, bringing out the lack in him by showing him that there is something he does not have that he *could* potentially want. (I am *not* saying that she does so intentionally, since I cannot know her motives.) What he comes away with is far more precious than any good or product or possession he could purchase: he comes away with an interest in life, a renewed desire for something. As Lacan says, "Desire is not a good [*un bien*] in any sense of the term" (p. 65); note that *bien* also means possession or commodity.

This is parallel to something that transpires in psychoanalysis. As Lacan puts it:

> If [the analysand] sets off in search of what he has, but does not know he has, what he discovers is what he is lacking in. [. . .] What he finds in analysis is articulated in the form of what he is lacking – namely, his desire. [. . .]
>
> You understand, of course, that when I say "realization of desire," I assume that it is clearly not possession of an object. Indeed, it involves the emergence of desire as such in reality. (p. 65)

Something similar to what happens to the rich man Lacan discusses in Seminar VIII might be said to occur between Mr. Darcy and Elizabeth Bennet in Jane Austen's *Pride and Prejudice*. Darcy is used to getting whatever he wants, and is depicted as plausibly expecting any woman to be more than willing to marry him. But Elizabeth flatly refuses his marriage proposal and tells him that he could not have solicited her hand in any more insulting and any less gentlemanly a manner. Even though she is from a much poorer family than his own, and the majority of the women depicted in the novel would be inclined to marry him simply for his money and status, Elizabeth manages to extract herself from the calculation of riches and monetary value, which, much to her embarrassment, is so central to her own mother's discourse. In doing so, she calls into question all phallically calculated values and insists upon an alternative "economy" (in this case, it is perhaps virtue that is juxtaposed to money).

Lacan (2015, p. 62) hypothesizes that Plato views Pausanias' discourse about "love as a value" as a load of hogwash. He arrives at this conclusion at least in part because of the interpretation he comes up with of something of which few commentators have ever ventured an interpretation: Aristophanes' hiccups. Recall that:

> When Pausanias finally [paused], it was Aristophanes' turn, according to Aristodemus. But he had such a bad case of the hiccups – he'd probably stuffed himself again, though, of course, it could have been anything – that making a speech was totally out of the question. So he turned to the doctor, Eryximachus, who was next in line, and said to him:
>
> "Eryximachus, it's up to you – as well it should be. Cure me or take my turn." (185c–d)

Based on a close reading of the Greek text, which includes repeated punning on Pausanias' name, Lacan (2015, pp. 60–2) concludes that Aristophanes – like Plato, no doubt – has found Pausanias' speech so ridiculous and has been laughing so hard that, in combination with all the food and drink he has been imbibing, he has gotten the hiccups. Far from this being a simple moment of comic relief in an otherwise serious text or an extraneous event that does not deserve any weight in our interpretation of it, Lacan suggests that it is absolutely crucial to an understanding of the more hidden or esoteric meaning of the text – the meaning that is not transparently visible to all comers. It is thanks to such mini-scenes or seemingly gratuitous events that we can divine Plato's own view of what he has one of his characters say. A psychoanalyst cannot help but be struck by a line like "he'd probably stuffed himself again, though, of course, it could have been anything," realizing that there would be no need to add the latter half if Plato were simply trying to tell us Aristophanes had stuffed himself. After all, who would know better why Aristophanes had the hiccups than the author?

Plato might be considered to be making fun here of his own narrator, Apollodorus, or of Aristodemus, the person who recounted what occurred at the banquet to the narrator (indeed, Aristodemus is perhaps doubly impugned, insofar as, although present at the symposium, he omits from his account the speech he himself must have given there). Plato may, in fact, have concocted some of the elaborate conditions of narration in his dialogues not solely in order to give them an air of accurate historical transmission but also to be able to have his narrators give the reader hints of this very kind.

Lacan (p. 61) tells us that his friend and teacher, Alexander Kojève, offhandedly remarked – in response to Lacan's mention that he was working on the *Symposium* – that Lacan would never understand the dialogue if he had not grasped the meaning of Aristophanes' hiccups; Lacan did not take the challenge lying down. He ends up venturing an interpretation that may perhaps shed a great deal of light on Plato's dialogues in general. Lacan takes quite far the notion (apparently shared by Kojève) that Plato often gives us little clues when he is ridiculing what his characters say – including Socrates!

Lacan argues, for example, that the whole concern with spheres found here in Aristophanes' discourse and in Plato's own dialogue, the *Timaeus*, is ridiculed in the *Symposium*. This might be viewed as a rather risky argument, considering that the *Timaeus* is thought to have been written circa 360 B.C., whereas the *Symposium* is thought to have been written circa 385–380 B.C. – that is, some 20 years earlier. But if it is true, it would show that Plato not only made fun, in one and the same dialogue, of some of the viewpoints expressed in it, but even in one dialogue of views expressed in another.

Lacan goes on to propose that the fascination with the sphere throughout so much of history has something to do with the refusal or denial of castration. The shape of the human breast, no doubt, plays a part in our fascination with circles and spheres, but Lacan suggests that what has really intrigued philosophers and scientists about the latter is not that they are, in and of themselves, perfect, harmonious, and lacking in nothing, but that they offer nothing to the forces of *castration*: they have no asperities, nothing that sticks out, and thus nothing that can be easily cut off or pruned. A sphere can be cut in two (as Zeus does to the primitive beings we supposedly once were), but cannot be castrated per se.

Eryximachus: Love as Harmony

Three cups of wine only do I mix for the temperate – one for
health, which they empty first, the second for sexual passion
(*Eros*) and pleasure, and the third for sleep, which men reputed
to be wise drink up and then go home.

Euboulos, fourth-century B.C. poet[3]

In the speech by Eryximachus, the physician, music is said to provide
the principle of harmony that regulates love: the same and the other –
that is, the two different partners – are resolved in harmony. Musical
harmony is taken by Eryximachus to be a fine metaphor for love –
the partners are not the same, they do not sound out the same note,
but they sound good together (Lacan, 2015, p. 72). Lacan comments
that, in our own times, we have gone beyond this, believing now in
the fecundity of contraries, contrasts, oppositions, and indeed disso-
nance (he is perhaps thinking of Bach or even quite modern music).

Insofar as harmony evokes Socrates' discussion of the immortality of the soul in the *Phaedo*, "the very idea of the soul qua
harmony" (p. 73), Lacan comments here that:

The idea that anything whatsoever that exists could participate
in the Platonic idea as incorporeal essence proves to be fictional
in nature, an illusion. Things go so far in the *Phaedo* that it
is impossible not to remark that there is no reason to believe
Plato was any less aware of this illusion than we are. Our claim
to be more intelligent than the person who wrote Plato's work
is quite unbelievable, unimaginable, and truly astounding.

In other words, Lacan sees clues, both here and in the *Phaedo*, that
Plato in no way thoroughly endorses the theory of forms – that is,
the Ideas that have become synonymous with his name! Lacan goes
on to add:

This is why, when Eryximachus sings his little song, without
it immediately having any obvious consequences, we can ask
ourselves what Plato meant by having this series of sallies take
place in this particular order in the *Symposium*. At least we
have realized that Pausanias' speech, which immediately precedes this one, is ridiculous. And if we keep in mind the overall
tone that characterizes the *Symposium*, we certainly have the
right to wonder whether what is at stake isn't consonant with
comedy as such. In discussing love, it is clear that Plato chose
the path of comedy. (p. 74)

Agathon's Speech

Once he recovers from his hiccups, Aristophanes, the comedian, gives a rather uncharacteristically serious speech (which we discussed briefly in Chapter 5), after which, Agathon, the tragedian, gives a rather playful, ludicrous speech. Agathon's speech is largely farcical; as he himself says at the end, he has offered it up partly in jest and partly in earnest (197e).

Agathon claims here that:

> Love is neither the cause nor the victim of any injustice; he does no wrong to gods or men, nor they to him. If anything has an effect on him, it is never by violence, for violence never touches Love. And the effects he has on others are not forced, for every service we give to love we give willingly. (196b–c)

Lacan points out that it is clear to everyone present at the banquet that love is violent and unjust, and that all kinds of injustices and violence are committed in the name of love, one minor example being the Trojan War. Love is anything but moderate, temperate, and sound-minded – indeed, it makes people go out of their heads! The fact that Socrates seems to take Agathon's words seriously, even though all the banqueters are aware he spoke tongue-in-cheek, casts a nebulous, dubious light on everything Socrates says thereafter.

Socrates' Speech and the In-Between (*Metaxú*)

Epistéme	*Dóxa*	*Amathía*
Coherent knowledge	Opinion	Ignorance
Mortals	Love	Immortals
Mortals	Daemon	Immortals
Agathon	Alcibiades	Socrates

By means of Diotima, Plato establishes an important relationship between love and knowledge (202a–b). Whereas Socrates sometimes employs a very simplistic binary dialectic in which whatever is not beautiful would seem to be ugly (201e), instead of considering the possibility that there may be things that are neither beautiful nor ugly (or something in between, as in: beautiful – plain – ugly), or that there may be a more complex system of negation,[4] Diotima establishes a tripartite logic or dialectic in which there is something μεταξύ (*metaxú*), some third term in between binary terms:

Epistéme	*Dóxa*	*Amathía*
Coherent knowledge	Opinion	Ignorance

As regards knowledge, her dialectic juxtaposes systematic, constructed, assured knowledge (ἐπιστήμη, *epistéme*, which is the root of our term "epistemology") – the kind of knowledge that Socrates' himself tries to establish through his usual form of argumentation – with ignorance (ἀμαθία, *amathía*), but her dialectic does not stop there. Diotima suggests that there is another kind of knowledge which cannot be proven, which cannot give reasons, for it does not have them, and yet which is apparently correct – she calls this δόξα (*dóxa*), opinion (combined with *ortho*, meaning right or correct, this has given us our terms "orthodox" and "orthodoxy"). *Dóxa* is not exact knowledge that is transparent to itself or that can be thoroughly explained, but, when it is "right opinion," it "hits the truth" (202a) or happens upon the truth (perhaps like psychoanalytic interpretation, which is neither exact knowledge nor, at least in the best of cases, total ignorance).[5]

This intermediary form of knowledge or quasi-knowledge is perhaps seen by Plato as especially relevant to the moral sphere, in which, although one is unable to prove that some action is right or wrong, one nevertheless feels or "just knows" that it is. The same goes for governing – certain statesmen seem to *know* which laws make the most sense, even if they cannot give irrefutable arguments for them and must resort primarily to persuasion through rhetoric. Is Plato trying to tell us that this quasi-knowledge is especially germane as regards love?

Regardless of what we might think of the category of *dóxa* in our "scientific age," Diotima locates love in a position between mortals and immortals, between gods and humans, that is similar to that of *dóxa* between knowledge and ignorance. Love cannot be a god because it is lacking in what it seeks – it lacks what it pursues and desires, which is beauty and virtue. Gods by their very nature have beauty, virtue, and happiness (202c) – therefore love cannot be a god. Obviously love is not a human being either. Hence, Diotima argues, it must be *metaxú*, halfway between the one and the other.

Mortals	Love	Immortals

There is something transparently specious about this reasoning: love could be related to something else, as it is for us in psychoanalysis, where it is related, for example, to hatred. It could be understood in terms of still other completely different categories, but Socrates, speaking under the aegis of Diotima, seems to make it at least momentarily plausible. Love then is "a great spirit, Socrates," she says. "Everything spiritual, you see, is in between god and mortal" (202d–e). Love thus remains personified here, in a sense: it is a kind of being, not a state of being, feeling, activity, or practice.

Love is described here as a messenger between the gods and men, as something that mediates between them, as something by which the gods send their messages to men (in Jowett's rendition of 202e, "Love interprets between gods and men"). When the Greeks fell in love with someone, they knew that their match had been made in heaven, so to speak – they would not have been able to fall in love were it not the gods' will, were it not destiny or fate.

To love was therefore to know that a god was involved; whether that god meant you harm or goodwill, was out to get you or looking out for you, was a separate question! In any case, you knew that you were meant, fated, or doomed to love this particular person. Today we hear many people wonder whether some particular partner was truly meant for them, is truly "the one" intended for them, for the gods no longer speak to us or send messages to us through our passions as they used to.

What sort of being is a messenger between gods and humans? Curiously enough, according to Diotima messengers are daemons, and thus she equates love with a daemon. Daemons are what she considers to be situated between mortals and immortals, between men and gods.

| Mortals | Daemon | Immortals |

Love, then, is a kind of daemon, or, in our more "modern" vocabulary, a vision, voice, or ghost that we believe conveys to us what God or the world wants us to do. In our times, we rarely talk about there being an attendant spirit who watches over each of us, except perhaps in the form of a "guardian angel," much less who communicates with us. (In contemporary movies, we sometimes see instead a little impish demon sitting on the hesitant main character's shoulder, telling him to do something lascivious or immoral, a tiny angel often alighting on his other shoulder and telling him to do the exact opposite.) Note that Socrates' daemon is said to stop him from doing something wrong, as if the daemon knew right from wrong better than the man himself.

In a Lacanian framework, we might think of the messages borne by such daemons as signifiers, as bits of language addressing commands, imperatives, recommendations, and so on to us. For thousands of years, people apparently thought of dreams as sent to them by the gods, whereas now we see them as products of the unconscious, as something within ourselves that is working all by itself when consciousness is switched off for the most part. People also thought of the different voices that they heard while waking as coming from something outside of themselves in reality, that is, as coming from the gods, whereas today we are more inclined to view them as intrapsychic and to associate them – at least in the case of neurosis – with the voice of conscience or with the superego. These voices often enunciate what we term "intrusive thoughts," which we understand now as coming to us from the preconscious or unconscious, from something within ourselves that we do not immediately associate with ourselves, from something that, in contemporary psychological parlance, is termed "ego-dystonic."

Love might then be understood as a kind of signifying process between the gods, who we now situate in the unconscious, and consciousness.[6] We do not know what lies in our unconscious in any direct or transparent manner, but love serves as a kind of messenger between the unconscious and consciousness. In most instances, we do not even want to know our own unconscious "conditions of love" – that is, what makes us tick, what makes us love one person instead of another, or what makes us love in one particular way rather than in another – we wish to ignore all of that. Some people even worry that if they knew the unconscious determinants of their love, their love would dissipate; that if they realized they had fallen in love with someone because of that person's similarities to a parent, they might stop loving him or her. Love, in such cases, does its job: it conveys its message without revealing to consciousness anything that is unconscious.[7]

Love, Diotima goes on, "is in between (*metaxú*) wisdom and ignorance as well" (203e), and tries to get the ignorant to love wisdom. The ignorant do not love wisdom because they do not even know that they are lacking in beauty, virtue, and knowledge (204a), and the gods do not love wisdom because, in her view, they already have it. Love here is thus closely aligned with *dóxa*.

Now, insofar as the exact same word *metaxú* is used by Plato to describe where Alcibiades, when he crashes the party drunk as a skunk, seats himself in relation to Agathon and Socrates, Lacan (2015, p. 133) concludes that Alcibiades himself is a daemon – indeed, that he is Socrates' daemon:

Agathon   Alcibiades   Socrates

This original thesis on Lacan's part relies on reading Plato to the letter: it is based on the fact that Plato uses the exact same word to talk about *dóxa*, love, and Alcibiades.[8] Of course, this also allows us to equate Alcibiades with love – as some sort of incarnation of love, perhaps of Socrates' love. And by a sort of Lacanian extension, we can perhaps think of Alcibiades as a signifier, as a message or interpretation that is conveyed between Agathon and Socrates, Lacan not failing to remind us that "it takes three to love, not just two" (p. 132). Here the third term is explicit, in the form of a third person, as we see in so many love triangles. Lacan suggests that a triangular structure is necessary for love (more strictly speaking, perhaps, for desire in the guise of love) in all cases, so we would have to assume that the third term is often implicit, as opposed to incarnate, as it is here.

Love Triangles Revisited

We will return to the Socrates–Alcibiades–Agathon love triangle momentarily, but note here that love does not always arise suddenly in one person when it is declared by another, as in Lacan's "miracle of love," but rather when it is declared for that other by someone who suddenly appears in between oneself and another and is perceived to be a rival. To give a literary example, in Jane Austen's novel *Emma*, Emma's love for Mr. Knightley bursts into flames when she hears her Pygmalion protégée, Harriet Smith, declare her feelings for Mr. Knightley. Regarding Emma's sentiments, consider the following passage:

> Till now that she was threatened with its loss Emma had never known how much of her happiness depended on being *first* with Mr. Knightley, first in interest and affection. Satisfied that it was so, and feeling it her due, she had enjoyed it without reflection; and only in the dread of being supplanted, found how inexpressibly important it had been. (Austen, 2004, p. 395)[9]

As Joni Mitchell once put it, you often "don't know what you've got till it's gone," and here Emma, thinking it possible that Harriet might be first with Knightley instead of herself, suddenly realizes how much she cares for him – indeed that she has always loved him and no one else.

Mr. Knightley in turn becomes ardent for Emma when faced with Frank Churchill's feigned affection for Emma, to which Emma is not indifferent:

> On [Mr. Knightley's] side, there had been a longstanding jealousy, old as the arrival, or even the expectation, of Frank

> Churchill. He had been in love with Emma, and jealous of
> Frank Churchill, from about the same period, one sentiment
> having probably enlightened him as to the other. (p. 412)

In such cases, one's own passions are first ignited when one's rival's
passions are ignited. One becomes impassioned when one sees one's
rival's hand reach out toward a flower, fruit, or log.[10] Here Mr.
Knightley's passions are aroused, first by Emma's obvious curiosity
about Frank Churchill, and then further by Churchill's apparent
fascination with Emma.

Returning to our triangle in the *Symposium*, recall that, right
at the beginning of the banquet, when Socrates sits down next to
Agathon, there is a whole discussion about which one of them
has knowledge and which one is ignorant; we are told the story
about the full vase and the empty vase (175d–e) and the potential
flow of knowledge from the one into the other like water along a
piece of yarn (could this be a kind of value that the one is hoping
to derive from the other, à la Pausanias?). Later in the dialogue,
as Lacan points out, Agathon admits under Socrates' questioning
that he obviously did not know what he was saying when he gave
his encomium – in other words, that he was ignorant – whereas
Socrates is presented as the one who knows something (about love).
The initial situation, whereby Socrates is purportedly ignorant and
Agathon knows, transforms into one in which Socrates knows and
Agathon is ignorant.

Agathon is presented here as Socrates' beloved and, with one
associated with ignorance and the other with knowledge, we can
quite specifically equate Alcibiades with the *dóxa*, daemon, or
love that comes or goes between them. Alcibiades might be viewed
here as a messenger (or signifier) telling Agathon and Socrates
something about their relationship, as a go-between or potential
rival designed to bring out their love for each other. (It is, admittedly, harder to imagine Alcibiades as embodying anything along
the lines of "right opinion," although opinion *tout court* might be
conceivable.)

What is said about knowledge in Socrates' speech is complicated
still further by the fact that Socrates, who supposedly knows about
love, does not tell us what he knows at the level of *epistéme*, but
has someone speak instead of him at the level of myth or *dóxa* – as
if he himself does not want to tell us what he knows and prefers
to let someone else present rather wild speculations about love.
He claims to know far less about love than Diotima does, but he
makes a couple of comments that allow us to think he is not quite
so impressed with what she says as he explicitly professes to be to

those present at the banquet. At one point during Diotima's speech he says "maybe" (206e), and at another point he says, "Most wise Diotima, is this really the way it is?" (208b), as if he is still quite doubtful. Indeed, we might get the sense he is rolling his eyes while she is spouting off her harebrained lucubrations! Here again, certain commentators have taken all of this at face value, whereas Plato seems to give many a hint that a different kind of reading is possible and perhaps even necessary.

If we take seriously what Socrates does here – giving the floor to Diotima, as if she were far more knowledgeable about love than him – we are, at the very least, forced to conclude that he does not believe that the nature of love can be approached through his elenctic method, but only through myth.

The Six Stages of Socrates' Speech

Let us now examine the structure of what Socrates says when he officially takes the floor. The whole progression of his speech is quite complex and problematic:

1. First he engages in his usual type of elenchus with Agathon, which ends with Agathon's "admission" that he must not have known what he was saying when he said that love is calm, moderate, harmonious, and never riotous or deceitful. Lacan (2015, pp. 105–14) suggests that this admission is rather tongue-in-cheek as everyone (except Socrates?) is well aware that Agathon has been joking all along.
2. There is a sort of raising of the Socratic elenchus to the second power, whereby Diotima refutes Socrates just as Socrates has "refuted" Agathon, the wise woman seemingly attempting to shift from a binary to a tripartite logic.
3. Diotima recounts the myth of the birth of Eros from Poros and Penia, a myth apparently found nowhere else in any of the texts from Antiquity that have come down to us thus far (new ones still being discovered in various archeological sites regularly).
4. Diotima and Socrates engage in more fairly typical Socratic-type dialogue.
5. Diotima launches into a long complicated discourse on the ladder of love.
6. We have the finale, complete with closing remarks.

As we examine each of these stages in turn, we should wonder about what motivates each shift in Socrates' speech.

Part 1: Changing the Agenda

There is a performative quality to everything Socrates says in the dialogue. He, for example, first announces that he was almost struck dumb by Agathon's Gorgian discourse: it was irresistibly powerful (198c) – something often said of Socrates' own words – and beautiful (201b). We might be led to conclude that Agathon contains object *a* for Socrates insofar as he is beautiful, intelligent, famous, and has a marvelous voice. But Socrates often pays his interlocutors very great compliments just before eviscerating them; so this may simply be sarcasm or designed to make Agathon fall all the harder when the blow comes.

We quickly encounter a shift in the type of discourse engaged in (201c, line 6), where the point is no longer to simply praise love: *Socrates himself changes the agenda of the symposium* well before Alcibiades' arrival does. He begins interrogating Agathon, his beloved, to disprove things he has said, and Agathon gives in, proffering, "Let it be as you say." You win.

Now, in a lovers' quarrel or argument, what is the likely effect of such a move, of saying something like, "Fine" or "Have it your own way"? It shifts things to a different level, to a different kind of discourse: "I am not going to argue with you about this," either because we are talking about apples and oranges or because you seem to be deaf to my point. This may reduce tension between us; it does not always work, because you will not necessarily let it go – you may insist on getting some sort of full retraction or admission of wrongheadedness from me. If my ploy does not calm things down, I can always try breaking down and crying to get you to give it a rest and shift to a different style of discourse. Crying instead of talking, and breaking lamps and plates instead of arguing, have a way of changing the "disk-course," a way of changing the record (Lacan, 1998a, pp. 32 and 34): stopping my interlocutor from endlessly harping on the same thing.

We can glimpse here the importance of changing discourses in relations between lovers, the importance of not engaging in battle on the terrain on which one is attacked or challenged, but shifting the discussion to other ground. Attack: "Why did you treat me the way you did? I am sure that reflects what you think of me, you bastard!" Instead of retorting, "You're the one who treated me badly" – which keeps things on the imaginary level (pointing to the projection: you actually did to me what you imagine I did to you)[11] – one could, for example, respond, "I was very upset that day about news I had received of an illness in my family." Rather than inciting rage, such a response might give rise to compassion, if not love.

As Lacan (1998a) says in Seminar XX, love arises when there is a shift in discourses: "love is the sign that one is changing discourses" (p. 21/16).

Such shifts can occur in the analytic setting too. In certain cases, when the analysand asks the analyst, "Why did you say what you said last time?" the analysand may be implying that it was wrong, stupid, or hurtful. Rather than attempt to defend or justify what he or she said, which keeps things within the discourse of argument and accusation that the analysand has introduced, the analyst could proffer a range of responses that shift ground or position. The analyst may answer with a question like, "What do you think I should have said?" or "Why do you think I said it?" and then follow up by trying to unpack the projections that went into the analysand's assumption as to what the analyst's words meant. The goal in this latter case is to get the analysand to articulate his or her presumptions – that the analyst is mean and critical of everything he or she says, just like the patient's parent was, for example – instead of to argue about the truth value of the analyst's statement or about the validity of the analyst's motives or intentions in saying it. Responses like "I didn't mean to be critical" do nothing but worsen the situation, for analysands are usually well aware that one can be critical without consciously meaning to be! Certain responses the analyst makes keep things at an imaginary level (e.g., the analysand imagines that you were thinking or feeling such and such, which is why you said what you said, and you reply that you were not thinking or feeling that), whereas other responses shift things to the symbolic level (e.g., what, in the analysand's own life and history, led him or her to imagine you were thinking or feeling such a thing in the first place). We have here the kind of change in discourse that is often highly appreciated by analysands (who sometimes realize they are rather foolishly looking for a fight, or just wanting to see if you will take the bait and prove your incompetence), since it is more likely to give rise to love than to further antagonism.[12]

Let us turn now to the *content* of this first stage of Socrates' speech. Socrates asks Agathon:

Is the love about which you spoke love of something? Does loving and desiring something mean having it or not having it? Can one desire what one already has? (199e–200a)

Socrates says that we cannot and this announces one of the biggest problems in love relations: for once the beloved has been conquered, in some sense, attached to oneself, can one continue to desire the beloved and vice versa? Can one continue to desire someone who has already succumbed to one's attempts at seduction?[13]

What Lacan (2015) points out here (pp. 113–15) is that, although ostensibly discussing love, Socrates has actually shifted the question to desire (this occurs in 200a–201c). For both Plato and Socrates, desire is based on or stems from lack. But love might well be something else. Indeed, it would seem quite possible to go on loving someone who has succumbed to one's attempts at seduction. Love, even if it is giving what you do not have, seems not to be dependent on lack in quite the same way as desire is.

Insofar as desire is always for something we do not have, in order for desire to persist in a relationship, there must always be something we do not have, that we do not yet have, or have not yet received from our beloved. As Lacan puts it (p. 124), desire can never have or possess anything other than lack, for as soon as it possesses its object, it disappears. To give oneself body and soul to one's beloved may then kill his or her desire; hence the difficulty and dance (à la Stendhal) around keeping the partner's desire alive. Socrates might perhaps have endorsed the notion that, for desire to persist, one must always try to maintain either an impossible desire (like Alcibiades' impossible desire for Socrates) or an unsatisfied desire, perhaps by deliberately steering clear of satisfaction (as it seems Socrates does). One cannot pine away for or waste away with desire for something unless one does not have it (at least not at that very instant), but it seems to me that one *can* love something one has.

Socrates' speech is built around a playing fast and loose with the terms "love" and "desire," and even replacing the former with the latter. Socrates reasons as follows: Love (as the god Eros) lacks what he desires; if Love desires beauty, Love must be lacking in beauty; if Love loves the good, it must be lacking in the good (201a–c); therefore Love is neither beautiful nor good (201e), since it lacks both.

The specious reasoning is quite blatant here, and Diotima equates love and desire still more completely in the part of her discourse that evinces a Socratic form of elenchus. She concludes that Love is not a god because he is lacking, that is, he has neither good nor beautiful things (202d), and that Love is neither a god nor a human, neither immortal nor mortal – love is "neither the one nor the other" (Lacan, 2015, p. 122).

By this point in Socrates' speech, the agenda of the symposium has changed: Love was initially taken to be a god and the goal was to praise him. But Diotima has "shown" love not to be a god, but rather a daemon (or signifier). Her name, curiously enough, might be understood to mean "she who honors Zeus," who is the highest of the gods; yet she begins her speech by knocking another god, Love, off his divine pedestal.

Part 2: The In-Between

As we explore Diotima's speech, let us note first the paradox (211b) of the fact that she, a woman, tells Socrates how to "love boys correctly"! Are we to conclude that love is the same for women as for men, or at least that women know all about love between men?

As I mentioned earlier, Socrates summarizes for us Diotima's discussion of *dóxa*, daemons, and love, shifting things from a binary to a tripartite logic. It would appear that Socrates' dialectical method suffices to take us up to a certain point regarding love – the point that desire, masquerading as love, stems from lack (Lacan, 2015, pp. 114–15) – but not beyond that. Diotima herself employs the Socratic method up to a certain point, but to go further into the nature of love she introduces a myth.[14]

We might thus conclude that there are two distinct fields: that of *epistéme* and that of myth (pp. 117–19):

Epistéme: knowledge contained within the   Myth:
signifying system   what people say

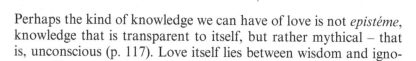

Perhaps the kind of knowledge we can have of love is not *epistéme*, knowledge that is transparent to itself, but rather mythical – that is, unconscious (p. 117). Love itself lies between wisdom and ignorance, like opinion (*dóxa*).

Rather than say that Diotima is a manifestation of Plato, who refuted his teacher Socrates, as many philosophical commentators do, Lacan proposes that she is a manifestation of Socrates: "the woman who is in him" (p. 118). Indeed, Lacan does not in any way try to claim things about Plato's personality, confining his remarks to saying that we would do well to assume that Plato knows what he is up to in the dialogue and that it would be a sign of hubris on our part to assume he did not and that we know better (this is not to say that the unconscious might not have been at work in Plato too). Note that this is the kind of credit Lacan gives to a great many authors that he reads: he assumes that, as confusing or seemingly self-contradictory as their claims may be, there is an internal logic to what they are saying and that this is what we need to elucidate. (If only commentators would lend Lacan the same credence!)

Part 3: The Myth of Love's Conception

According to Diotima (as Socrates tells us, if we are to believe Apollodorus, who, let us not forget, heard it from Aristodemus [173b]), Eros is the son of Poros, he who possesses resources, expedients, and know-how (he is one of the "haves"), and of Penia, who embodies poverty, lack, and abject misery. She is Aporia, lacking in resources (she is one of the "have-nots").

In the story of the conception of Love (Lacan, 2015, p. 130), Penia is depicted as the desiring party. Poros is the beloved, who is passive and is somehow made to conceive Eros with Penia while he is asleep, drunk after a banquet. Certain women were seen as desirous at that time, and, indeed, a number of scholars suggest that men were sometimes afraid of women's sexual desire.[15] But Lacan points out that this myth depicts the logical time *prior* to the birth of Love; this might suggest that after the birth of Love, positions shift and men more often become desirous and women passive. The fact remains that lack (Penia, Aporia) and unconsciousness or ignorance (Poros is asleep and thus does not know what is happening) are said here to precede the birth of love.

Love is the child or product of an impasse, an aporia. Penia – his mother – is characterized as Aporia, without resources, expedients, or tricks. Is love, then, a solution to a problem? The solution to an impasse? If so, what might that impasse be? What, if anything, does love "cure" in our patients? (Is it the stagnation of the libido in depression, or the pain of separation?)

As Diotima "corrects" Socrates' viewpoints about love in the course of her speech, note that she contradicts what Alcibiades later says about Socrates. She declares that Socrates "thought love was being loved, rather than being a lover" (204c) – in other words, that everything Socrates thought about love was from the position of the beloved (that of receiving love instead of showing one's own lack to someone else). Why does she say this? Does Plato want to hint that she is completely wrong about Socrates? It would seem to be Alcibiades, not Diotima, who tells us the truth about Socrates, insofar as Socrates seems to insist upon being the lover, not the beloved. (Indeed, he explicitly states that he is the lover of Alcibiades in the *Gorgias*, 481d–482b.) Why, then, would Socrates conceptualize love solely from the perspective of the beloved?

Note that Eros himself, the product of the most unlikely union

between Poros and Penia, is depicted as part bum (hopeless romantic) and part brave, resourceful hunter or philosopher (203c–d),
which is very similar to how Alcibiades describes Socrates later on
in the dialogue.

Part 4: Love and Immortality

Having equated love and desire, trying to pass the latter off as the
former, Diotima highlights the one thing desire still does not have
even when it possesses its object (the beloved): it does not have the
knowledge or guarantee that it will be able to continue to possess its
object forever. This leads her to conclude that "Love is wanting to
possess the good forever" (206a, lines 10–11). In her book, love *must*
desire immortality (207a).

Bards and love-letter writers often evoke the everlastingness of
their love. In poetry, for example, love must profess to its eternity,
if only in death. In the words of Elizabeth Barrett Browning, for
example, "if God choose, I shall but love thee better after death";
and in those of Tao-Sheng, "In life we share a single quilt./ In death
we will share a single coffin."[16] It seems that, to poets at least, love
must be affirmed to be immortal, transcending death itself.

Lack, insofar as it is permanent, can only be filled up or con-
soled by immortality, Diotima claims, and reproduction of the
species (out of love, like animals) is the mortal form of immortality.
Diotima concludes, "It is for the sake of immortality that everything
shows this zeal, which is Love," thereby turning Love into a means
(to immortality), not an end in itself. Here Socrates professes his
amazement and queries, "Well, most wise Diotima, is this really the
way it is?" – allowing us to wonder whether he is taking anything
Diotima said seriously. He adds that she went on "in the manner
of a perfect sophist" (208b), which is hardly a flattering description
coming from Socrates.

According to Diotima, people will do just about anything to
achieve immortality, in the sense of being remembered forever after
their physical death. To our psychoanalytic ears, this smacks of
obsessionality, for obsessives very often do not live in the present or
for any kind of lived jouissance but only for the Other with a capital
O, only for the record books, only to leave a trace in history. In
saying this, Diotima appears to be calling into question all so-called
heroic gestures, seemingly suggesting that they are calculated to
ensure immortality as opposed to being done for the explicit reasons
attested to by their doers. It is as if someone were to say to you, "It
wasn't really out of friendship that you helped your friend out of

a terrible fix but merely because you wanted other people to hear about your kind deed, merely because you wanted your kindness to go down in history."

If we take her seriously, she is essentially impugning the motives behind virtually all ethical acts (even Antigone burying her brother; see Sophocles' *Antigone* and Lacan's extensive commentary on it in Seminar VII). To be generous, we could say she is indicating that they are overdetermined, but her language would seem to suggest that she believes immortality to be their *primary* motive, which would seem to imply that they are not ethical acts at all. I find it hard to believe that either Socrates or Plato would have found such a view palatable.[17]

Part 5: The Ladder of Love (scala amoris)

Diotima portrays a flight of "rising stairs" (211c) to us as "the final and highest mystery" (209e). Lacan (2015) claims that whereas at first, in Diotima's discourse, beauty serves desire as a guide, guiding us toward objects, beauty surreptitiously becomes an aim – indeed, an end in itself (pp. 127–8). Recall that the connection between love and beauty stems from the fact that Love was conceived the day Aphrodite was born:

> That is why Love was born to follow Aphrodite and serve her: because he was conceived on the day of her birth. And that's why he is also by nature a lover of beauty, because Aphrodite herself is especially beautiful. (203c)

Lacan (2015, pp. 120–2) considers this to be part of the speciousness of Diotima's argument, where something shifts from being a simple expedient to being the very goal aimed at. My own sense is that in Diotima's argument beauty does *not* shift from being a means to an end but rather that, whereas beauty is at first the aim, it becomes a means.[18]

The progression would seem to me to be as follows: we begin with an interest in a beautiful boy; then in all beautiful boys; then in beauty itself; then in the beauty of the soul, and of activities, laws, customs, and knowledge; and then in knowledge of beauty (210d). We see in the last item in this list that knowledge has supplanted beauty as the goal. Beauty has become a means toward the end of knowledge.

The goal now seems to be to celebrate knowledge (of beauty) and not to celebrate beauty or even love at all. Diotima tells us that her goal is to get Socrates to stop going "out of [his] senses," as she says he does (211d) – and one might well wonder how she would know! – not to be so smitten by good-looking boys. Socrates did, after all, have a reputation for falling hard for young boys like Critobulus, the one whose shoulder he brushed up against, as Xenophon tells us, Socrates having complained of being sore for a whole week thereafter.[19] Does she feel he should learn to love in some other way? Or not at all? To love calmly? Moderately? Someone seems to be making fun of his susceptibility to such instantaneous passions here! (Might it be Plato?)

The larger question that is raised by this passage is whether beauty or love is an end in itself. Diotima shifts from discussing our love of beauty to beauty's claim to be an aim in its own right, but quickly moves on to the importance of knowledge of beauty. In the course of this discussion, Diotima has to tell Socrates to pay attention, as if he had nodded off or as if his eyes had glazed over. She then dives into full-blown metaphysics, speaking of the "goal of loving" (210e), as if loving had a goal or purpose other than itself! Having demoted Eros from the lofty post of god to the lowly rank of messenger, it seems that love for her is no longer an end in itself but merely a means to the end of knowledge. She is joined in this view, it would seem, by recent generations of psychoanalysts for whom the love elicited in the transference is valued only for its use in bringing about "self-knowledge," the goal of analysis as they see it being to know thyself, as if one could be cured by gaining knowledge of oneself (see Fink, 2014a).

Freud's goals of "love and work" leave "knowledge" conspicuously out of the picture, and he explicitly indicated that patients who had some of the most successful analyses he had conducted could not even remember what had been said in sessions, much less formulate what had happened in the course of the treatment. Many practitioners today seem to have reversed Freud's goals and made some sort of knowledge (a facsimile of "self-knowledge," presumably involving conscious knowledge of the unconscious) more important than love or libido. Lacan returns to Freud in this regard, as in others, claiming that the analyst is there to further the analysand's Eros – "I am not there, in the final analysis, for a person's own good, but in order that he love" (Lacan, 2015, p. 15). The analysand's ability to love is an end in itself for Lacan, not a means to his knowledge of anything whatsoever, whether of beauty, virtue, the unconscious, or psychoanalysis. To paraphrase what Lacan (1998a, p. 3) says of jouissance in Seminar XX, *Encore* – "Jouissance is what serves no purpose" – we might say that *love is something that serves no purpose, it just is*. In psychoanalysis, love is an end in itself.

This is not to say that the goal with each and every analysand is to increase his or her Eros or libido quantitatively. There are, after all, analysands who suffer from too much libido (manic ones, for example) or uncontrolled libido that repeatedly gets them in trouble with the law (voyeurs, for example); those who are psychotic or perverse rarely if ever need us to help free up their libido, often seeking help limiting it instead. The goal in these latter cases is to enhance their ability to love and allow them to feel Eros in a qualitatively different way than before.

Does the fact that Socrates cannot stay awake or attentive during this part of Diotima's speech indicate that Plato finds it ridiculous that Diotima makes knowledge an end in itself instead of love? If love of beauty gives way, in Diotima's speech, to love of knowledge, must we not conclude that the last stage is knowledge of love? We will return to this question shortly, but let me suggest that neither Socrates' instantaneous crushes on attractive boys nor Diotima's fixation on knowledge goes unscathed here – both are perhaps being joked about in the *Symposium*.[20]

Part 6: Finale, Closing Remarks

We explored beauty in Chapter 7, especially in connection with Lacan's discussion of it in Seminar VII where he relates it to death. Here let us turn to the end of Socrates' speech: by the time Diotima steps down from the podium, we have been told that Love is a mere means to immortality: "human nature can find no better workmate [or helper] for acquiring [immortality] than Love" (212b). Even knowledge is perhaps subordinate to the goal of immortality, which appears to be an end in itself – indeed, the goal of goals.

In the final analysis, Socrates has, via Diotima, praised not Love itself, but "the power and courage of Love" as a means to the end of true virtue and immortality. As I mentioned earlier, this destroys the entire premise of the *Symposium* up until that moment, each participant having been asked to praise Love as a god, as an end in itself, not to praise something else love might be good for. What, we might wonder, is so great about immortality in this sense, about being remembered for all times by others we do not know? What can that possibly do for us here and now? There may be satisfaction in the present at the thought that we will be passing something valuable (a good example, a lesson, a stance, or what have you) on to future generations, but we can never really know in advance what will be found valuable by future generations.[21] Isn't there something rather absurd about mortals wanting to become immortal and godlike?

When Socrates says at the very end, "Consider this, then, Phaedrus, if you wish, a speech in praise of love. Or if not, call it whatever and however you please to call it" (212b–c), there seems to me to be *something supremely ironic here*!

After Socrates' Speech

After the applause that greets the end of Socrates' rambling speech, Aristophanes tries in vain to interject something in response to the comment Socrates made about the folly of seeking our other half, claiming that we should seek our other half only if it is good, not simply because it belongs to us personally (205d–e); if my arm is diseased, I should cut it off (here he foreshadows the biblical injunction, "If your hand offend you, cut it off" (Mark 9:43; cf. Matthew 5:29–30)). Rather than being fascinated by the uncastratable sphere, Socrates says, "castrate thyself" for the sake of the good: do not seek your other half (or, we might interject, your object *a*) if it is morally corrupt.

As opposed to Aristophanes' myth of a return to a prior uncastrated state where there has been no loss, Socrates proposes a kind of *ecstatic Stoicism* (although this might well be an oxymoron): courage and fortitude, abstinence, sublimated sexuality, seeking beauty for the sake of virtue, and, in short, constant desire without satisfaction. This appears not to involve a return to some mythical past state of bliss, but rather a forward-looking adventure.

The Scene Alcibiades Makes

Alcibiades makes quite a scene when he comes in, proving perhaps that there is no harmony in a group of people supposedly admiring beauty together, or basking in the glow of Agathon's beauty. There is no calm, joint contemplation of beauty here (Lacan, 2015, p. 133); indeed, Alcibiades and Socrates seem almost to come to blows over access to or possession of Agathon! If there is such a thing as the quiet shared contemplation of beauty as Diotima depicted it, it certainly does not occur at this dinner party.

When Alcibiades enters, instead of lofty speeches about transcending the world of human bodies and incarnations of beauty, reality suddenly takes center stage. His appearance there changes anew the agenda of the banquet, it now being decided that Alcibiades (the only one who has not yet given a speech) will eulogize Socrates, since according to Alcibiades Socrates will allow him to eulogize no one else in his presence, not even a god. Note that the Good, virtue, and beauty have no place in his speech: Alcibiades does not say, I have got to have Socrates because he is good for me; he says, I have got to have him whether he is good for me or not, whether it will be toxic or not! "Alcibiades is a man imbued with desire [*l'homme du désir*]," full of desire, overflowing with desire, as Lacan puts it (p. 157).[22] In his later discussion of the *Symposium* in "Subversion of the Subject," Lacan (2006a, pp. 825–6) comments that "Alcibiades is by no means a neurotic; [. . .] he is the epitome of desirousness, and a man who pursues jouissance as far as possible." Lacan thereby leaves us to wonder if he means that Alcibiades has somehow gone beyond neurosis or that he falls into some other diagnostic category, such as perversion. What Alcibiades says and does seems, in any case, to demonstrate the inanity of many of the prior speeches about love.

Alcibiades' Speech

Alcibiades tells us that he thought Socrates really wanted *him*, but Socrates wanted something else, something beyond him (217a). Yet Alcibiades, like most of us, wanted to be wanted for himself. By frustrating Alcibiades, Socrates turned Alcibiades from his beloved into a lover (217c). As Alcibiades puts it, "He presents himself as your lover, and, before you know it, you're in love with him yourself" (222b). Socrates drove Alcibiades crazy and apparently did not make him a better person in the process.

Alcibiades tells us that it is not what is outside (beauty) but what is inside that counts; and what is inside Socrates is *ágalma* (Lacan, 2015, pp. 137–8). It is owing to Alcibiades' passion that he is able to see what is hidden inside Socrates (pp. 138–9). Only a lover has access to this, only a lover can see or experience what the other has inside – other people cannot glimpse it, other people think we are crazy to be so beside ourselves or so head over heels about someone who seems so ordinary to them. This is a discourse of passion, not affection or quiet attachment.

Leaving to the wayside his position as beloved for others to lust after, Alcibiades becomes completely helpless next to the *agálmata* he perceives in Socrates. We no longer have here the simple positions of lover and beloved: Alcibiades characterizes himself as a slave, someone who will slavishly carry out Socrates' will (if only Socrates will issue commands). We see here "the fetishistic function of the object" (p. 140), which leads to fixation, submission, and subservience. Alcibiades is conquered by the object he sees in Socrates;

he grovels before it. He is reduced to begging! Alcibiades begs for a sign of Socrates' desire, a sign of his lack insofar as it is specifically related to Alcibiades (e.g., an erection caused by Alcibiades) as opposed to a lack that is general and structural (p. 137). In refusing to give any such sign, Socrates' assumption is perhaps that to do so would allow Alcibiades to reduce Socrates from the Other with a capital *O* (the subject-supposed-to-know that Alcibiades believes he is) to the other with a lowercase *o*.

Note, however, that Socrates does not describe Alcibiades as a slave, but rather as a very bossy beloved who will not allow Socrates to address so much as "two words to anyone else" or even to look at an attractive man without flying "into a jealous rage" and slapping him around. "The fierceness of his passion terrifies me," Socrates continues (213c–d).

Ágalma

> Any extremely useful idea that can only be explained in very
> simple terms will necessarily be scorned in France.
>
> Stendhal, 2004, p. 267/232

How are we to understand the *ágalma* Alcibiades sees in Socrates? In Greek, the word's meanings include shine[23] and brilliancy; *ágalma* is something admirable or charming (Lacan, 2015, pp. 151–2); it is a trap for gods – it draws or attracts their eyes (those of Athena in Homer's *Odyssey*, for example); it is an uncanny object or charm – the Trojan horse, for example, is referred to as *ágalma*.

Lacan associates *ágalma* with the partial object as adumbrated by Karl Abraham and developed by Freud. He indicates that psychoanalysts very quickly ran from the importance of the discovery,[24] being disturbed by the notion that we view our partners in love as a collection of objects that we get pleasure and jouissance from rather than as subjects. Analysts were willing to admit that at the oral and anal stages, children are selfish and do not recognize their mothers, for example, as persons in their own right – that is, as separate subjects. But analysts hypothesized that at the genital stage, lo and behold, a vast synthesis occurs and we begin to recognize the other as another person in her own right. A perfect complementarity develops whereby our own satisfaction is incomplete without the other's satisfaction, the goal being completely harmonious, simultaneous orgasm.

Their idea here was that rather than being selfish, we become altruistic and all-giving ("oblative"), our own satisfaction being intimately connected with giving satisfaction to our partner. Implicit in this notion was that a kind of perfect reciprocity and harmony could be achieved through genital relations (see Fink, 2004, pp. 148–50). In this sense, partial objects kept getting totalized, and completion was insisted upon, as if the fascination with the apparent perfection of circles and spheres was too strong to ever be given up. The partial object had to be transcended in favor of some sort of "total object," as it was sometimes called in the psychoanalytic literature.

In 1953, Lacan (2006a, p. 263) critiqued the insistence by analysts on bringing about some such complete harmony, claiming that it was like "bind[ing] heavy burdens, hard to bear, and lay[ing] them on men's shoulders" (Matthew 23:4), it not being clear to Lacan that any such harmony is even theoretically possible, much less achievable through psychoanalysis. By Seminar XVIII, Lacan went further and formulated a nonrelationship between the sexes – "There's no such thing as a sexual relationship" – as a way of combating the perennial belief in the possibility of perfect complementarity between the sexes.

There would seem to be something not castratable about this total, whole person who one was supposed to love as a total genital object; the appeal to analysts of the notion was perhaps that, although the subject is inevitably castrated, at least the object (who could be likened to a perfect circle or sphere) remains unscathed. Nevertheless, any analyst who has taken the trouble to elicit and listen attentively to the fantasies of actual, living, breathing, human beings is aware that what turns people on in their partners is not the "total person" but something far more partial and specific (e.g., "It's the way he looks at me," "the way he holds me," "the sound of her voice," or a particular body part seen from a certain angle or in a certain light).[25] This is what Alcibiades seems to be getting at: there is something he sees in Socrates; it does not matter if no one else sees it; all that counts is that Alcibiades sees it and that it drives him wild.

The "Mystery" of the Relationship between Socrates and Alcibiades

It is because Socrates knows that he does not love.

Lacan, 2015, p. 153

Alcibiades (who might be equated with love, being seated in between Agathon and Socrates, in between knowledge and ignorance) knows that Socrates appreciates his looks and knows he is loved by Socrates. But that is not enough for him. What more does he want?

One possible answer is that he feels a need to reduce Socrates from the Other with a capital *O* to the small other, from the idealized Other whom he looks up to and who judges, criticizes, and upbraids him, to an object (another person like himself) to get off on, a substitutable object that is no better than any other.[26] He perhaps believes that if he can get Socrates to have sex with him, he will cut him down to size, reduce him to the status of an ordinary lascivious mortal, and have him at his mercy. The "problem of love [is] that the subject can only satisfy the Other's demand by demeaning the Other, turning this Other into the object of his desire" (Lacan, 2015, p. 219).

Up until this point in Lacan's work, one's partner in love can occupy but one of two possible positions: other (*a*) and Other (A). In his early seminars, *a* is simply the other like oneself – one's semblable, the little brother, sister, or neighbor who is about the same age and about the same strength as one is oneself (as we saw in Chapter 5; this *a* is nothing like object *a*, the cause of desire). This other is no better than oneself, no more virtuous or ideal a figure, and is far easier to deal with than someone on a pedestal.

The latter is a forbidding godlike figure. One cannot have a relationship with such a person (unless one is Judge Schreber, and even then it is unbearable, or a mystic), unless one is convinced this Other is always satisfied with one's performance in life, which is rare indeed. To be borne, this Other has to be cut down to size. Hence the jubilation on the part of certain people when a "big daddy" like former President Clinton has an affair with Monica Lewinsky, when former New York State Governor Eliot Spitzer falls from grace with a call girl, or when presidential hopeful John Edwards falls from his lofty family values position because it turns out that, behind his ill wife's back, he has fathered a "love child" with another woman. Presumably the satisfaction some obtain from such revelations is related to the idea that a figure who is supposed to be (or claims to be) morally superior turns out to be ultimately no better than they are, no more virtuous than anyone else.

Socrates infuriates Alcibiades because he does not allow himself to fall from grace in this manner. He does not seem to be tempted into satisfying his "base, animal needs" despite being under the covers with the handsomest of men. In a word, Socrates cannot be taken down to Alcibiades' own level.

Lacan refers to this taking the Other down a notch as part of "the game of love" (Lacan, 2015, pp. 152–3), as one of the maneuvers endemic to the dance of seduction. He argues that since Socrates knows what the game is and how it works, he does not allow it to happen. In the game of seduction, the seduced party falls from a lofty position and is no longer worshipped or loved for being unlike all others. The seduced party becomes a sex partner like any other and can then be compared to other sex partners – as someone who is a more or less good lover, not as good as certain others perhaps, but better than this one or that. Instead of being in a class of his own, he becomes one of many.

Socrates does not fall into the trap of the "game of love." He refuses to be reduced to an other like any other for Alcibiades. Is it because he is anxious to hold on to a certain position of power he occupies in the relationship? We will discuss that further on. Is it because he insists upon remaining the cause of Alcibiades' desire, object *a*, rather than one in a series of objects of Alcibiades' desire? Because he absolutely must be the singular object that will put an end to the metonymic slippage of Alcibiades' desire? This is not exactly how Lacan formulates it in Seminar VIII (although there are, as we shall see, some hints of it), and this, I would suggest, is because he has not yet fully formulated the concept of object *a* as we see it in his subsequent work. Although the letter *a* is present in Lacan's work from very early on, it refers there exclusively to the imaginary other (or other with a lowercase *o*). It is right around the time of Seminars VII and VIII that *a* first shifts from the imaginary to the real in Lacan's work, his earliest names for object *a* arguably being "the Thing" in Seminar VII and *ágalma* in Seminar VIII. In *Transference*, Lacan formulates the situation between Socrates and Alcibiades not in terms of object *a* but in terms of aspects of love he brings out in the course of his reading of the *Symposium*. And he does not rely on one explanation alone.

Here is what he proposes. First of all, like the Greek gods, Socrates refuses to "enter into the scale of the desirable" (Lacan, 2015, p. 161) and such entry necessarily occurs when one allows oneself to be loved – that is, to become someone else's *erómenos* or beloved. Socrates is willing to occupy only one position: that of *erastés*, the lover. This means that although Socrates regularly turns his beloveds into lovers, into men who begin to love him and the knowledge they believe he has, he himself can never undergo the metaphor (or miracle) of love because he refuses to occupy the initial position: that of the beloved.[27]

Is this because, like the Greek gods, he is concerned only with his own passion? Lacan suggests that Socrates not only does not know (like all beloveds) what he has in him that another could possibly find lovable – he refuses to believe that there is anything lovable about him. Even though he accuses Alcibiades of asking him for "gold in exchange for bronze" (218e) – the *agálmata* Alcibiades claims to see in Socrates in exchange for the younger man's good looks – Socrates goes on to disclaim, "Still, my dear boy, you should think twice, because you could be wrong, and I may be of no use to you" after all (219a). Lacan takes this to imply two things: (1) Socrates believes he contains nothing within himself that is of value or that can do Alcibiades any good; he feels he truly is empty; (2) Socrates certainly will not give Alcibiades anything that he does not feel would be for Alcibiades' own good, and it would do Alcibiades no good to have sex with Socrates.[28]

Lacan (2015) suggests that for Socrates to give Alcibiades a sign of his love (in the form of an erection) would be to show that he has shifted from being Alcibiades' beloved to his lover; but to do so would mean that Socrates would have to admit to having first been Alcibiades' beloved, "an object worthy of Alcibiades' desire, or of anyone else's for that matter" (p. 155). Socrates was clearly enamored of Alcibiades' looks but could not or would not allow himself to enter into the metaphor of love.

Everyone seems to agree that Alcibiades was the love of Socrates' life (after all, Socrates says so himself in the *Gorgias*, 481d–482b, and in the *Alcibiades I*, 103a and 131c–e), but Socrates is presented to us as a lover who has never gone through the metaphor of love. We might say that he loves without wishing to be loved in return, indeed, without being able to accept love in return. He is perhaps like the analyst in this regard, the analyst insofar as he or she is working as an analyst (not insofar as he or she functions as an individual outside of the consulting room). This brings us to Socrates' so-called interpretation.

Socrates' "Interpretation"

Taking notice of the seemingly incidental remark Alcibiades makes at the end of his speech – to the effect that Agathon should beware Socrates and be wary of his devious ways – Socrates says to Alcibiades that it is

> As if your speech [. . .] had but the following goal: to enunciate that I should be in love with you and no one else, and that for his part, Agathon should let himself be loved by you and by no one else. (*Symposium*, 222c–d)[29]

Socrates' "interpretation" is that what Alcibiades secretly wants is for Socrates to love him and for Agathon to be Alcibiades' beloved.

In other words, he wants a nonreciprocal circuit of love or desire. "Socrates says to Alcibiades, 'What you want, in the final analysis, is to be loved by me and to have Agathon be your object'" (p. 158).

Socrates → Alcibiades → Agathon

Alcibiades does not want to see Socrates manifest desire for him so that he will know their feelings are mutual; he wants to see Socrates manifest desire for Alcibiades so that he will then be free to pursue another man. If Socrates manifests sexual desire for Alcibiades, Socrates will have become just another notch in Alcibiades' belt and Alcibiades will be able to move on. Socrates seems to make Alcibiades out to be a sort of Don Juan: as soon as the partner succumbs to his seductive ploys, he loses interest and looks elsewhere.

At the end of the *Symposium*, Socrates shows his love for Agathon, not Alcibiades, and is on the verge of praising Agathon publicly when the second interruption occurs. Socrates' interpretation seems to say to Alcibiades, "Although you have been proclaiming unparalleled love for me, you actually love Agathon." It could, of course, be the case that Alcibiades loves both Socrates and Agathon, but Socrates is perhaps hoping to rid himself of an importunate suitor by fobbing him off on Agathon. We do not know whether Socrates believes he is genuinely exposing the "truth" of Alcibiades' desire or whether he is saying something strategic when he declares: "You think I have *ágalma*, but I do not, Agathon does." (Might this be akin to what the analyst does – seeking the object of the analysand's affections outside of the consulting room even when the analysand seems to want to locate the object of his or her affections inside the consulting room?)

Socrates' "Mistake"

Alcibiades demonstrates the presence of love, but only insofar as Socrates, who knows, can be mistaken about its presence, and only accompanies him in being mistaken. The deception [*leurre*] is mutual. Socrates is just as caught up in the deception – if it is a deception and if it is true that he is deceived [*leurré*] – as Alcibiades is.

But which of them is the most authentically deceived, if not he who follows closely, and without allowing himself to drift, what is traced out for him by a love that I will call horrible?

Lacan, 2015, p. 163

Lacan claims that, with this interpretation, Socrates is mistaken. Does he mean by this that Socrates' mistake resides in the fact that Alcibiades does not really love Agathon, Socrates merely putting the idea that he does into his head? This would seem unlikely, given that from the very moment he arrives at the banquet Alcibiades calls Agathon "the cleverest and best-looking man in town" (212e) and kisses him as he places ribbons on his head (213b).

Or is Lacan suggesting that Socrates genuinely confuses what Alcibiades wants with what he himself wants – man's desire being the Other's desire – and tells Alcibiades that Alcibiades is in love with Agathon, whereas it is in fact Socrates who is in love with Agathon? Or that Socrates comes to believe he himself is in love with Agathon when it is Alcibiades who is?

My sense is that Lacan believes Socrates' mistake involves refusing to see himself as the true object – or at least one of the true objects – of Alcibiades' desire. Lacan (2015) says that, in order not to be deceived as to the true state of affairs, Socrates would have to admit that, unbeknown to himself, he is in fact Alcibiades' beloved. Socrates would have to admit that unconsciously he is beloved (pp. 154–6), that there is something that he does not know about himself that he nevertheless contains.

As we saw in Chapter 3, ignorance – the "he didn't know" – is at the heart of love, and Socrates does not know he is worthwhile. Although he professes to know about the art of love, he does not know why he is lovable, but, worse still, he does not even know *that* he is lovable (indeed, he refuses to admit that he is).[30] Lacan seems to be pointing to something unconscious in Socrates: insofar as the unconscious is the Other's desire, this might imply that Socrates cannot become aware of the true nature of Alcibiades' desire; he cannot become aware that it is not the kind of desire that will disappear if satisfied, because for Alcibiades Socrates is the *cause* of his desire and not just one object among many. Mistakenly thinking he is an other like any other for Alcibiades, Socrates overlooks his own position as object *a* for Alcibiades, his own position as the object qua cause that *can* put an end to the metonymic slippage from one man to the next. Socrates goes astray by thinking that he has come to know all about the game of love and all about himself, whereas we must always recognize that we never completely know ourselves.

Unlike Socrates, the analyst must be aware of his position as the object that causes the analysand's desire; if he sees himself as an ordinary object for the analysand like any other, he may well go astray in his interpretations like Socrates did. The analyst may feel as empty of value as Socrates apparently did, but must realize (1) that love is giving what you don't have, not what you do have,

and (2) that it is the analyst's very desirousness – his or her unflag-
ging desire that the analysand come to sessions, recount dreams and
fantasies, and free associate – that brings out the analysand's desire
and keeps the analyst an object unlike any other in the rest of the
analysand's life. One might say that Lacan comes to understand
desirousness itself as a manifestation – indeed, the quintessential
manifestation – or avatar of object *a*, and this is the form of object *a*
that the analyst is most often seen to embody.

Whereas to love, pure and simple, may often be seen as a sign
of weakness – as indicative of lack and castration on the lover's
part – to desire, pure and simple, is often seen as a sign of strength.
Indeed, such desire is something that men often envy in other men –
their will to achieve things, whether in the world of work, career,
research, business, or sexual conquests – and that women often find
a real turn-on in men, their very desirousness being thrilling, as long
as it does not direct itself exclusively to them (it must embrace other
women too). It is often referred to as "drive" (as in, "I admire his
drive").

Whereas to declare love (especially in words, all speech being a
demand for love in return) may be viewed as an expression of weakness, scarcity, or powerlessness – in a word, having nothing to offer
(Penia, lack) – manifesting desire is often viewed as an expression
of strength, power, or possession – in a word, having something,
whether it is said to be cheek, gumption, nerve, moxie, or balls. The
lover who is most successful in his suit is far less often he who has
"the most to offer" than he who most manifests desire.

Alternatively, we could hypothesize that Lacan believes Socrates'
mistake stems from confusing love and desire: perhaps Alcibiades
desires Socrates but loves Agathon and Socrates desires Alcibiades
but loves Agathon (or vice versa). Might this be the way in which
"the deception is mutual" (Lacan, 2015, p. 163)? Or might it be that
Socrates loves but does not desire, whereas Alcibiades desires but
does not love? These questions must go unanswered . . .

In any case, Socrates seems to fail to realize where his power
over someone like Alcibiades comes from; he believes that it derives
from his ability to occupy the position of the all-knowing Other
(or subject-supposed-to-know), whereas it actually stems from
Alcibiades' ability to see object *a* in him.[31] Like many psychoanalysts, Socrates conceptualizes things as involving a power struggle
between himself and Alcibiades, whereby Alcibiades wishes to cut
him down to size, knock him off his pedestal, or turn him into an
other who knows no more about virtue than Alcibiades does.[32]
Insisting on continuing to play the subject-supposed-to-know for
Alcibiades, he overlooks the other position he already occupies

for Alcibiades: that of the singular, nonfungible object that causes Alcibiades' desire.

Parting Shot

Love is beautiful and beauty belongs to love, but Socrates is ugly.
Love is a god, yet God is love. Paradoxes?

Socrates never stops talking, and never stops bringing out the lack in men.[33] As the curtain falls on the banquet, Socrates tells the two interlocutors who have managed to stay up all night discoursing with him, "authors should be able to write both comedy and tragedy." Note that his interlocutors are Aristophanes, who only writes comedies, and Agathon, who only writes tragedies. Socrates cannot pass up the occasion to point out that they are each lacking in some way! (Note, however, that at the banquet itself, the comedian gave a rather serious speech while the tragedian gave a rather comical one.)

Which is the *Symposium*? A comedy or a tragedy? Does it highlight the tragicomedy of Socrates' position?

IX

Some Possible Conclusions about Love

How many people does it take to love? For Onan and Narcissus, it takes only one. For Aristophanes, it takes two who become one. For Kierkegaard, we love another in a third, so, like for Lacan, it takes three. But Freud holds the record; for him it takes at least six: the two partners and their two sets of parents as well.

A number of at least provisional conclusions – which are perhaps not all consistent with each other – might be said to grow out of Lacan's discussion of the *Symposium*:

1. Love is a comical feeling, perhaps at least in part because what each partner is looking for in the other is not necessarily felt by the other to be in him or her; "every time this love [. . .] manifests itself as love pure and simple, and not as dark love or jealous love, it is irresistibly comic" (Lacan, 2015, p. 109).
2. "It takes three to love, not just two" (p. 132) – that is, love is not solely imaginary (except perhaps in psychosis); the coming into play of the Other's desire shifts things into the symbolic register.[1]
3. Love, like desire, is the Other's love: Lacan's myth of reaching for the fruit, flowers, or log implies this (the "miracle of love").
4. Feelings are often (if not always) mutual: the beloved is likely to burst into flames when the lover declares his or her love.
5. Love arises when there is a change in discourses.
6. Love is a signifier or messenger from the unconscious (p. 122).[2]
7. The height of love – at least from the lover's perspective – is the reversal in positions that takes place when one's beloved becomes a lover (the metaphor of love).
8. Love constitutes a demand to be loved in return ("to love is to want to be loved").

9. To declare that one loves is to declare that one lacks, that one is castrated. Love is giving what you don't have.[3]

10. When we are enamored, we tend to overlook the true nature of the beloved, seeing instead what we want to see: there is a big "difference between the object of our love insofar as our fantasies cover it over, and the other's being" (p. 47).

11. To occupy the position of the beloved for someone is to enter automatically into the scale of the desirable (p. 95) and to be found more or less lovable than other people – unless one becomes the incomparable, irreplaceable object *a* for one's lover.

12. It is not enough for each of us to be the object of our partner's desire; we want to be the cause of his or her desire (*a*), not just the object or envelope: *i(a)*. "For each of the partners in the relationship, [. . .] it is not enough to be subjects of need or objects of love – they must hold the place of the cause of desire" (Lacan, 2006a, p. 691).

13. The fact that "love is giving what you don't have" (i.e., giving what is all the more valuable precisely because you do not have much or any of it) doesn't mean that you should give people what they *explicitly request* that you give; as Lacan (1965–6, class given on March 23, 1966) puts it: "It is not always what people ask you for that is precisely what they desire you to give them."[4]

Unanswered Questions

How do I love thee, let me count the ways:
I love thee to the depth and breadth of thy conscious,
preconscious, and unconscious,
To the furthest reaches of thy id, ego, and superego,
Thy body, soul, heart, mind, and spirit,
Thy ideals, fantasies, urges, and drives.
                    (With apologies to Elizabeth Barrett Browning)

As we draw to a close here, I would like to recall to mind a few broad questions we are left with regarding love.

What Does it Mean to Love Another?

Who and what is the other person we endeavor to love or are expected to love? Do we love everything about him or her –

fantasies, drives, superego, unconscious?[5] Or only some of it? Lovers often seem to wish they had a line-item veto, like the governors of 43 out of 50 states have in America – and which a number of U.S. Presidents have requested to no avail – so that they could expunge from their lover the one thing they do not and feel they cannot love. "If only it weren't for that!" they cry. "That I cannot abide!"

We see evidence of this in the growing number of those who add clauses to their prenuptial agreements so that he cannot stop taking care of himself and become flabby and soft, so that she cannot gain more than 20 pounds, so that he cannot start gambling again, so that she cannot have more than one drink a day, or so that neither can decide to go in some life direction the future partner abhors. The very fact that spouses-to-be are tempted to set such conditions seems to imply that they are well aware of such propensities in their partners and that such propensities lie perhaps at the crux of their partners, not at the periphery, being essential, not extraneous to them. Indeed, it is perhaps their spouses' very abhorrence of those propensities that leads such "faults" to gravitate toward the center and not remain peripheral!

Is Love Particular or Universal?

Emma: "I suppose there may be a hundred different ways to be in love."

Austen, 2004, p. 45

Emma: "One half of the world cannot understand the pleasures of the other."

Austen, 2004, p. 77

Is there a "perfect love story" for all of us, one that we would *all* find compelling? I seriously doubt it. There are love stories found in poems, songs, novels, and films that appeal to many, but none that appeal to all of us without exception. Insofar as what I feel to be the "perfect love story" is one that corresponds to my conscious and unconscious fantasies, it is likely to differ from the "perfect love story" for others. And insofar as my conscious fantasies are inevitably at odds with my (unconscious) fundamental fantasy, I may well feel repulsed by the love story that I simultaneously find most compelling.

In one and the same culture, different people's conscious fantasies are likely to overlap to some degree, given that large numbers of people hear the same stories, read the same books, and watch the same shows and movies. Yet our fundamental fantasies remain radically different, even if there is perhaps not an *infinite* variety of fundamental fantasies and thus a specific fundamental fantasy might well be shared by a number of people – consider, for example, the one Freud (1955c) discusses in "A Child Is Being Beaten" – even if not all of them develop it for the same reason or in the same way (see Fink, 2014b, Chapter 13).

Perhaps the experience of love, although colored by all of culture, history, and language – not to mention by psychoanalysis itself – is influenced at least as much by each person's own unconscious. Perhaps love cannot be defined in any universal way but is instead largely dependent on the particularity of each subject who loves. Whereas psychology and psychiatry in recent decades have bent over backwards trying to determine what is "normal" for everyone and to legislate to everyone what is normal and what is abnormal, psychoanalysis (in the best of cases, that is) focuses on what is unique about each person's experience. As Lacan (2015, p. 319) puts it:

> Personally, I have never, in fact, believed I was so strong or clever not to feel my pen shake a little whenever I would broach the topic of what a normal person is. But Ernest Jones wrote a whole article about it. He certainly was not lacking in courage. [. . .] Be that as it may, it is truly only through subterfuge that we can bring into play in psychoanalysis any sort of notion of normalization. It is a theoretical view that considers only part of the picture, like when we talk, for example, about "instinctual maturation," as if that were the only thing involved. In such cases we give ourselves over to the kind of extraordinary vaticinations bordering on moralizing preaching, that are so likely to inspire distrust and make people recoil. To unthinkingly bring in the idea of a normal anything in our praxis – whereas we discover in it precisely to what degree the so-called normal subject is anything but normal – should arouse in us the most radical and the most assured suspicion as to its results. We should first ask ourselves whether we can employ the notion of normal for anything whatsoever connected with our practice.

I would suggest that what applies to our psychoanalytic practice here applies to our "love practice" as well. Often it may seem that we ordinary mortals – but we analysts too – are willing to love only what we consider to be "normal" in our partner, excluding anything "bizarre," "perverse," "weird," or "abnormal," excluding, indeed, all that is specific to our partner's subjectivity. Our partner's present-day experience of things is based on a whole prior life of relations with others, making her flee other people just as she gets close to them, leading him to enslave himself to other people, or inclining her or him to desperately pursue people who are inaccessible. In what might be the best of cases, we are of two minds about what we find out-of-the-ordinary in our partners: we, for example, like our partner's ideals consciously and dislike them unconsciously; we admire our partner's uncommon uprightness but feel uneasy living alongside someone we view as a bit of a boy scout or girl scout; or we consciously think our partner's urges and pleasures weird and abnormal, but secretly they intrigue us and turn us on.

While there may be certain commonalities among many people's experiences of love, such that large numbers of people can relate to an author's depiction of her love affair in a novel, poem, or country-music song, the fact that people see themselves in someone else's love affair does not make it paradigmatic for everyone. It just means that their subjective experience of some of their love affairs (not necessarily all of them) coincides to some degree with that author's depiction of one of hers.

For although an individual's love stories tend to follow a certain pattern – especially those individuals who have not undergone analysis – each love unfolds in its own way because each of our love objects has its own specificity. A love object, encountered in most cases partly if not entirely by chance, may conform to an earlier model (that of a beloved figure in one's past), may initially seem to match it and later prove diametrically opposed to it, or may conform to it in some perhaps superficial respects but not in other more profound ones. A love object initially chosen for its apparent aloofness may turn out to have been merely shy or awkward with strangers and anything but aloof once the partners get to know each other.

In such cases, although our choice of a love object is dictated by a past relationship, love steals over us before we can see through our own misreading (or wishful, projected reading) of the object and may well persist despite the lack of similarity between the beloved and the earlier model. Although our tendency in past relationships may have been to fixate on people who did not return our love, our misreading of our current beloved may be such that we find our love being returned when we least expect it.

Many is the writer or bard whose depiction of one love story differs vastly from his depiction of another. From suffering and torment with one object, love may turn into something quite different with another, because the object may be so different in psychological complexion. Hence the oft-heard regret for the one lover who got away, the one who was unlike all the others, the one whom one ought to have stayed with or won back. Apart from the fact that "the one who got away" may seem to be "the One" precisely because he or she got away, we often feel there was one person who is or truly was "the love of my life" and forever regret that we were unwilling or unable to make it work when we were with that person. We might infer that we cannot so easily see or locate object *a* in certain of our partners as in others, and that a partner in whom we were clearly able to perceive it retains a considerable afterglow!

In the era of arranged marriages, the character and appeal of the potential love object was often rather random, socioeconomic status generally prevailing over good character, looks, temper, charm, and humor in the arrangers' choice of a spouse. Even now (in those countries where arranged marriages are few and far between), there is a certain randomness to our encounters, we stumbling upon people at times simply because we happen to take the same bus at the same time, go to the same school, or work in the same office. We prefer to talk about fate – believing we were destined to meet our partners – but the recent success of the locution "this random guy" or "some random girl" perhaps belies the degree to which we believe our encounters are truly "meant" to be.

Love and Psychoanalysis

In Chapter 3, I cited Lacan's (1975, p. 16) comments about what changes in the analysand's love life owing to analysis:

> Transference is based on love, a feeling that takes on such a new form in analysis that love is subverted by this form. [Transference love] is no less illusory [than the more usual forms of love] but it brings with it a partner who has a chance of responding, which is not the case in the other forms. This brings me back to the question of good fortune [that is, of having the good fortune, the incredible luck of meeting the right person], except that this [good] fortune comes from me in this case and I must furnish it.

The analyst must serve, for a time, as the "right person" so that the analysand can stop merely repeating everything she did with previous partners. Transference love works to disrupt that repetition, making something new possible.

In Seminar XVI, Lacan (2006b, p. 204) asks, "Has anyone ever learned from psychoanalysis how to treat his wife well?" Certainly not directly, through the analyst's instruction, in any case, Lacan suggests. But "one likes to think that, by the end of an analysis, the pathways that stopped a man from holding onto [*tenir*] her the right way [that is, from handling her the way one should handle a woman, something she reproaches him for not doing] have been cleared."[6] In other words, impediments and obstacles have been cleared away without the analyst giving explicit instructions of any kind.

In concluding my discussion of love in this book, which is less a finished reflection than an ongoing one, I would opine that when practitioners mistake themselves for love doctors, taking it as one of their primary concerns to *directly* solve the problems of the analysand's love life through advice and suggestions, they go astray, forgetting that their job is to track and trail the unconscious through thick and thin, and allow themselves to be led around by the nose by it (Lacan, 1973–4). All we can aspire to offer to those who have become mired in their own private Love Canal (a toxic waste site in Niagara Falls that became infamous in the 1970s) is a halt to repetition, and the *potential* to find love and jouissance differently than before.

Notes

Preface

1 See Jekels and Bergler (1949, p. 339), where they write, "All loving is the equivalent of being loved. In the last analysis there is only the wish to be loved"; here, perhaps unbeknownst to themselves, they were following Plato's *Alcibiades*. See also their comment, "Behind the beloved object there is one's own ego – basking in the manic intoxication of being loved" (p. 337).

2 "Is love then a consequence of a feeling of guilt? This opinion may seem peculiar, but we maintain it" (Jekels & Bergler, 1949, p. 337). Lacan (2015) states their conclusion more generally: we love in order to escape feeling guilty; indeed, we hope to be loved by the person who can make us feel guilty! Lacan himself disagrees with their perspective (pp. 337–8).

3 He called it the "full genital" organization, maturity, or object relation.

4 Freud himself wrote of "a capacity for enjoyment and efficiency [or efficacy]" (Freud, 1916–1917/1963, p. 457) and the "capacity for work and enjoyment" (Freud, 1912/1958, p. 119). In other words, at least in his published work, love seems not to have been part of the equation.

5 Freud, 1905/1953b, pp. 150–1.

6 Freud, 1921/1955d, pp. 111–12.

7 "Cupid pierces one's heart with his arrows and brandishes his torches – he wounds whoever he touches"; this has also been rendered as: "To me Love shall yield, though he wound my breast with his bow, and whirl aloft his brandished torch. The more violently Love has pierced and branded me, the better shall I avenge the wound that he has made" (Ovid, *The Art of Love*, I. 21–4). Curiously enough, Cupid was also depicted as blind, he being known as the blind archer, blind child, blind god, blindfolded one, and little blind. His golden arrow was reputed to make you fall in love and his lead arrow to make you fall out of love.

8 Capellanus, 1990, p. 31.

9 The question whether we can or cannot enjoy (*jouir de*) what we love is a profound one, which will only be tangentially broached in this book.

10 Kierkegaard (1847/1995) writes, "It is the same love that loves and hates" (p. 34).

11 Stendhal (2004, p. 180/162) extols the virtues of what he calls the Italian model of love affair in which lovers spend hours together every day, yet knows – and seems to wish to know – nothing of it. The quote from *Pride and Prejudice* can be found in Austen, 2000, p. 17.

12 Aristotle, *Rhetoric*, 1380b35.

13 Lacan, 1980, p. 256.

Introduction

1 This version of the story comes from Freud and Ernest Jones (see Jones, 1953, pp. 222–6) and is repeated by Lacan; but it is contested by Breuer's biographer Albrecht Hirschmüller (1989). Hirschmüller admits, however, that Jones had access to letters that he himself never saw, and his arguments strike me as generally quite weak. The only points he makes that I find convincing are that, whereas Jones claims that the result of the sudden second honeymoon in Venice was the conception of Breuer's youngest daughter, Dora, she was actually born on March 11, 1882, thus three months *before* Anna O.'s treatment ended; and that Dora committed suicide not in New York, as Jones (1953, p. 225) claims, but just before the arrival of the Gestapo in Vienna (Hirschmüller, 1989, pp. 337–8 n. 194). Mario Beira (in a talk given March 29, 2008, at the APW conference held in Philadelphia on the theme of love) suggests that Breuer did not rush off to Venice but, rather, remained in Vienna during all of July of 1882; nevertheless, not much seems to be known about Breuer's whereabouts during the second half of June or the month of August.

The referral to Robert Binswanger (Ludwig's son) is confirmed in Breuer's letters to Robert Binswanger (Hirschmüller, 1989, pp. 293–6). Freud's letter of June 2, 1932, to Stefan Zweig asserts that Breuer told Freud that when Bertha's parents called him urgently back to her sickbed the day he broke off the treatment, he "found her confused and writhing in abdominal cramps. Asked what was wrong with her, she replied: 'Now Dr. B.'s child is coming!'" (Freud, E. L., 1960, letter 265, pp. 412–13). Breuer apparently did not confess to Freud that Bertha was having an hysterical pregnancy (pseudocyesis), but Freud put two and two together; he claims in the same letter that his deduction was confirmed by Breuer at a later date through his youngest daughter.

In what is perhaps the most tendentious take on the case of Anna O. in print, Mikkel Borch-Jacobsen (1996) argues that the entire case is a sham and that Freud made up stories about it, sometimes getting Breuer to do so as well. Borch-Jacobsen argues the following: Pappenheim was not really ill – it was sheer simulation, encouraged by Breuer (he fails to explain why her family would have called in a well-known nerve specialist for "a lingering cough" [p. 81], the only symptom he acknowledges at the outset, apart from her suffocating "family atmosphere" [p. 83]); there were no amorous, much less erotic, feelings between Breuer and Pappenheim (indeed, Borch-Jacobsen seems to think there never are between therapists and patients, making one wonder how he would account for the overwhelming evidence of affairs between them); there was no hysterical pregnancy; Breuer's wife made no suicide attempt; Pappenheim did not remember events from the year before with remarkable accuracy; Pappenheim was in no way helped by her work with Breuer; there is no such thing as the unconscious or transference; the list goes on and on. His evidence is often sketchy, including portions of private letters shown him by the notoriously unreliable historian Elisabeth Roudinesco and indirectly by Jeffrey Masson. He assumes that Breuer would normally have written in his report to Binswanger all the same things – many of which he believed to be crazy at the time – he said when discussing the case at great length with Freud, which any clinician referring a patient to another practitioner would find implausible, to say the least. And complex problems of the will (related to "faking," "simulation," and being dimly aware of what one is doing) are glossed over by him as though all mental illness were a matter of mere Sartrian bad faith!

Even if Borch-Jacobsen's facts were correct – and they would be very difficult to substantiate – his conclusions do not follow, for psychoanalytic concepts like transference and the unconscious, and the benefits of talking do not, in any way, collapse if one particular case was not what it was made out to be.

2 A song by the band Queen.

3 La Rochefoucauld (1967) wrote that *"la plus juste comparaison que l'on puisse faire de l'amour, c'est celle de la fièvre"* (love can best be compared with fever). The expression perhaps goes back to a 1657 play entitled *Amour malade, ballet du Roy*, by Jean Baptiste Lully and Francesco Buti. The term *maladie de l'amour* ("malady of love" or "love as a malady") is found in the *Journal d'un Voyage à Paris en 1657–1658* by Philippe de Villers. But Hélisenne de Crenne, the author of *Torments of Love*, had already depicted love as a "lamentable illness" and a most cruel calamity, in the Renaissance. The French also used the term *maladie de l'amour*, at times, to characterize various sexually transmitted diseases. Shakespeare referred to love as "a madness most discreet" in *Romeo and Juliet*. The Greeks had, however, already compared love to illness: in Longus' (1973) *Daphnis and Chloe*, when Daphnis received his first kiss from Chloe, he felt as if he had been bitten. He became pale, neither ate nor drank, fell silent, was no longer interested in playing his pipes or tending to his flock, "and his face was greener than the grass in summer" as he cried, "Oh strange illness whose name I don't even know" (p. 31).

Chapter I – Freudian Preludes: Love Triangles

1 Freud, 1912/1957b.

2 For examples, see Fink, 1997, Chapter 8; 2014a, Chapters 10 & 11.

3 Freud, 1910/1957a, p. 166.

4 See, for example, Lacan, 2006a, p. 632.

5 Those who go much further in their fascination with the other man – going so far as to wonder "What's he got that I ain't got?" and

constantly comparing himself with this other man in order to learn from him how to be a "real man" – might well be hysterical, not obsessive.

6 See Freud's (1900, pp. 146–51) discussion of the witty butcher's wife, and Lacan's (2006a, pp. 620–7) and my commentaries on it (Fink, 1997, pp. 125–7; 2004, pp. 20–3).

7 Lacan (2006b, p. 386) indicates that, in his view, hysterics are not necessarily women and obsessives are not always men.

8 Lacan, 2006a, p. 626.

9 Naturally, it is often quite enough that the girl perceive some love for the mother on the father's part, not a genuine preference for the mother. And there are fathers and mothers who sleep in separate bedrooms, and some fathers do discuss their wives' "misbehavior" with their daughters.

10 The recent fascination with dangerously thin body types is obviously extremely complex, involving cultural factors like the development and power of the media, who has control over the fashion industry, and the current tendency to repudiate femininity in Western culture, as well as the unconscious desires that fuel the kind of self-deprivation involved in anorexia. The hysterical link is probably but one factor in a much larger equation.

11 "Desire is man's very essence, insofar as it is conceived to be determined, from any given affection of it, to do something" (Spinoza, 1994, p. 188).

12 Plato, *Symposium*, 200a–201c.

13 Of course, Frau K. is also the wife of Herr K., who courts Dora quite assiduously. But it is not clear that Herr K. is of much interest to Dora – he is perhaps primarily of interest to Freud (1905/1953a)!

14 Should a man see in his father the key to "the secret of masculinity," we are likely talking about hysteria rather than obsession. For in obsession, it is not clear that masculinity is a secret – rather it seems to be something everyone knows the components of.

15 When a woman would never have noticed a man had a girlfriend of hers not been interested in him, we may thus be dealing with obsession, not hysteria. But insofar as "desire is the Other's desire," this is hardly conclusive.

Chapter II – Freudian Conundrums: Love Is Incompatible with Desire

1 "Attachment theory," a school of psychoanalysis that began in the late 1950s with John Bowlby (1982), might suggest that anaclisis is involved in all object-choice, not in just some (not just, for example, in a child's love for its primary caretaker or someone like that caretaker later in life). Perhaps virtually all object-choice when one is an adult includes both narcissistic and anaclitic elements.

2 Consider, for example, young children's fascination with urine, feces, and flatulence, which most go on to find disgusting later in life.

3 Freud suggests here that in "normal love" only a few characteristics of the mother as a prototype are found in the object chosen by the man. However, in the "male love" of the type he outlines in this article, the

mother-surrogates are very much like the mother (though perhaps primarily due to their structural situation).

4 Or at least no sexual desire for the mother herself, although there perhaps was for a nursemaid, governess, or babysitter?

5 The situation is obviously complicated when one is raised, for the most part, by governesses and other kinds of childcare helpers.

6 Freud, 1910/1957a, pp. 168–70. This perhaps explains the logic of the colloquialisms: "Scratch a virgin, find a whore" and "Treat a lady like a whore and a whore like a lady."

7 Let me raise a few questions about Freud's formulation here that involve material discussed in Chapter 4: the mother had been imbued with sizable quantities of his libido and then lost a lot; do the "fallen" women he becomes interested in thereafter not have much libido invested in them and need to have it restored? Or is it that after the mother's fall, all of his libido went to the old ideal image of her and the male tries to redirect some of that to himself? If he rescues a woman, does he himself become worthy of love again? He was no longer worthy because of his mother's fall? When she fell he fell?

8 Although the expression "castration complex" can be found in *The Interpretation of Dreams* and the *Three Essays* (as later interpolations), the earliest detailed discussion is found in "On the Sexual Theories of Children" (Freud, 1908/1959a, pp. 216–17) and the first published mention in the case of Little Hans (Freud, 1909/1955f, p. 8, and elsewhere). Nevertheless, the castration complex is not explicitly formulated as putting an end to the Oedipus complex in boys until considerably later in his work.

9 One might almost say, in the most literal translation of Freud's meaning, that the boy either gives up a woman or becomes one.

10 Here is an example of a related but somewhat different scenario: one of my analysands had for many years been married to a woman whom he viewed as strong, domineering, and decisive like his father. He loved her and hated her and almost never made love to her. One day he came home from work to find her under the sink, attempting to repair the plumbing. Seeing her in a position that he took to be hardly dignified and, indeed, degrading, she suddenly shifted out of the position of the phallus for him, which he felt she held in his eyes owing to his own less-than-stellar performance in life, and into the position of the trampy partial object, cause of his desire – a position she had not occupied since the very earliest days of their marriage. He shocked himself by making passionate love to her three times that evening.

11 Which is not to say that there must not usually be one false note in the realizing or playing out of a fantasy in order for it not to become terrifying. As Lacan says in Seminar VIII, "You can easily find the passage [in Jean Genet's work] where he admirably indicates what call-girls know full well, namely that, whatever the fanciful ideas of men may be who are thirsting to have their fantasies fulfilled, one feature is common to all of them: in the enactment, there must be one feature that seems *untrue*, because otherwise, perhaps, were it to become altogether true, they would no longer know which way is up. The subject

would perhaps no longer have any chance of survival" (Lacan, 2015, p. 392).

12 In Lacanian terms, we might say that the obsessive is faced here with a forced choice like "your money or your life" (Lacan, 1973a, pp. 191–3/210–3): your desire or your wife. More accurately stated, the forced choice is between love and desire, where love must always be lost if desire is to be found in an actual relationship with a woman. The more common solution is to choose love in an actual relationship with a woman and desire in virtual or short-lived extramarital relationships.

13 Freud's (1912/1957b) implicit assumption here seems to be that if love and desire fuse, not when one is a child, but later in life (on the post-Oedipal, not pre-Oedipal object), there is no need to repress one of them or leave one of them out of the Eros equation. Qualifying the more usual case, however, Freud says, "where they love they do not desire and where they desire they cannot love" (p. 183). A decade later, Freud (1921/1955d, p. 112) makes it clear that he thinks this fusion often takes place in adolescence, thus well after the resolution of the Oedipus complex; but what then brings about the fusion? Hormones? Socialization? Freud does not tell us.

14 I assume he does not mean that a man must lose all respect for women, although some might disagree with me here; does respect for a woman automatically put her in a class with the mother and sister?

15 As one of my analysands once put it in referring to her father, "I worked hard to shore him up."

16 A young girl's sensual bond with her father is thus often much weaker than a young boy's with his mother, and this may lead to a difference in the importance of the incest taboo between boys and girls.

17 Perhaps more commonly, the mother remains loved, to at least some significant degree (though perhaps also debased?), and the father becomes desired, to at least some significant degree. When we add identification(s) to the picture, things become more complicated still; for if a girl identifies with the good girl she believes her father loves in her mother (mom$_1$, as it were), all sensuality may be excluded and she may only be able to enjoy sex when it is more or less forced upon her, she being required then to take no responsibility for an enjoyment she considers sinful or disgusting. Indeed, she may feel she is sinning against or betraying her mother, father, or both when having sex and require a considerable counterforce for enjoyment to ensue; and even then her enjoyment may be quite mixed or tainted with displeasure.

18 Stendhal's âme-tendre (sensitive soul) wants to be wanted, but the "brute," prosaic man (a foul-mouthed captain sporting a mustache) does not seek to be wanted. He wants tout court: he knows what he wants and goes for it. He is not tortured by the question of whether or not he is loved in return. Stendhal (2004) wonders why such men have more success with women than sensitive souls like himself, asking, "is it due to modesty and the mortal boredom that it must impose upon many women that most women value nothing in a man more than effrontery?" (p. 85/86). Modesty, in his view, enflames tender souls (men's) but women want men who couldn't care less about modesty

and who don't ask permission to kiss them or court them. Further on he adds, "A little rudeness and indifference in one's first contact, if the drug is administered naturally, is almost a sure means by which to get oneself respected by a spirited woman" (p. 144/131).

Ovid perhaps lends some support to Stendhal's viewpoint here when he says, "What she asks you for, she is afraid of receiving; what she does not ask for, she wants: for she actually likes your persistence. Persist and soon all you want will be yours" (*The Art of Loving*, I. 484–5).

19 Is it that the prohibition of incest, for such women, has not been very strong and must be evoked or provoked?

20 Although jouissance is sometimes rendered as "enjoyment," Lacan (1965–6, class given on April 20, 1966) once commented that "enjoyment does not have the same resonances as jouissance and we would, in a sense, have to combine it with the term *lust*, which would be a bit better." Lacan was no specialist in English, but one could argue that "enjoyment" does, indeed, sound cleaner or more aseptic in English than *jouissance* does in French (it is often, I think, better rendered as "getting off").

21 *La Carte du Tendre* is a seventeenth-century map of the tender or amorous sentiments – perhaps a forerunner to Adam Smith's *Theory of Moral Sentiments* – drawn by Madeleine de Scudéry. It purported to trace out all the stages of love, all the stages of development of the tender feelings, as well as all of the obstacles and problems one might encounter along love's path, such as jealousy and despair. It was included in her ten-volume novel *Clélie*, published between 1654 and 1660 (see Scudéry, 2001, p. 179). The map can more readily be found in DeJean, 1991.

22 Cf. Freud's (1933/1964, p. 134) comment: "One forms the impression that the love of man and the love of woman are separated by a psychological phase-difference."

23 This is after the formulation of the second topography. See, especially, Chapter 8 entitled "Being in Love and Hypnosis" (Freud, 1921/1955d, pp. 111–16).

24 Freud (1921/1955d) suggests that "earthly love" is uninhibited in its aim. When sensual aims are prohibited, they become repressed and often give rise to "aim-inhibited drives" (pp. 111–12); he refers to affectionate love (as opposed to "earthly love") as just such an aim-inhibited drive. Freud again indicates here that a synthesis between the two currents (love and desire) normally occurs in adolescence, in other words, not prior to the resolution of the Oedipus complex.

25 Fink, 1997, p. 67. As we shall see in Chapter 7, Stendhal celebrates the severe strictures placed upon sexuality as the very things that make civilized love sublime.

26 Here Freud would seem to agree with Stendhal, although Freud's argument here revolves around sex, whereas Stendhal's revolves around love.

27 Herbert Marcuse (1955) argued that capitalism imposes too much prohibition and far too many limitations, leading to what he called "surplus repression."

Chapter III – Lacan's Reading of Plato's *Symposium*

1 See Lacan, 2006a, pp. 11–61; and Fink, 1995c; 2014c.
2 Much the same might be said of Kierkegaard's "In Vino Veritas" (in *Stages on Life's Way*, 1988) and *Works of Love*; as Kierkegaard (1995, p. 409) himself says, "When I have first presented one aspect clearly and sharply, then the other affirms itself even more strongly." In other words, once he has let one voice speak or let one strand of his thought express itself fully, he can move on to the next. Hence the shifting, dialogical nature of his work; this may be true of most thinkers (and analysands) if we consider the evolution of their work over time.
3 One could argue that love is somehow found, too, in the twists and turns in Marguerite de Navarre's *Heptameron* and in Kierkegaard's "In Vino Veritas."
4 Lacan had perhaps formulated this notion before 1960, as it appears in "Direction of the Treatment" (Lacan, 2006a, p. 618), which was first given as a talk in 1958, but not published until 1961. In Seminar VIII, Lacan points to a specific formulation provided in the *Symposium* by Diotima, when she discusses *dóxa* (often rendered by "true opinion"): ἄνεν τοῦ ἔχειν λόγον δοῦναι (*áneu tou échein lógon doúnai*) [202a]. In this formulation, says Lacan, Diotima "characterizes *dóxa* as giving an answer without having one, echoing the formulation I myself have proposed here that love is giving what you don't have" (Lacan, 2015, p. 129). See, also, Socrates' question to Alcibiades in *Alcibiades I* (possibly penned by Plato, although its authorship is debated): "Could one give something one does not have?" (Plato, 2003, 134c). On "unprovoked denials," see Fink, 2007, pp. 41–2.
5 According to Lacan, Diotima introduces the notion that desire is essentially a kind of metonymic slippage from one object to another. This comes up in her discussion of love for beauty. As we shall see in Chapter 8, Diotima talks about beauty as what helps man get over the difficult hurdles that lie in his path on the way to eternity. Beauty, to her, is a transition, a point of passage – it is a *guide toward the immortal*. Then there is a transition point in Diotima's discourse, whereby beauty stops being a medium.

Her Don Juanesque perspective involves a sort of infinite passage beyond any one single object – it moves from generation to love of a handsome young man, to love of all young people, to the essence of beauty, and then on to eternal beauty. *Each object gives way to the next in a metonymic slippage which itself finally seems to be the real aim. Lacan calls this the metonymic function in desire. In this sense, desire has no object.*

As a partner in love, each of us wants to be the object to end all objects, the object that puts an end to the other's endless metonymic slippage that seems to be desire's real aim (Lacan at first calls this wanting to be the phallus for the other, later wanting to be the object that causes the other's desire). For desire, as such, seems to have no object, wanting only to go on desiring. Love, however, does have an object.

Fixation on object *a* as the elective cause of desire (Lacan, 2015, p. 170) can put a stop to the potentially infinite metonymic slippage of objects. This object is overvalued and we may fade in relation to it ($\$0a$), but it saves "our dignity as subjects" (p. 171). Believing he had found such an object, one of my analysands once said, "This is a woman for whom I could abandon all other women."

6 Certain hysterics manage to show their lack to almost everyone they meet, and one might argue that this is what analysts do, too.

7 *Il "se suffit de sa jouissance"* (Lacan, 1973–4, class given on February 21, 1974).

8 As we shall see, love requires not only an admission of lack, but also the raising up of the beloved to the status of an object (i.e., object *a*) that puts an end to the exchangeability of partners, an end to the metonymic slippage from one to the next. Here object *a*, the object that quintessentially causes one's desire, becomes associated with one single partner.

9 As we shall see in Chapter 8, Kierkegaard would characterize this as the wrong kind of love – that is, as essentially selfish (or "erotic") love as opposed to Christian love.

10 Lacan suggests that male homosexual relations in ancient Greece emphasized love, noting that Aristotle, in the *Prior Analytics* (68a–b), remarks that a man prefers a situation (or at least should?) in which his beloved loves him in return, even if he does not grant him sexual favors, to a situation in which his beloved grants him sexual favors but does not love him in return. In other words, it is possible that Greek homosexuality placed greater emphasis on being loved than on sex. Greek homosexuality might, in that sense, be said to be feminized, in contrast to certain forms of male homosexuality that we see around us today, in which certain male homosexuals accumulate sexual conquests just like male heterosexuals sometimes do.

11 This is perhaps why Lacan (2015, p. 32) qualifies the feminine as the *active* party or principle in relationships in Seminar VIII. One might wonder, however, whether showing and declaring one's lack is more specifically feminine or hysterical. Note that the French *amour* (love) was sometimes a *feminine* noun in earlier centuries, especially in the plural.

12 Nor is it based on anatomy.

13 Freud would have read this completely differently, for in his view it is men who love and women who simply want to be loved. Men like Freud perhaps focus far less on women's expressions of love than on the implicit demand to be loved in return that such expressions bring with them.

14 The song "Show Me," including the lyrics "Don't talk of love . . . show me," sung by Eliza Dolittle in *My Fair Lady*, was not surprisingly written by a man, in this case, by Alan Jay Lerner. The more typical male attitude is expressed in Marvel's "To His Coy Mistress."

15 Note that Lacan occasionally says still more concrete things about it: for example, that André Gide gave his wife Madeleine what he did not have when he gave her immortality through his writing (Lacan, 2006a, pp. 754–5). I would propose that psychology be distinguished from psychoanalysis as follows: whereas the psychologist gives what he (like most everybody else) has – namely, advice (and it may be useless or useful, but it is still advice), the analyst gives what he doesn't have.

It should be noted that although Žižek and many others cite Lacan as adding, after "love is giving what you don't have," "to someone who doesn't want it," it is clear in the original transcripts of Seminar VIII that this cynical addendum was made by someone in the audience, not by Lacan, and that it was not endorsed by Lacan. Lacan did, however, take it up once in his own name in Seminar XII (class given on March 17, 1965) in the limited context of Socrates and Alcibiades. The original formulation can be found in numerous Seminars (IV, V, VI, VIII, X, XII, XIII, XVII, XVIII, XXII, etc.), whereas the longer version appears only once, to the best of my knowledge.

16 The appearance of the phallus also leads to comedy, according to Lacan, and perhaps this plays a role here as well. Soler (2003) suggests that love is a comical feeling insofar as a man begins to believe everything his wife says – not simply that it says something about her but that it is also true for him: he believes her like the psychotic believes what his voices say. He is constantly saying, "My wife says that . . ."

17 See also Lacan, 2015, pp. 68–9. Lacan suggests that, of all the stories in Antiquity about men killing their fathers and sleeping with their mothers (and they are plentiful), Freud picked the story of Oedipus because of Oedipus' ignorance: *he did not know* he had killed his father and was sleeping with his mother (pp. 99–100).

18 Socrates, too, raises this question, but not in the context of love, in the *Alcibiades I*, in Plato, 2003, 128e–130c; his answer is, naturally, that it is the soul (*psuche*).

19 As Lacan (1974–5, class given on February 18, 1975) says, "I define the symptom as the way in which each person gets off on the unconscious."

20 This perhaps suggests that love at the time was rather different than in our times, or that what such men felt was more akin to what we would call desire than to love. But see Aristotle's *Prior Analytics* (68a–b).

21 Putting the signifiers beloved and lover in the formula for metaphor that Lacan (2006a, p. 515) provides in "Instance of the Letter," we see that the additional meaning generated by the metaphor (lowercase *s*) is love.

$$f\left(\frac{\text{Beloved}}{\text{Lover}}\right) \text{Lover} = \text{Lover} (+) \text{ love}$$

In such cases, there is a reversal, whereby the man who Socrates seems to have adopted as his beloved takes the place of Socrates the lover – that is, he puts himself where the lover was before.

22 Might these correspond to Joni Mitchell's "both sides" in "Both Sides Now"?

23 For example, Socrates is supposed to give an encomium, not of Eros but of Agathon, a speech singing the praises of Agathon, at the end of the *Symposium*. He is interrupted before he is able to do so, a fact that is perhaps quite telling – Socrates' love is perhaps a pure love with no unique beloved; see 222e and 223a–b.

24 Lacan (1998a, p. 16) says that "love is the sign that one is changing discourses."

25 It is not clear to me, however, which, if any, of Lacan's four discourses we could situate the beloved in before and after the metaphor of love occurs.

26 Rather he provides an image which could almost be associated with the graph found under the formulas of sexuation in Seminar XX, in which an arrow from the masculine side goes toward object *a* on the feminine side and an arrow from the feminine side goes toward the phallus on the masculine side, each reaching, as it were, for something different in the other person (Lacan, 1998a, p. 78).

27 Lacan's image here is perhaps not unrelated to one Ovid provides, with which Lacan was undoubtedly familiar: "Now having seen Narcissus, she [Echo] was struck by his beauty, enamored, followed along behind him, going from bush to bush, eager for yet a closer look at this marvelous creature. The closer she came, the more ardently she burned, as a torch with its coating of sulfur will burst into flames from another torch that is held nearby" (*Metamorphoses*, III. 372–8).

28 Lacan seems to have had an appreciation for this aspect of love that Freud did not have. For here there is no zero-sum game of libido (see Chapter 4); rather, object-libido and ego-libido increase hand in hand, leading to a greater "constant," a greater quantum of energy, than there was at the outset. But, then again, perhaps there is simply an increase in object libido on both sides here . . .

29 See Lacan, 1988, p. 32; this can also be found in Lacan, 1973–4 (classes given on November 13, 1973, and June 11, 1974). Lacan (1988, pp. 32–3) first formulates this regarding anger that arises in the analytic setting, it being one party's anger that can elicit the other's (see Fink, 2007, pp. 152–3).

30 The Greek gods did not seem to worry whether they were loved or not: they did not enter into that scale of comparison (the God of the Old Testament seemingly did, however, stating "I am a jealous God"). If one enters into the scale of comparison, there is always the possibility that there might be another object that is more worthy of love than oneself. Where one enters into the scale of comparison, all love objects are fungible, since one object can always be left behind or exchanged for a "better" or "superior" one; there is no possibility here of being someone's "one and only," one's "sole and unique"; our worry is that everyone will naturally love he or she who is most worthy.

31 The analyst's love must not burst into flames, but smolder instead, like a wet log thrown on a fire (see Allouch, 2009).

32 We are people who, owing to our training, should fully realize that we do *not* possess the knowledge of what makes the analysand tick. We know we are lacking in knowledge. The analysand, however, often begins by believing he knows a great deal – about himself, about his motives and reasons for doing things that he has done, major decisions he has made, career choices, choices of partners, and so on. Like Socrates, we try to lead the analysand from a position of believing in his own fullness of knowledge to believing in his own lack of knowledge. In this sense, there is a reversal of the usual communicating vases image, which is mentioned when Socrates sits next to Agathon at the symposium, Socrates suggesting that Agathon's knowledge will flow into Socrates who does not possess knowledge. In the analytic

situation, it is not a fullness of knowledge but rather a lack of knowledge that flows from the one (analyst) into the other (analysand); this is one way in which we give what we don't have. Using a kind of Socratic elenchus (or refutational approach), we get the analysand to call into question his purported knowledge of himself and others, just as we have called into question our own.

33 "The psychoanalytic object is the something that is the aim of desire as such, the something that emphasizes one object among all the others as incommensurate with the others" (Lacan, 2015, p.146). An early version of object *a* (as *ágalma*) is found in what Lacan calls the "Thing" in Seminar VII (Lacan, 1992). For a detailed discussion of object *a*, see Fink, 1995a, Chapter 7.

34 He also says that Socrates is "bursting with figures of virtue inside" (222a); and that Socrates is like a statue of Silenus, the satyr, that is "full of tiny statues of the gods" (215b). Reeve (2006) provides a striking alternate translation in his essay, "Plato on Love," that precedes the translation of the *Symposium* that I have relied on here: "I don't know whether anyone else has seen the figures within *(ta entos agálmata)* when he is serious and opened up, but I saw them once, and I thought that they were so divine and golden, so marvelously beautiful, that I just had to do whatever Socrates told me" (p. xxv).

35 This is Lacan's paraphrase of what Freud says in his "Autobiographical Study" (1925/1959b, p.27) about the time a woman threw her arms around his neck and kissed him upon awakening from hypnosis: "I was modest enough not to attribute the event to my own irresistible personal attraction." See also Freud, 1916–1917/1963, p.450.

36 Analysts, insofar as they encourage analysands to delve into their desires, which often run counter to societal norms and standards, are relegated, like Socrates, to a kind of *atopos*, nowhere, having no established place within society.

37 In friendships, we often do crave questions, hoping our friends will express as much interest in knowing about us as we express in them.

Chapter IV – Freudian Preludes: Narcissism

1 See John Keats, "My love is selfish – I cannot breathe without you" (letter to Fanny Brawne, October 13, 1819; available at: <http://englishhistory.net/keats/letters/love-letter-to-fanny-brawne-13-october-1819/>).

2 A rather different perspective is expressed by Shakespeare's Juliet when she says, "My bounty is as boundless as the sea,/ My love as deep; the more I give to thee,/ The more I have, for both are infinite"; and by Lacan's "miracle of love."

3 Freud implicitly agrees with Cicero (1971, p. 80) here, who says, "Every man is by his very nature dear to himself"; and with Saint Bernard of Clairvaux (1995, p.25), who says that "Love is not imposed by a precept; it is planted in nature. Who is there who hates his own flesh?" But as any analyst knows, there are plenty of people who hate their own flesh, and who cut it and subject it to all kinds of ill-treatment.

4 Freud presumably associates secondary narcissism with schizophrenia

because he hypothesizes that schizophrenics have suffered a severe, irreparable early object loss, making genuine cathexis of any other object impossible and making relating to others unfeasible and/or uninteresting to them. Secondary narcissism is more commonly associated with ordinary physical illness which makes one decathect or divest from those around one and focus all of one's attention upon oneself, as does a person with a toothache, Freud (1914/1957c, p. 82) tells us; although we can say of the latter that he becomes self-absorbed, I do not think that we can say that he has, like the schizophrenic, suffered a severe, irreparable loss.

5 More complex configurations may exist in the case of homosexual object-choice, for the object chosen resembles oneself and may also resemble an early caretaker.

6 This would seem to be the obsessive's unwitting goal. He loves them because he can rest assured that they will not love him back. He cannot then be overwhelmed by their love, something the obsessive is often likely to be. Since women are defined by Freud as wrapped up in themselves, they can be loved safely by obsessives (anaclitically). Yet the basis for anaclitic love is object-choice based on a past loving figure. This leads to a paradox: the man who makes an anaclitic choice essentially selects a woman based on her similarity to his mother, but with the important difference that this woman cannot love him, for she simply wants to be loved. The contradiction is that she will not give him the real satisfactions that were, as we shall see, presumably at the basis of his object-choice.

7 We could also speculate about what phobic, perverse, and psychotic theories of love might look like.

Chapter V – Lacan's Imaginary Register

1 Lorenz's contributions to the study of animal behavior were immense, he having been among the first to emphasize the importance of the direct observation of animal behavior under natural conditions. One of Lorenz's earliest contributions was the concept of *angeborener Auslösemechanismus* (the "innate releasing mechanism" or IRM). Already in 1935, Lorenz had coined the term *Prägung*, or "imprinting," to denote the rapid process of learning during the sensitive period in early development (although certain authors claim that Oscar Heinroth was first to use the term). Lacan was familiar with Lorenz's work on animal behavior – aggressive and other – and with developmental approaches that compare animals and humans; he had perhaps read Lorenz's 1949 book, *Er redete mit dem Vieh, den Vögeln und den Fischen* (Vienna: Borotha-Schoeler), which was published in English in 1952 as *King Solomon's Ring*, and *On Aggression*, published in German in 1963 and in English in 1966, and regularly uses the term *Prägung*.

2 In the realm of human behavior we refer to this kind of display as "posturing"; it includes bearing or display behaviors like strutting and posing.

3 Note that, to the best of our knowledge, these postures are never used

to *dupe* the adversary: a dog never adopts a submissive posture to lure another dog into being off guard, only to attack it a moment later. In other words, these postures are not signifiers but, rather, signs with a generally clear and unambiguous meaning to other dogs.

4 In short, they argue that Darwin was wrong in thinking that the bared-teeth grin of a Sulawesi macaque is an expression of being pleased, something that Darwin (1899) argued in his study on the emotions. They claim that it is, instead, an expression of fear or a message to a potential aggressor that one accepts the other's dominant position and has no intention to resist.

5 Certain therapists seem to take this as a rule of thumb in their interpretative strategy with patients, as do certain politicians in their foreign policy; they can be understood to be trapped in the imaginary dimension, in this respect, not situating their work at the symbolic level.

   Regarding nonrecognition of qualitative difference in the animal kingdom, note that a lion in the wild will not "interpret" a child's gesture to pet its face as fundamentally nonaggressive. If it resembles an act of aggression coming from a non-lion species, it will be "read" that way in all cases. Even lion tamers who have worked with their lions for years have to be very careful not to get too close to them; if they inadvertently get into a lion's attack range, based on its fight-or-flight instinct (when an enemy is far enough away, a lion will run, when the enemy has snuck up too close, it will attack; Lorenz, 1966), they may well find themselves in mortal danger. The lion does not shift attitudes and come to regard the lion tamer as fundamentally a friend who should be allowed all things. All individuals encountered are viewed as ultimately the same: *sameness here means that every individual encountered is sized up in the same way* – that is, in terms of dominance and submission.

6 Note, however, that ethologist Sarah Brosnan believes she has found indications of "an instinctual sense of fair play" in the capuchin monkeys she studies at Yerkes National Primate Research Institute in Atlanta, Georgia; she suggests that "it traces to the kind of emotional sense of fairness that may promote the high level of cooperation needed in species that hunt or otherwise work closely together" (cited in Sachs, 2005, p. 37). African hunting dogs *do* hunt together later in life; whether they show signs of fair play at that stage, I cannot say . . .

7 See, for example, Hartmann, Kris, & Loewenstein (1946) and my commentary on it (Fink, 2004, pp. 40–2).

8 Freud (1921/1955d, p. 105) refers to an extremely early identification between a boy and his father.

9 If the ego is alienating, that seems to be because it misrecognizes, misunderstands, or simply *misses* the subject. The ego is a kind of mask or face presented to the world: a social self, a socially presentable self. It even takes on the features of a kind of character armor, as Wilhelm Reich (1933/1972, p. 97) called it, an alienating identity.

   The fiction known as the ego is thus alienating, insofar as the ideal ego, which forms during the mirror stage, is at its core. Lacan (1988, p. 16) goes so far as to say that the ego is "the mental illness of man": it is a problematic but necessary fiction. (It is a double-edged sword – it leads to stasis and resistance, but without it there is psychosis.)

Now, if the ego as an agency is essentially fictional in structure – it is based on a fiction, something which is essentially *not true* or not representative of the child in question – whatever the "subject" is, it seems "truer to life" than the ego is. This "subject" is a sort of black box or *x*. Lacan's choice of the term "fictional" to describe the ego immediately implies its opposite: the ego is a fiction while the subject is real or true. (Analogously, in Hinduism the ego is considered to be an illusion, whereas Atman is considered to be the soul or true essence.)

10 Lacan views this "ideal ego" as the "psychotic core" found in all of us, it being psychotic insofar as it involves a delusion of perfection and power that has yet to be achieved. It is, moreover, extremely sensitive to any perceived attempt to cut it down to size, to suggest that it is not as perfect as all that. Such attempts may well bring on paranoid reactions.

11 See Fink, 1995b.

12 Sibling rivalry can exist in families to varied degrees, of course, and can operate at both imaginary and symbolic levels. In families where the rivalry is primarily for symbolic recognition from the parents, each child somehow feeling that the other is loved, appreciated, or respected more by a parent, relations between siblings often improve markedly very shortly after they move away from the parental home; where the rivalry is primarily imaginary, it tends to remain forever intact.

13 The term *semblable* is often translated as "fellow man" or "counterpart," but in Lacan's usage it refers specifically to the mirroring of two imaginary others (*a* and *a'*) who *resemble* each other (or at least see themselves in each other). "Fellow man" corresponds well to the French *prochain*, points to man (not woman), the adult (not the child), and suggests fellowship, whereas in Lacan's work *semblable* evokes rivalry and jealousy first and foremost. "Counterpart" suggests parallel hierarchical structures within which the two people take on similar roles, that is, symbolic roles. "Semblable" was formerly used in English, for example, in *Hamlet*, V.ii: "his semblable is his mirror; and who else would trace him, his umbrage, nothing more."

14 One might wonder whether the fact of having older siblings of the opposite sex from oneself – to whom one is compared by one's parents and with whom one compares oneself, using their image as a foundation of one's own – inclines one to have more of what are often referred to as "gender confusion" or "gender identity" issues in the course of one's life.

15 The film – made by Arnold Lucius Gesell (1880–1961), a man who apparently knew nothing of Lacan's mirror stage – was entitled *La découverte de soi devant le miroir* (*The Discovery of Oneself in Front of the Mirror*); it was shown by Lacan on May 19, 1953, when he gave a talk entitled "The Mirror Stage in Action," and discussed in Seminar I (Lacan, 1988, p. 168).

16 Freud (1921/1955d) uses the term to talk about what allows numerous different individuals to identify with a leader (a trait like Hitler's toothbrush mustache, for example).

17 Projection in general is imaginary, whereas introjection in general is symbolic (Lacan, 1998b, p. 402).

18 Lacan associates ratification of the mirror image with what Freud calls the ego-ideal (*Ichideal*): assuming that a child has been sufficiently

invited into its parents' world, a child usually internalizes its parents' ideals and judges itself in accordance with those ideals. The child is slowly induced by its parents, in most cases, to give up certain satisfactions in life in exchange for recognition, approval, esteem, and love which is fundamentally conditional, not unconditional. It is the child's interest in such recognition, in such ratification of its being, that leads the mirror image to be assumed in an important way.

A child whose parents have not sufficiently invited their child into their world may not be terribly interested in recognition or ratification of its being by those parents and the mirror image may not be assumed in the same way. At one point, Lacan even proffers that the psychotic is someone who has given up looking for recognition from the Other, which is why analytic work with psychotics is so different from such work with neurotics. When there is an adequate invitation, we come to rely on the Other to see ourselves: our self-image can only form as mirrored back to us by the Other, as mediated.

As mentioned earlier, the nod of recognition is dubbed the "unary trait" (or S_1) by Lacan (corresponding to the *einziger Zug* in Freud's work), and is considered to be the point of origin of the ego-ideal and of the symbolic. It does not suffice to completely instate the symbolic, but the outline or first step is there. When the symbolic is fully instated (after the operation of the Name-of-the-Father), a whole new order is instated: a reorganization (or first organization) takes place in the early chaos of perceptions and sensations, feelings and impressions. The imaginary register – that of visual images, auditory, olfactory, and other sense perceptions of all kinds, and fantasy – is restructured, rewritten, or we might say "overwritten" by the symbolic, by the words and expressions the parents use to express their view of their child. As Lacan (1993, p. 9) puts it, "While images also play an important role in our field, that role is entirely reworked, recast, and reanimated by the symbolic order." A new symbolic or linguistic order comes into being which supersedes the former imaginary order, which is why Lacan talks about the dominance and determinant nature of language in human existence.

The overwriting of the imaginary by the symbolic – which is the "ordinary neurotic" path – leads to the suppression or at least subordination of imaginary relations characterized by rivalry and aggression to symbolic relations dominated by concerns with ideals, authority figures, the law, performance, achievement, and guilt. The assimilation of the ego-ideal solidifies and firms up the boundaries of the ideal ego – the confusion of self and other seen in transitivism no longer occurs and the child must now begin the long and more difficult process of attempting to mentally put himself in someone else's shoes, to empathize, instead of being the other in a more direct way.

In psychosis, on the other hand, *this rewriting does not occur*. We can, at the theoretical level, say that this is due to the unsuccessful establishment of the ego-ideal, the non-functioning of the paternal metaphor, the non-initiation of the castration complex, and a variety of other things. The point here is that the imaginary continues to predominate in psychosis, and that the symbolic, to the extent to which it is assimilated, is "imaginarized": it is assimilated, *not* as a radically different order which restructures the first, but simply by imitating other people. The essential structure of language is not assimilated, only its forms. (Another way of saying this might be that language never becomes symbolic in psychosis; it remains real, as is true for the schizophrenic.)

19 For a different sort of gloss on the ideal ego, see Lacan, 2015, pp. 339–40.

20 Freud (1922/1955b) also describes here another way in which homosexual object-choice may come about: he mentions a boy who is fixated on his mother and who, a few years after puberty, comes to identify with her and takes as his love object a boy around his age at the time the identification occurred. For many years thereafter, perhaps, it is boys of that age that attract him. (In one case of my own, a homosexual male was particularly attracted for some 20 years to boys between around 15 and 17 years old, his moral scruple being that they were minors, under age.) Freud qualifies this as a solution to the Oedipus complex which involves remaining true to his mother while retiring in favor of his father by not competing with him for his mother's love (pp. 230–1); this is similar to the explanation he provides in a reversed form regarding the famous case of the "young homosexual woman" (Freud, 1920/1955e).

21 Note that there is a gain in ego-libido here: object-libido attached to the mother returns to the subject who falls in love with someone like himself.

22 He adds, "The future victim [a famous actress of the time] is not her only persecutor. Just as certain characters in primitive myths turn out to be doublets of a heroic type, other persecutors appear behind the actress, and we shall see that she herself is not the final prototype. We find Sarah Bernhardt, who is criticized in Aimée's writings, and Mrs. C., a novelist whom Aimée wanted to accuse in a communist newspaper. We thus see the value, which is more representative than personal, of the persecutor that the patient recognized for herself" (p. 164).

23 C. de la N. seems to be a play on words, insofar as it sounds just like c'est de la haine (it is hatred). Lacan goes on to say, regarding Miss C. de la N., that "the person thus designated was both her dearest friend and the dominating woman she envied; she thus appears as a substitute for Aimée's sister" (p. 233).

24 Lacan even goes so far as to use the expression "internal enemy" (p. 237), at one point, to designate the person she attacked (although the context is slightly different).

25 Lacan (1932/1980) also suggests that "narcissistic fixation and homosexual drive thus stemmed in this case from points of libidinal evolution that were very close to each other" (p. 264). Whereas Freud took paranoia to result from "repressed homosexuality" (p. 301) or a "defense against homosexuality," Lacan seems to see it here as related to passion tied to the image of someone who closely resembles oneself.

26 He mentions something quite similar in Lacan, 1938/1984, p. 49.

27 In this sense, Aimée strikes out at the person who is her own ideal – not her ego-ideal (she does not put her sister in the place of her ego-ideal the way a soldier might with his general), but her ideal ego. Her sister does not seem to be adopted as a symbolic ideal but is rather a concrete image of perfection that she herself has been unable to attain. See

Darian Leader's in-depth discussion of the case of Aimée in Chapter 9 of his fine book entitled *What Is Madness?* (London: Penguin, 2011).

28 He also refers to it as the "fraternal complex" in his thesis (Lacan, 1932/1980, p. 261) and in "Family Complexes" (1938/1984, p. 47).

29 Weaning presumably puts an end to the initial "mother–child unity" more often in situations where weaning occurs by age one or so, than in cases where breastfeeding goes on to age five, as it does in certain non-Western cultures and in certain instances within Western culture. Note that the mirror stage occurs between the ages of six and 18 months, which is precisely when most breastfed children are weaned in the West. This would seem to imply that the mirror stage supervenes in order to provide a sense of unity that was lost owing to weaning. Our prematurity at birth and weaning are thus the two major sources of fragmentation (or lack of unity) in humans that are overcome in the mirror stage through the internalization of the parent's nod (S_1).

30 In this sense the term "identification" is once again a misnomer, since identification involves establishing that two different objects are identical; here one can hardly say that there are two different objects involved that at some later point become equated.

31 As I put it elsewhere (Fink, 1997, p. 249 n. 40), if we think of the self (or ego) as like a balloon – borrowing an image from Corday (1993) – the ego-ideal is the thread or string that ties the balloon shut and keeps it from deflating.

32 In "Family Complexes," Lacan (1938/1984) lists three stages or complexes: the weaning complex, the intrusion complex, and the Oedipus complex.

33 Lacan's 1957 formulation might be seen as foreshadowing his later notion of woman as Other to herself (Lacan, 1998a, pp. 81–9); see Chapter 6.

34 Cf. Lacan, 2015, pp. 204–6.

35 The expression comes from a play entitled *The Mourning Bride* (1697) by William Congreve. The complete quote is "Heaven has no rage like love to hatred turned / Nor hell a fury like a woman scorned."

36 The more they feel castrated by her, the more she seems to embody the ideal ego – or is it the phallus? – for them. They perhaps partner with her partnering with their castration . . .

37 See Stéphane Mallarmé (1994, p. 40), where the French "*De la langueur goûtée à ce mal d'être deux*" has been translated as "Bruised in the languor of duality."

38 Curiously enough, the well-known expression "decided desire," is used by Lacan (1974, p. 67) to talk about someone's desire to enter analysis, not the desire he or she has upon finishing analysis; it has since been used by Lacanians to refer almost exclusively to the latter, not the former.

39 Consider the refrain from the song "I'd Wait A Million Years" by The Grass Roots, and the refrain from "Ain't No Mountain High Enough" by Diana Ross.

40 See the L Schema (Lacan, 2006a, p. 53). One question to raise in this regard is whether the narcissistic passion that seems quite clearly involved in all forms of "falling in love," even among neurotics, is at least in part based on the ideal ego. Although an important part of the

narcissistic passion involved in falling in love seems based on the ego-ideal, as we saw earlier in our discussion of Freud's work, perhaps some of the intensity of the experience derives from other sources as well. We do not necessarily find only our ego-ideal in the other but perhaps something involving our ideal ego as well.

41 On alienation and separation, see Fink, 1997, Chapters 7–9.

42 Note, however, that the title of a recent psychoanalytic book by Eric Brenman (2006), *Recovery of the Lost Good Object*, makes it sound as though such a thing is possible.

Chapter VI – Love and the Real

1 He adds, "The Greeks perceived the experience of erotic desire as the onset of a pathological disease" (p. 43), and suggests that there was a "popular belief that erotic seizure is caused by the attack of a 'small, young god who holds burning torches'" (p. 45). "Literary and iconographic evidence corroborate the impression that Eros [a.k.a. Cupid] began his career as a frighteningly demonic figure. Indeed, his standard weapons – the whip, the torch, and the bow and arrow – all connote violence or torture" (pp. 45–6).

2 The sixteenth-century novelist Hélisenne de Crenne (1996, p. 10) seems clearly to have had firsthand experience of love at first sight.

3 Freud (1905/1953b, p. 229 n. 1) refers here to "the compulsive character of the process of falling in love."

4 He said this in reference to a language in which one might say, *j'aime à vous*, instead of *je vous aime*.

5 Did he then do to Regina what he felt his mother had done to him – preferring another (his father or brother?) to him – by betraying her trust and destroying the relationship? His fascination with repetition might suggest this. A major section of his book *Stages on Life's Way* is entitled "Guilty?"/"Not Guilty?"; was he wondering if he was guilty or not guilty for what he (repeating his mother's action) had done? Could it have been less his father's blasphemy (when his father was quite young he cursed God for the lack of success of his family's shepherding business and that blasphemy was supposedly felt by Kierkegaard to have left a curse on the entire family, leading to the death of all of his other siblings at very young ages, except one brother, and of his mother at a young age as well) than his mother's typically Oedipal "betrayal" that plagued him so?

6 The author of this statement that Lacan attributes to a poet has, to the best of my knowledge, never actually been determined, although some propose Galen of Pergamon.

7 It is this Other jouissance that may be related to what both male and female mystics (whom Lacan would characterize as having "feminine structure") refer to as a kind of ecstatic experience of love of God. Lacan (1998a) himself refers to Saint John of the Cross and Hadewijch d'Anvers (p. 76).

8 See Lacan, 1998a, pp. 81–9.

9 And since he had been referring to anxiety as the medium of or intermediary between desire and jouissance shortly before that in the same

seminar, perhaps he is suggesting there that where anxiety was, love must come to be.

10 This Other cannot be put to the work of the One, that is, of economic efficiency, whether in the form of capitalism or communism.

Chapter VII – Languages and Cultures of Love

1 Words like "cool" and "awesome" may suffice, early in one's life, to cover what it will later take 20 different words to say.

2 Faraone (1999) discusses the gradual change in Greek usage from preference of the verb *philein/philia* for affectionate love at the time of Antiphon and Aristotle to preference for the verb *agapan/agapasthai* (p. 117 n), based on *agape*.

3 Using terms discussed further on, I would be inclined to propose that whereas animals share with humans two forms of love, they do not share two others. They share the (1) attachment and dependency sort of love (for the being that gives warmth, affection, and nourishment), and (2) lust or physical/carnal sort of love, but they do not share (3) Eros as we find it in the intensity and excitement of being in love, or (4) agape (or "Christian love") as love for one's neighbor, for another being who is fundamentally different from oneself. This is not to say that all humans (if, indeed, any) are truly capable of this fourth sort.

4 In ancient Greece, there was a strong emphasis on like-mindedness (*homonoia*) and friendship (*philia*) between marital partners. According to Faraone (1999, p. 118 n. 75), Xenophon says "that adultery destroys the *philia* between a husband and wife – he makes no mention of *eros* or jealousy; and Aristotle (*Ethics*, 1161a and 1162a15) describes marriage as a partnership based on *philia*."

5 This story is recounted in Decaux (1998, pp. 13–15). The king's daughter was known as Gyptis, according to Justin, and as Petta, according to Aristotle.

6 Tolstoy's comment that "Happy families are all alike; every unhappy family is unhappy in its own way" (Leo Tolstoy, *Anna Karenina*, first line) is perhaps germane here. Note that Jane Austen occasionally devotes a page to descriptions of marital felicity – she, for example, describes the daily togetherness and happiness of Admiral Croft and his wife in *Persuasion* (Austen, 2003, pp. 158–9).

7 Other examples include partners on the police force, where the goal seems to be to show that their bond is stronger than other allurements (money, drugs, or sex).

8 *Philia* seems to have become associated in Catholic theology with the idea of brotherly love, Christian love, altruism, and, as Saint Thomas Aquinas puts it, dilection (pious love).

9 Under the guise of the Good, parents generally treat their children: (1) the way they themselves were treated; (2) the way they wish they had been treated; (3) the way they have come to think children ought to be treated; (4) some oscillation among these; or (5) some combination of these.

10 Some might quibble and say that Lacanians thus believe that helping analysands love is for their own good; Lacanians might retort that they

strive to promote analysands' ability to love, whether it is for their own good or not, taking that as an end in itself, not as a means to any other end.

11 Note that Shakespeare's Juliet implores Romeo not to swear about his love for her.

12 Freud (1930/1961a, p. 110) says he would *not* take exception to a commandment like "Love thy neighbor as thy neighbor loves thee," a commandment that smacks strongly of the imaginary and would hardly be useful to analysts in their work with patients!

13 See Lowrie, 1970, p. 212.

14 Erotic love or passion is inherently jealous, to him: "Passion always has this unconditional characteristic – that it excludes the third – that is, the third means confusion" (p. 50).

15 Aware of the narcissism involved in the choice of a partner, Kierkegaard (1995, p. 56) writes, "the similarity by which [the lover and beloved] are different from other people" is used as a basis for love.

16 Much the same might be said for healthcare workers of all ilks, and even educators. Lacan, nevertheless, allows that analysis is not for everyone, in particular not for those he refers to as *la canaille*, which might be understood as referring to scoundrels or bastards (Hitler comes to mind).

17 As Balmary (2005, p. 171) puts it, the analyst "*se refuse à jouir de son patient*" (the analyst "refuses to get off on his patient"). Some analysands believe their analysts to be as rich as Croesus, imagining that they only take the trouble to analyze people out of love, to support the psychoanalytic "cause," or to advance analytic theory and practice.

18 See Lacan's comment that the analyst may occasionally hear "the subject pronounce before him the very words in which he [the analyst] recognizes the law of his own being" (Lacan, 2006a, p. 359).

19 Later Lacan perhaps qualified this still further with his claim that "*il y a du psychanalyste*," implying that we find in certain people what it takes to be an analyst, but it is never present even in them 100 percent of the time.

20 "Chemical communication" can supposedly explain the tendency of the menstrual cycles of female roommates to synchronize or the attraction of women to the scents of T-shirts worn by men whose immune systems are supposedly genetically compatible with theirs. Human pheromones are thought by some to include androstenol, a chemical component of male sweat that may heighten sexual arousal in women, and female vaginal hormones called copulins that some researchers believe raise testosterone levels and increase sexual appetite in men (see Tierney, 2011).

21 Certain of my patients similarly describe a sense of disgust with themselves and their partners after sex.

22 Lacan (1992, pp. 279/238 and 291/248–9) borrows the idea that beauty extinguishes desire from Aquinas and the idea that it disrupts us "from any and every object" from Kant's *Critique of Judgment*.

23 Lacan (1992, pp. 291/248–9) tempers this a bit further on in the seminar, saying that beauty does not *completely* extinguish desire. Yet one of my patients indicated that the more beautiful he found his mistress, the more he needed Viagra® to be able to have intercourse with her.

24 A number of patients have told me that in certain porn videos, when a

man is about to reach orgasm, he will sometimes move so as to ejaculate on the woman's face, saying words like, "I'm going to mess up your beautiful face," as if her beautiful face would get in the way of his satisfaction and thus *has* to be sullied.

25 Freud might have characterized Gide's supposedly pure, spiritual form of love as anaclitic, affectionate, or attachment-based; another example might be Goethe's Werther who, in *The Sufferings of Young Werther*, instantly fell in love with a girl, Lotte, who was tending to her younger siblings in a maternal fashion (cf. Lacan, 1988, p. 142).

26 Beauty remains unfazed by outrage, Lacan (1992, pp. 279–80/238) says, *outrage* in French also meaning rape, attack, harm, damage, blot, stain, and slander.

27 Elsewhere in Seminar VII, Lacan (1992) links beauty with the second death (p. 302/260), and says that beauty involves the hero going beyond a certain limit or *Até* (*Até* – being the daughter of Eris and Jupiter who induces rash and ruinous actions in gods and men, in Bulfinch's [1979] words, "the goddess of discord" – seems to refer in this context to destiny or perdition). Beauty is related to the ideal and has to do with "*un passage à la limite*," "going to an extreme" (pp. 344–5/298). In Kant's work the form of the human body is, according to Lacan, a divine form. "It is the envelope of all possible fantasies of human desire. The flowers of desire are contained in this vase whose sides [*parois*] we are trying to establish" (p. 345/298). Regarding the vase in the mirror schema in the paper on Lagache, it is similar to a pot: "the existence of emptiness at the center of the real that is called the Thing"; alongside it are the flowers of desire (p. 146/121). See Kant's *Critique of Judgment* and Georges Bataille's (1957) *Erotisme*.

28 For an example, see Fink, 2014c, pp. 19–24.

29 "Erectile dysfunction" can stem from numerous causes, another of which is when a man fails to accept and reckon with his own aggression toward women and refuses to give them jouissance by means of intercourse (in cases in which they want it).

30 He may also be understood to be saying that, although there is no such thing as a sexual relationship between a man, insofar as he is a man, and a woman insofar as she is a woman, there is such a thing as a love relationship, and that love can in certain ways reconcile jouissance (woman) and desire (man).

31 Gaston Paris (1883, p. 519) is the person who came up with the name "courtly love" for this set of love practices. The term found in texts of the time is *fin'amour*.

32 As we shall see, this may only be partially true, according to the historical record.

33 Recall Freud's (1921/1955d, pp. 111–12) notion that affectionate love arises from the extended deferral of sexual gratification.

34 This was also true in the Arab tradition that perhaps preceded it, as we see in John Jay Parry's introduction to Capellanus (1990, p. 11).

35 Capellanus argues – implicitly recognizing that there were at least occasionally sexual relations between courtly lovers – that a woman must be careful not to lead men on: she must not, he says, make promises that she then refuses to keep (Chapelain, 2004, p. 57/166).

36 Note too that, as reported in Padraic Colum's introduction to the complete English edition of *Tristan* (Bédier, 1960, p.xiii), an inscription was found by archaeologists in Cornwall that gave the name Tristran as the son of Mark, suggesting that the Oedipal rivalry over a woman may have been even more direct than it is in the story as it has come down to us. Scholars are not sure of the reliability of the inscription (presumably as concerns its date), but if it is trustworthy – if it refers to a true historical personage – the story would originally have been of a son in love with his father's new young wife-to-be (and perhaps with his biological mother too).

37 Such poetry would perhaps be harder to write today, for we live in a less metaphorical time, a more concrete time. For someone in the Middle Ages, everything had a double meaning: worldly and other-worldly. A donkey was always both a farm animal *and* a reference to Christ going to Jerusalem on Palm Sunday, for example.

38 See John Jay Parry's introduction to Capellanus, 1990, pp. 7–12.

39 Echoing the title of Norman Brown's (1959) well-known book.

40 The well-known Latin reads: "*Nondum amabam et amare amabam et secretiore indigentia oderam me minus indigentem. Quaerebam quid amarem, amans amare.*"

41 "We believe, though, that any man who devotes his efforts to love loses all his usefulness. Read this little book, then, not as one seeking to take up the life of a lover, but that, invigorated by the theory and trained to excite the minds of women to love, you may, by refraining from so doing, win an eternal recompense and thereby deserve a greater reward from God. For God is more pleased with a man who is able to sin and does not, than with a man who has no opportunity to sin" (Chapelain, 2004, pp. 95–6/187).

42 Note that he himself divorced not long after writing this particular book.

43 Those familiar with Alain Badiou's work may be interested to note the similarity of his language to Rougemont's here, both employing the same terms: "event," "decision," and "intervention." "*Fidelité*," which is translated in the English edition of Rougemont's book as "keeping troth," is the exact same term that Badiou (1999, 2006) uses constantly throughout his work in such expressions as "fidelity to the event."

44 As many as 600 people participated in *la court amoureuse* founded by the Duke of Burgundy on Valentine's Day in 1401, which was governed "principally by the conduct, strength, and certainty of the highly praised virtues – namely, humility, honorability, praiseworthiness, and service of all ladies and demoiselles" (Favier, 1967, p. 132).

45 In the case of the book entitled *The Rules*, it is made clear that such rules are not recognized as amorously binding by men, but that they must nevertheless be enforced by women and their mothers. Ignoring the rules will lead to wrack and ruin, which in the American context means no tying of the knot.

46 Even if certain male and female members of the animal kingdom pair for life, there is obviously no such thing as the *institution of marriage* among them, and therefore marriage cannot be the ultimate telos of

their activity. (For a nineteenth-century account of love courts, see Stendhal, 2004, pp. 318–30/275–83.)

47 Writing in the early 1600s, Cervantes depicts Don Quixote as reading far too many of the novels that abounded at that time about the knights of the Round Table and about incredible deeds performed by knights for their ladies. Naturally, such books began to be produced *after* there were essentially no longer any knights errant, or any reason for their being, in a kind of nostalgic gesture – why bother to write about it, after all, if you can simply experience it yourself? But novels like *Amadis of Gaul* were among the first to circulate in Europe and turned the heads of many young men to lofty ideals and a pining for a long-lost lifestyle.

48 Sapho adds that she wants only a slave. We can only imagine Prince Tisander's psychological make-up, to have fallen in love at such a declaration! It was perhaps not so different from Jean-Jacques Rousseau's, Rousseau having apparently fallen in love instantly upon seeing a woman on horseback in riding boots carrying a whip (although Rousseau's condition for falling in love was perhaps more imaginary than symbolic).

49 Perhaps they are seeking to experience anew the kind of intense passion most often experienced in early childhood, but which is considerably tempered if not outright lost with alienation and separation. One might wonder whether the Amish ever experience the kind of intense romantic passion so familiar to us, since their narcissism (narcissism playing such an important role in passion, as we have seen) seems considerably tempered in early childhood (Kraybill, 2001).

50 Stendhal (2004) contrasts *amour-passion* or "passionate love," the kind that arises from falling in love – which comes to one like a lucky chance or accident (*tuché*) – with what he calls *amour-goût* or "mannered love," which is calculated and is primarily about delicacy and good taste, not passion: one has affairs because one is supposed to, because that is "what is done." He suggests that love triangles are of importance only in mannered love, where it is important to a woman what other women think of her man. In passionate love, what other women think is important for but five minutes (p. 47/58).

He also contrasts passionate love with what he calls *amour-vanité* or "vanity love," where one choses a "trophy" partner (a phallus, one might say, embodying rank, fame, fortune, power, and the like) who one believes reflects well on one and raises one up in the eyes of others. Parading around with such a partner increases one's self-esteem. If we subtract the vanity, Stendhal tells us, there is little left (pp. 27–8/43–4). One is happy when one has such a trophy and upset when the person who seems so valuable leaves. When the latter occurs, one begins to convince oneself that one has a great passion for that person even though one's vanity has simply been wounded.

51 This first crystallization (or love at first sight) might be related to what Freud calls "primary process" thinking, in which a perceptual identity is established between an early image (of a parent, for example) associated with a pleasurable discharge and a new image (e.g., that of a new partner). In such primary process thinking, we picture to ourselves a desired state of affairs (identity) in the present.

Chapter VIII – Reading Plato with Lacan: Further Commentary on Plato's *Symposium*

1 This is a lot more precise and limited than knowing all about love: Socrates can detect it in others and guess their beloved. Whether he could do it any better than Mrs. Jennings in Jane Austen's *Sense and Sensibility* is an open question!

2 It is not clear to me that sexual difference is not part of the equation when it comes to homosexual love: as in all domains, what is "left out" of it or set aside may well be as important to its nature as what is included in it. Just as heterosexuality is, at least in part, defined by what it excludes – homosexuality – homosexuality is, at least in part, defined by what it excludes.

3 Cited in Faraone, 1999, p. 126.

4 See, for example, that developed by Aristotle and formalized in Apuleius' so-called logical square (in which there is both the beautiful and not beautiful and the ugly and the not ugly).

5 See my comments on this in Fink, 2007, pp. 74–80.

6 See Seminar XI, where Lacan (1973a, p. 58/59) says that God is unconscious, and Seminar XXII where he says that "God [. . .] is repression in person" (1974–5, class given on December 17, 1974). See also Regnault (1985).

7 Patients will, for example, occasionally say, "I think my unconscious is trying to tell me something."

8 But see the *Alcibiades I*, where Socrates' daemon/guardian is said by Socrates to have not allowed him to see Alcibiades for a while prior to the dialogue (124c–d).

9 I do not believe we could say that Harriet Smith incarnates Woman for Emma the way Frau K. does for Dora.

10 The movie *Clueless*, based loosely on *Emma*, involves similar scenarios with a slightly different cast of characters.

11 Jane Austen (2004, p. 425) was alive to the ruses of projection long before the invention of psychoanalysis; she puts the following thoughts about Frank Churchill in Mr. Knightley's mouth as he addresses Emma: "His own mind full of intrigue, that he should suspect it in others."

12 If we depict the analysand's complaint or reproach as proceeding from a' to a along the imaginary axis in Lacan's (2006a, p. 53) L Schema, a response in kind on the analyst's part would proceed from a to a' along the same axis, whereas a response that changes discourses would proceed from A to S on the symbolic axis (and would perhaps retroactively read the initial reproach as having proceeded from S instead of from a').

13 Certain authors suggest that people, instead, lose interest at that point; indeed, their love "often turns into hatred and disgust" (Aragona, 1547/1997, p. 34). And as Marcel Achard (1962, p. 52), the author of the play *Turlututu*, puts it, "It is easier to keep a dozen men who wonder if you will be theirs interested in you than it is to hold onto just one who no longer wonders any such thing."

14 Lacan (2006a, pp. 846–8) later does much the same regarding libido, formulating the myth of the lamella in "Position of the Unconscious."

15 Faraone (1999) discusses the ancient Greek belief that men are

naturally wild and sexually aggressive while women are naturally self-controlled; this explains, in his view, the use of magic by men to make women more like men (so that the women will want to have sex with them). But Faraone also mentions other scholars who have implied that men in ancient Greece were afraid of the natural wildness and promiscuity of women, suggesting that this was a primary cause of ancient Greek misogyny (pp. 162, 166, and 169–72).

Faraone suggests that women were perhaps seen "as wild and lascivious only during the period of adolescence when they must of necessity make the transition from their roles" as daughters to wives (p. 170). It was perhaps only during adolescence that "Greek males actively secluded their women." "The sometimes violent sexual desire of adolescent females [. . .] was variously explained as a natural sign that it was time for young women to marry and have children, that God was angry at them or their family and had to be appeased, or that they were the victim of a magical attack" (p. 171).

16 The poems cited here can be found in Pockell, 2003, pp. 78 and 85.

17 Consider how Socrates responds to Agathon's professed fear of speaking in front of the few good men at the banquet versus presenting his ideas onstage to a large public audience (194b). Regarding Diotima, we might say that rather than emphasizing the immortality of love (as do poets), she praises the love of immortality – or immortality *tout court*, love perhaps dropping out of the equation altogether.

18 Beauty appears to me to be a primary aim when Diotima says that, if we are pregnant in our souls from early youth with virtue, moderation, and justice, and we are lucky enough "to find a *soul* that is beautiful and noble and well-formed" (209b), we "instantly teem with speeches about virtue" in the endeavor to educate this noble soul. "When [a man] makes contact with someone beautiful and keeps company with him, he conceives and gives birth to what he has been carrying inside him for ages. And whether they are together or apart, he remembers that beauty" (209c).

19 See Xenophon, 1996, p. 150; the passage is from *Symposium*, Chapter 4, 27–8.

20 Theology has, Lacan mentions, apparently criticized Plato for saying that, in climbing the ladder of love, *the lover seeks only his own perfection*. In the movement of the lover of beauty from possessing goods or objects to communing with beauty itself, the lover becomes a lover of beauty and virtue and thereby becomes lovable or desirable himself (Lacan, 2015, p. 128). Lacan claims, however, that this is not Plato's ultimate message; it is just one small part of one speech in the dialogue. As mentioned in Chapter 3, analysts harness love to get analysands to do the work of exploring the unconscious, and in that respect love is a means to an end in psychoanalysis. But love is also the end aimed at by the speaking of what was unconscious.

21 This seems to be the kind of immortality that is referred to in the *Symposium*, but perhaps it is instead some sort of ecstatic oneness with the Platonic forms.

22 Whether Alcibiades should be referred to here as a man or a boy is open to debate, as some commentators suggest he may have been only 15 or 16 at the time of the banquet – that is, still more or

less beardless, which was the preferred state for many older Greek suitors. Nevertheless, many accounts place Alcibiades' birth around 451 B.C. and the date of the symposium in 416 B.C., which would make Alcibiades about 35 at the time. His relationship with Socrates apparently began long before the symposium, however; the dialogue between Socrates and Alcibiades in the *Alcibiades I*, for example, takes place when Alcibiades is 20 years of age and makes it clear that they have known each other for some time already (Plato, 2003).

23 Cf. Freud's (1927/1961d, pp. 152–7) fetishistic patient who was fascinated by the "shine on the nose."

24 Later in the Seminar, Lacan (2015, Chapter 26) reminds us that Abraham did not actually talk about "partial objects" but rather about "partial love for objects." This was apparently too subtle for analysts, who quickly preferred the former to the latter.

25 And, indeed, we see in dreams and fantasies that men are often interested in everything about a woman except her genitalia, and that women often picture to themselves men's bodies without including their genitalia. Lacan (2015, pp. 378–81) comments on Karl Abraham's notion that the genitals are what are the least cathected in the partner, one's own genitals attracting the lion's share of the available cathexis.

26 This might be understood as akin to the turning of a virgin into a whore.

27 We could imagine, nevertheless, that from the beloved's (or object's) vantage point, different lovers could be compared to each other and placed on a scale from best to worst, and thus that scales *can* exist for both lovers and beloveds.

28 Socrates, unlike certain psychoanalysts (such as Reich), did not feel that he could make people better or teach them how to love by having sex with them. Note that in the *Alcibiades I*, Alcibiades blames himself for not having learned more or become a better person: "I think that I am responsible myself because I did not put my mind to it" (118e).

29 This is Lacan's (2015, p. 158) own rendering.

30 Socrates' situation here is quite different from that of one of my patients who nonchalantly declared one day, "I like all the girls who are interested in me."

31 Note, however, that Aeschines, in his *Alcibiades* (Plato, 2003, p. 97), quotes Socrates as saying, "I, though knowing no lesson through which I could benefit a man by teaching, nevertheless believed that by being together with this man I could make him better through love." Assuming the quotation is not apocryphal, Socrates proves not to have read Bruno Bettelheim's (1950) *Love Is Not Enough*!

32 Regarding relationships as power struggles, consider the following anecdote from Xenophon's (1961, p. 44) *Symposium*: Socrates is saying, after seeing a young girl who is dancing and throwing hoops into the air, that women are not inferior to men except in physical strength and vigor, and he adds, "Those among you who have a wife should not hesitate to teach her what you would like her to know." Antisthenes then retorts: "How is it then, Socrates, that with such ideas you don't take the trouble to teach Xanthippus [Socrates' wife], instead of putting up with living with a woman who is the most disagreeable of women today

and even, in my opinion, of all women both past and future?" Socrates replies (ironically?): "It is because I see that people who want to be good horseback riders get themselves not the most docile horses but the most difficult ones; they figure, in fact, that if they're able to master such steeds, it will be easy for them to handle other horses. Similarly, in my desire to converse with human beings and frequent them, I took this wife, knowing full well that if I managed to put up with her, my relations with the rest of humanity would be easy."

33 Lacan says that Socrates (like psychoanalysts) has a desire for infinite discourse, which he characterizes as somewhat delusional (Lacan, 2015, pp. 101–2).

Chapter IX – Some Possible Conclusions about Love

1 Similarly, as every experienced firebuilder knows, three logs make for a lasting fire. One log alone burns not; two logs can burn but briefly; "it takes three to burn or love" enduringly.

2 Does this imply that love – like knowledge for Plato, which is always already there in the soul, just waiting to be drawn out – is always already there in the unconscious? Might Socrates' midwifery apply, then, at least as much to love as to knowledge?

3 The idea of giving what you don't have (or out of your Penia or lack) can be found in Mark 12: 41–44. "For they [the rich people] put in [to the treasury] out of their abundance, but she [a poor widow] out of her poverty put in all that she had, her whole livelihood."

4 If I tell my lover what I want her to do to show she loves me and then she does it, I will not be satisfied because, although she has complied with or satisfied my request to the letter, she might have done so merely to appease me or shut me up. In other words, as it is no more than what I asked for, it does not tell me who I am for her or what I mean to her. I would have preferred that she do it without me asking or that she surprise me by doing more than I would have asked.

5 Lacan (1998a, p. 144) might be understood to suggest that we have to love our partner's unconscious ("All love is based on a certain relationship between two unconscious knowledges"), but few people do; few want to know much about it. As he says:

> There's no such thing as a sexual relationship because one's jouissance of the Other taken as a body is always inadequate – perverse, on the one hand, insofar as the Other is reduced to object *a*, and crazy and enigmatic, on the other, I would say. Isn't it on the basis of the confrontation with this impasse, with this impossibility by which a real is defined, that love is put to the test? Regarding one's partner, love can only actualize what, in a sort of poetic flight, in order to make myself understood, I called courage – courage with respect to this fatal destiny. But is it courage that is at stake or pathways of recognition? That recognition is nothing other than the way in which the relationship said to be sexual – that has now become a subject-to-subject

relationship, the subject being but the effect of unconscious knowledge – stops not being written.

6 *Traiter* (treat) might perhaps also be rendered here as "to deal with." *Tenir* can be understood here as "to hold," "hold onto," "keep," "maintain," or "handle."

References

Achard, M. (1962). *L'amour ne paie pas* [Love doesn't pay]. Paris: La Table Ronde.

Allouch, J. (2009). *L'amour Lacan* [Love, Lacan]. Paris: EPEL.

Aquinas (1952). *The* Summa Theologica *of Saint Thomas Aquinas*. Chicago, IL: Encyclopaedia Britannica.

Aragona, T. d' (1997). *Dialogue on the infinity of love* (R. Russell & B. Merry, trans.). Chicago, IL, & London: University of Chicago Press. (Original work published 1547.)

Aristotle (1952). Complete works. In *Great Books of the Western World*. (R. M. Hutchins & M. J. Adler, eds.; W. D. Ross, trans.) Chicago, IL: Encyclopaedia Britannica with University of Chicago Press.

Augustine (1961). *The confessions of Saint Augustine*. New York: Collier.

Austen, J. (1970). *Sense and sensibility*. London: Oxford University Press.

Austen, J. (2000). *Pride and prejudice*. New York: Modern Library.

Austen, J. (2003). *Persuasion*. New York: Barnes & Noble Classics.

Austen, J. (2004). *Emma*. New York: Barnes & Noble Classics.

Badiou, A. (1999). *Manifesto for philosophy* (N. Madarazs, trans.). Albany, NY: SUNY Press.

Badiou, A. (2006). *Being and event* (O. Feltham, trans.). New York: Continuum.

Baker, R. R., & M. A. Bellis (1995). *Human sperm competition: Copulation, masturbation and infidelity*. London: Chapman & Hall.

Balmary, M. (2005). *Le Moine et la psychanalyste* [The monk and the psychoanalyst]. Paris: Albin Michel.

Bataille, G. (1957). *L'Érotisme* [Eroticism]. Paris: Editions de Minuit.

Bédier, J. (1960). *The romance of Tristan and Iseult*. New York: Heritage Press.

Bettelheim, B. (1950). *Love is not enough: The treatment of emotionally disturbed children*. Glencoe, IL: The Free Press.

Bettelheim, B. (1961). *Paul and Mary*. New York: Doubleday.

Bettelheim, B. (1967). *The empty fortress*. New York: The Free Press.

Borch-Jacobsen, M. (1996). *Remembering Anna O*. New York: Routledge.

Bowlby, J. (1982). *Attachment and loss*, Vol. 1. New York: Basic.

Brown, N. O. (1959). *Life against death*. Middletown, CT: Wesleyan University Press.

Bulfinch, T. (1979). *Myths of Greece and Rome*. New York: Penguin.

Cervantes (1995). *Don Quijote* (B. Raffel, trans.). New York: Norton.

Chapelain, André le [a.k.a. Andreas Capellanus and Andrew the Chaplain] (2004). *Comment maintenir l'amour* (F. Lemonde, trans.). Paris: Payot & Rivages. (Original work published c.1185.) [In English, see Capellanus (1990). *The art of courtly love* (J. J. Parry, trans.). New York: Columbia University Press.]

Chauvin, R. (1941). Contribution à l'étude physiologique du Criquet pélerin et du déterminisme des phénomènes grégaires [Contribution to the physiological study of grasshoppers and the determination of gregarious traits]. *Annales de la Société Entomologique de France*, *1*, 1–137; *3*, 133–272.

Cicero (1971). *On old age and on friendship*. Ann Arbor, MI: University of Michigan Press.

Clairvaux, Bernard of (1995). *On loving God: An analytical commentary by Emero Stiegman*. Kalamazoo: Cistercian Publications.

Corday, R. (1993). *Losing the thread* (videotape). Insight Media.

Crenne, H. de (1996). *Torments of love* (L. Neal & S. Rendall, trans.). Minneapolis, MN: University of Minnesota Press. (Original work published 1538.)

Darwin, C. (1899). *The expression of the emotions in man and animals*. London.

Decaux, A. (1998). *Histoire des françaises* [History of French women]. Paris: Perrin. (Original work published in 1972.)

DeJean, J. (1991). *Tender geographies: Women and the origins of the novel in France*. New York: Columbia University Press.

Duby, G. (1992). The Courtly Model. In *A history of women in the West, Vol. 2: Silences of the Middle Ages* (pp. 250–66). G. Duby, M. Perrot, C. Klapisch-Zuber, eds. Cambridge, MA.: Belknap Press, 1992.

Erikson, E. (1963). *Childhood and society*. New York: Norton. (Original work published 1950.)

Faraone, C. A. (1999). *Ancient Greek love magic*. Cambridge, MA: Harvard University Press.

Favier, M. (1967). *Christine de Pisan, Muse des cours souveraines* [Muse of Sovereign Courts]. Lausanne: Editions Rencontre Lausanne.

Fein, E. and Schneider, S. (1995). *The rules: Time-tested secrets for capturing the heart of Mr. Right*. New York: Grand Central Publishing.

Fielding, H. (1979). *The history of Tom Jones, A foundling*. Norwalk, CT: The Easton Press. (Original work published 1749.)

Fink, B. (1995a). *The Lacanian subject: Between language and jouissance*. Princeton, NJ: Princeton University Press.

Fink, B. (1995b). Logical time and the precipitation of subjectivity. In B. Fink, R. Feldstein, & M. Jaanus (eds.), *Reading Seminars I & II: Lacan's return to Freud* (pp. 356–86). Albany, NY: SUNY Press.

Fink, B. (1995c). The nature of unconscious thought or why no one ever reads Lacan's Postface to the "Seminar on 'the purloined letter.'" In B. Fink, R. Feldstein, & M. Jaanus (eds.), *Reading Seminars I & II: Lacan's return to Freud* (pp. 173–91). Albany, NY: SUNY Press.

Fink, B. (1997). *A clinical introduction to Lacanian psychoanalysis: Theory and technique*. Cambridge, MA: Harvard University Press.

Fink, B. (2004). *Lacan to the letter: Reading* Écrits *closely*. Minneapolis, MN: University of Minnesota Press.

Fink, B. (2007). *Fundamentals of psychoanalytic technique: A Lacanian approach for practitioners*. New York: Norton.

Fink, B. (2014a). *Against understanding*. Vol. 1: *Commentary and critique in a Lacanian key*. London: Routledge.

Fink, B. (2014b). *Against understanding*. Vol. 2: *Cases and commentary in a Lacanian key*. London: Routledge.

Fink, B. (2014c). *The purloined love: An Inspector Canal mystery*. London: Karnac.

Firestone, S. (1970). *The dialectic of sex*. New York: Farrar, Straus and Giroux.

Freud, E. L. (ed.). (1960). *Letters of Sigmund Freud*. New York: McGraw-Hill.

Freud, S. (1953a). Fragment of an analysis of a case of hysteria (Dora). In J. Strachey (ed. & trans.), *The standard edition of the complete psychological works of Sigmund Freud* (Vol. 7, pp. 7–122). London: Hogarth Press. (Original work published 1905.)

Freud, S. (1953b). Three essays on the theory of sexuality. In J. Strachey (ed. & trans.), *The standard edition of the complete psychological works of Sigmund Freud* (Vol. 7, pp. 130–243). London: Hogarth Press, 1953. (Original work published 1905.)

Freud, S. (1953c). The interpretation of dreams. In J. Strachey (ed. & trans.), *The standard edition of the complete psychological works of Sigmund Freud* (Vols. 4 & 5). London: Hogarth Press, 1953. (Original work published 1900.)

Freud, S. (1954). *The origins of psychoanalysis: Letters to Wilhelm Fliess, drafts and notes, 1887–1902.* New York: Basic.

Freud, S. (1955a). Notes upon a case of obsessional neurosis. In J. Strachey (ed. & trans.), *The standard edition of the complete psychological works of Sigmund Freud* (Vol. 10, pp. 155–318). London: Hogarth. (Original work published 1909.)

Freud, S. (1955b). Some neurotic mechanisms in jealousy, paranoia and homosexuality. In J. Strachey (ed. & trans.), *The standard edition of the complete psychological works of Sigmund Freud* (Vol. 18, pp. 223–32). London: Hogarth. (Original work published 1922). [Sur quelques mécanismes névrotiques dans la jalousie, la paranoïa et l'homosexualité (J. Lacan, trans.). *Revue Française de Psychanalyse*, 3 (1932).]

Freud, S. (1955c). A child is being beaten: A contribution to the study of the origin of sexual perversions. In J. Strachey (ed. & trans.), *The standard edition of the complete psychological works of Sigmund Freud* (Vol. 17, pp. 179–204). London: Hogarth. (Original work published 1919.)

Freud, S. (1955d). Group psychology and the analysis of the ego. In J. Strachey (ed. & trans.), *The standard edition of the complete psychological works of Sigmund Freud* (Vol. 18, pp. 69–143). London: Hogarth. (Original work published 1921.)

Freud, S. (1955e). The psychogenesis of a case of homosexuality in a woman. In J. Strachey (ed. & trans.), *The standard edition of the complete psychological works of Sigmund Freud* (Vol. 18, pp. 147–72). London: Hogarth. (Original work published 1920.)

Freud, S. (1955f). Analysis of a phobia in a five-year-old boy (Little Hans). In J. Strachey (ed. & trans.), *The standard edition of the complete psychological works of Sigmund Freud* (Vol. 10, pp. 5–149). London: Hogarth. (Original work published 1909.)

Freud, S. (1957a). A special type of choice of object made by men. In J. Strachey (ed. & trans.), *The standard edition of the complete psychological works of Sigmund Freud* (Vol. 11, pp. 165–75). London: Hogarth. (Original work published 1910.)

Freud, S. (1957b). On the universal tendency to debasement in the sphere of love. In J. Strachey (ed. & trans.), *The standard edition of the complete psychological works of Sigmund Freud* (Vol. 11, pp. 179–90). London: Hogarth. (Original work published 1912.)

Freud, S. (1957c). On narcissism. In J. Strachey (ed. & trans.), *The standard edition of the complete psychological works of Sigmund Freud* (Vol. 14, pp. 73–102). London: Hogarth. (Original work published 1914.)

Freud, S. (1958). Recommendations to physicians practising psycho-analysis. In J. Strachey (ed. & trans.), *The standard edition of the complete psychological works of Sigmund Freud* (Vol. 12, pp. 111–20). London: Hogarth Press. (Original work published 1912.)

Freud, S. (1959a). On the sexual theories of children. In J. Strachey (ed. & trans.), *The standard edition of the complete psychological works of Sigmund Freud* (Vol. 9, pp. 209–26). London: Hogarth Press. (Original work published 1908.)

Freud, S. (1959b). An autobiographical study. In J. Strachey (ed. & trans.), *The standard edition of the complete psychological works of Sigmund Freud* (Vol. 20, pp. 7–74). London: Hogarth Press. (Original work published 1925.)

Freud, S. (1961a). Civilization and its discontents. In J. Strachey (ed. & trans.), *The standard edition of the complete psychological works of Sigmund Freud* (Vol. 21, pp. 64–145). London: Hogarth Press. (Original work published 1930.)

Freud, S. (1961b). The ego and the id. In J. Strachey (ed. & trans.), *The standard edition of the complete psychological works of Sigmund Freud* (Vol. 19, pp. 12–66). London: Hogarth Press. (Original work published 1923.)

Freud, S. (1961c). Female sexuality. In J. Strachey (ed. & trans.), *The standard edition of the complete psychological works of Sigmund Freud* (Vol. 21, pp. 225–43). London: Hogarth Press. (Original work published 1931.)

Freud, S. (1961d). Fetishism. In J. Strachey (ed. & trans.), *The standard edition of the complete psychological works of Sigmund Freud* (Vol. 21, pp. 152–7). London: Hogarth Press. (Original work published 1927.)

Freud, S. (1963). Introductory lectures on psycho-analysis. In J. Strachey (ed. & trans.), *The standard edition of the complete psychological works of Sigmund Freud* (Vols. 15–16). London: Hogarth Press. (Original work published 1916–17.)

Freud, S. (1964). New introductory lectures on psycho-analysis. In J. Strachey (ed. & trans.), *The standard edition of the complete psychological works of Sigmund Freud* (Vol. 22, pp. 5–182). London: Hogarth Press. (Original work published 1933.)

Hartmann, H., Kris, E., & Loewenstein, R. (1946). Comments on the formation of psychic structure. *The Psychoanalytic Study of the Child*, Vol. 2 (pp. 11–38). New York: International Universities Press.

Hesiod (1973). *Hesiod and Theognis* (D. Wender, trans.). Middlesex: Penguin.

Hirschmüller, A. (1989). *The life and work of Josef Breuer: Physiology and psychoanalysis*. New York: New York University Press, 1989. (1989 is the 2nd revised edition; original work published 1978.)

Huxley, A. (1932). *Brave new world*. New York: Harper.

Jekels, L. and E. Bergler (1949). Transference and love. *Psychoanalytic Quarterly*, *18*: 325–50.

Jones, E. (1953). *The life and work of Sigmund Freud*, Vol. I. New York: Basic.

Kierkegaard, S. (1954). *Fear and trembling* and *The sickness unto death* (W. Lowrie, trans.). Princeton, NJ: Princeton University Press. (Original work published 1843.)

Kierkegaard, S. (1965). *The concept of irony* (L. M. Capel, trans.). Bloomington, IN: Indiana University Press. (Original work published 1841.)

Kierkegaard, S. (1988). *Stages on life's way* (H. V. Hong & E. H. Hong, eds. & trans.). Princeton, NJ: Princeton University Press. (Original work published 1845.)

Kierkegaard, S. (1995). *Works of love* (H. V. Hong & E. H. Hong, eds. & trans.). Princeton, NJ: Princeton University Press. (Original work published 1847.)

Kraybill, D. B. (2001). *The riddle of Amish culture* (revised ed.). Baltimore, MD: Johns Hopkins University Press.

Lacan, J. (1933–4). Le problème du style et la conception psychiatrique des formes paranoïaques de l'expérience and Motifs du crime paranoïaque: le crime des soeurs Papin. *Le Minotaure*, 3–4. [In English, see Lacan, J. (1988). The Problem of Style and the Psychiatric Conception of Paranoiac Forms of Experience *and* Motives of Paranoiac Crime: The Crime of the Papin Sisters (J. Anderson, trans.). *Critical Texts*, *5*(3): 4–11.]

Lacan, J. (1953). Some reflections on the ego. *International Journal of Psycho-Analysis 34*(1): 11–17.

Lacan, J. (1965–6). *Le séminaire de Jacques Lacan, Livre XIII: L'objet de la psychanalyse* [The Object of Psychoanalysis] (unpublished).

Lacan, J. (1973a). *Les quatre concepts fondamentaux de la psychanalyse (1964)*. (J.-A. Miller, ed.). Paris: Seuil. [In English, see Lacan, J. (1978). *The Four Fundamental Concepts of Psychoanalysis (1964)*. (J.-A. Miller, ed., & A. Sheridan, trans.). New York: Norton.]

Lacan, J. (1973b). L'Étourdit. *Scilicet*, *4*: 5–52.

Lacan, J. (1973–4). *Le séminaire de Jacques Lacan, Livre XXI: Les non-dupes errent* [Those who are not dupes go astray] (unpublished).

Lacan, J. (1974). *Télévision*. Paris: Seuil. [In English, see *Television: A challenge to the psychoanalytic establishment* (D. Hollier, R. Krauss, & A. Michelson, trans.). New York: Norton, 1990.]

Lacan, J. (1974–5). *Le séminaire de Jacques Lacan, Livre XXI: R.S.I.* (unpublished).

Lacan, J. (1975). Introduction à l'édition allemande d'un premier volume des *Écrits* [Introduction to the first volume of *Écrits* in German]. *Scilicet, 5*: 11–17.

Lacan, J. (1976). Conférences et entretiens dans des universités nord-américaines [Lectures and meetings at North American Universities]. *Scilicet, 6–7*: 5–63.

Lacan, J. (1980). *De la psychose paranoïaque dans ses rapports avec la personnalité* [The relationship between paranoiac psychosis and personality]. Paris: Seuil. (Original work published 1932.)

Lacan, J. (1984). *Les complexes familiaux*. Paris: Navarin. (Original work published 1938.) [In English, see the partial translation: Lacan, J. (1988). The Family Complexes (J. Anderson, trans.). *Critical Texts, 5*(3): 13–29.]

Lacan, J. (1988). *The seminar of Jacques Lacan, Book I: Freud's papers on technique (1953–1954)* (J.-A. Miller, ed., & J. Forrester, trans.). New York: Norton. (Original work published 1978.)

Lacan, J. (1992). *The seminar of Jacques Lacan, Book VII: The ethics of psychoanalysis (1959–1960)* (J.-A. Miller, ed., & D. Porter, trans.). New York: Norton. (Original work published 1986.)

Lacan, J. (1993). *The seminar of Jacques Lacan, Book III: The psychoses (1955–1956)*. (J.-A. Miller, ed., & R. Grigg, trans.). New York: Norton. (Original work published 1981.)

Lacan, J. (1998a). *The seminar of Jacques Lacan, Book XX, Encore: On feminine sexuality, the limits of love and knowledge (1972–1973)* (J.-A. Miller, ed., & B. Fink, trans.). New York: Norton. (Original work published 1975.)

Lacan, J. (1998b). *Le séminaire de Jacques Lacan, Livre V: Les formations de l'inconscient (1957–1958)* [The seminar of Jacques Lacan, Book V: Unconscious Formations] (J.-A. Miller, ed.). Paris: Seuil.

Lacan, J. (2004). *Le séminaire de Jacques Lacan, Livre X: L'angoisse (1962–1963)* [The seminar of Jacques Lacan, Book X: Anxiety (1962–1963)] (J.-A. Miller, ed.). Paris: Seuil.

Lacan, J. (2006a). *Écrits: The first complete edition in English* (B. Fink, trans.). New York: Norton. (Original work published 1966; page numbers given here are those found in the margins that correspond to the pagination of the original French edition.)

Lacan, J. (2006b). *Le séminaire de Jacques Lacan, Livre XVI, D'un Autre à l'autre (1968–1969)* [The seminar of Jacques Lacan, Book XVI: From one Other to another (1968–1969)] (J.-A. Miller, ed.). Paris: Seuil.

Lacan, J. (2013). *On the names-of-the-father* (B. Fink, trans.). Cambridge, UK: Polity. (Original work published 2005.)

Lacan, J. (2015). *The seminar of Jacques Lacan, Book VIII: Transference (1960–1961)* (J.-A. Miller, ed., B. Fink, trans.). Cambridge, UK: Polity. (Original work published in 1991 and the second, revised edition in 2001.)

Leader, D. (2011). *What is madness?* London: Penguin.

Lévi-Strauss, C. (1969). *Elementary structures of kinship* (J. H. Bell & J. R. von Sturmer, trans.). Boston, MA: Beacon. (Original work published 1949.)

Longus (1973). *Daphnis et Chloé* (P. Grimal, trans.). Paris: Gallimard.

Lorenz, K. (1966). *On aggression.* New York: Viking. (Original work published 1963.)

Lowrie, W. (1970). *Kierkegaard*, Vol. 1. Gloucester, MA: Peter Smith.

Lucretius (1990). *The way things are* [more commonly known as *On the nature of things*]. Chicago, IL: Encyclopaedia Britannica.

Mallarmé, S. (1994). *Collected poems: A bilingual edition* (H. M. Weinfield, trans.). Berkeley & Los Angeles: University of California Press.

Marcuse, H. (1955). *Eros and civilization: A philosophical inquiry into Freud.* Boston, MA: Beacon.

Matthews, C. (2004). Love at first sight: The velocity of Victorian heterosexuality. *Victorian Studies, 46*(3): 425–54.

Matthews, L. H. (1939). Visual stimulation and ovulation in pigeons. *Proceedings of the Royal Society*, Series B, *126*: 557–60.

Mews, C. (2001). *The lost love letters of Heloise and Abelard: Perceptions of dialogue in twelfth-century France.* New York: Palgrave Macmillan.

Ovid (1979). *The art of love and other poems.* Cambridge, MA: Harvard University Press.

Ovid (1994). *The Metamorphoses of Ovid* (D. R. Slavitt, trans.). Baltimore, MD: Johns Hopkins University Press.

Paris, G. (1883). L'Amour courtois [Courtly love]. *Romania, 12.*

Plato (and Aeschines) (2003). *Socrates and Alcibiades: Four texts* (D. M. Johnson, trans.). Newburyport, MA: Focus Publishing/ R. Pullins.

Pockell, L. (2003). *The 100 best love poems of all time.* New York: Warner.

Reeve, C. D. C. (2006). *Plato on love.* Indianapolis, IN, & Cambridge, MA: Hackett.

Regnault, F. (1985). *Dieu est inconscient* [God is unconscious]. Paris: Navarin.

Reich, W. (1972). *Character analysis* (V. R. Carfagno, trans.). New York: Simon & Schuster. (Original work published 1933.)

Rochefoucauld, F. duc de La (1967). *Maximes*. Paris: Garnier Frères. [In English, see *The maxims of La Rochefoucauld*. New York: Random House, 1959.]

Rougemont, D. (1983). *Love in the western world*. Princeton, NJ: Princeton University Press (revised ed.; original work published in French in 1940.)

Rousselot, P. (1907). *Pour l'histoire du problème de l'amour au moyen âge*. Münster: Aschendorffsche Buchhandlung. [In English, see *The Problem of Love in the Middle Ages: A Historical Contribution*. Milwaukee, WI: Marquette University Press, 2001.]

Sachs, J. S. (2005, October/November). Why do animals do that? *National Wildlife* (magazine). Reston, VA.

Saussure, F. de (1959). *Course in general linguistics* (W. Baskin, trans.). New York: McGraw-Hill.

Sautoy, M. du (2008). *Symmetry: A journey into the patterns of nature*. New York: HarperCollins.

Scudéry, M. (2001). *Clélie: Histoire romaine*, Vol. 1. Paris: Honoré Champion.

Scudéry, M. de (2003). *The story of Sapho*. Chicago, IL: University of Chicago Press.

Slater, P. (1970). *The pursuit of loneliness*. Boston, MA: Beacon.

Soler, C. (2003). *Ce que Lacan disait des femmes*. Paris: Editions du Champ lacanien. [In English, *What Lacan said about women* (J. Holland, trans.). New York: The Other Press, 2006.]

Soler, C. (2009). *Lacan, L'inconscient réinventé*. Paris: Presses Universitaires de France. [In English, see *Lacan – The unconscious reinvented*. London: Karnac, 2014.]

Soler, C. (2011). *Les affects lacaniens*. Paris: Presses Universitaires de France. [Forthcoming in English as *Lacanian affects: The function of affect in Lacan's work* (B. Fink, trans.). London: Routledge, 2015.]

Solomon, R. C., & Higgins, K. (eds.). (1991). *The philosophy of (erotic) love*. Lawrence, KS: University Press of Kansas.

Spinoza, Benedict de (1994). *A Spinoza reader* (E. Curley, ed. & trans.). Princeton, NJ: Princeton University Press.

Stendhal (2004). *Love*. London: Penguin. (Original work published 1822.) [The French edition referenced here is Stendhal (1980). *De l'amour*. Paris: Gallimard.]

Sulloway, F. J. (1996). *Born to rebel: Birth order, family dynamics, and creative lives*. New York: Pantheon Books.

Tierney, J. (2011, February 21). The threatening scent of fertile women. *The New York Times*.

Urfé, H. d' (1935). *L'Astrée*. Paris: Larousse. (Original work published between 1607 and 1633).

Waal, F. B. M. de, & Tyack, P. L. (eds.). (2003). *Animal social complexity: Intelligence, culture, and individualized societies.* Cambridge, MA: Harvard University Press.

Webster's third new international dictionary (Unabridged) (1986). Chicago, IL: Encyclopaedia Britannica.

Winnicott, D. W. (1949). Hate in the counter-transference. *International Journal of Psycho-Analysis, 30*(2): 69–74.

Winnicott, D. W. (1965). The theory of the parent-infant relationship. In *The maturational processes and the facilitating environment* (pp. 37–55). London: Hogarth Press. (Original work published 1960.)

Winnicott, D. W. (1978). *The Piggle: An account of the psychoanalytic treatment of a little girl.* London: Hogarth Press.

Woodley, S. (February 2009). *Duquesne University Times.*

Xenophon (1961). *Banquet. Apologie de Socrates* [Symposium and Apology]. Paris: Belles Lettres.

Xenophon (1996). *The shorter Socratic writings* (R. C. Bartlett, ed.). Ithaca, NY: Cornell University Press.

Index